D0754544

IN THE COURT OF
PUBLIC OPINION

IN THE COURT OF
PUBLIC OPINION

Winning Your Case with Public Relations

JAMES F. HAGGERTY, ESQ.

WILEY

John Wiley & Sons, Inc.

Copyright © 2003 by James F. Haggerty. All rights reserved.

Published by John Wiley & Sons, Inc., Hoboken, New Jersey.
Published simultaneously in Canada.

No part of this publication may be reproduced, stored in a retrieval system, or transmitted in any form or by any means, electronic, mechanical, photocopying, recording, scanning, or otherwise, except as permitted under Section 107 or 108 of the 1976 United States Copyright Act, without either the prior written permission of the Publisher, or authorization through payment of the appropriate per-copy fee to the Copyright Clearance Center, Inc., 222 Rosewood Drive, Danvers, MA 01923, 978-750-8400, fax 978-750-4470, or on the web at www.copyright.com. Requests to the Publisher for permission should be addressed to the Permissions Department, John Wiley & Sons, Inc., 111 River Street, Hoboken, NJ 07030, 201-748-6011, fax 201-748-6008, e-mail: permcoordinator@wiley.com.

Limit of Liability/Disclaimer of Warranty: While the publisher and author have used their best efforts in preparing this book, they make no representations or warranties with respect to the accuracy or completeness of the contents of this book and specifically disclaim any implied warranties of merchantability or fitness for a particular purpose. No warranty may be created or extended by sales representatives or written sales materials. The advice and strategies contained herein may not be suitable for your situation. You should consult with a professional where appropriate. Neither the publisher nor author shall be liable for any loss of profit or any other commercial damages, including but not limited to special, incidental, consequential, or other damages.

For general information on our other products and services, or technical support, please contact our Customer Care Department within the United States at 800-762-2974, outside the United States at 317-572-3993 or fax 317-572-4002.

Wiley also publishes its books in a variety of electronic formats. Some content that appears in print may not be available in electronic books. For more information about Wiley products, visit our web site at www.wiley.com.

Library of Congress Cataloging-in-Publication Data:

Haggerty, James F., 1965–
    In the court of public opinion : winning your case with public relations / James F. Haggerty.
        p.   cm.
    Includes index.
    ISBN 0-471-30742-4
    1. Public relations and law—United States.   2. Public relations consultants—Legal status, laws, etc.—United States.   I. Title.
    KF390.5.P8 H34 2003
    347.73'504—dc21

                                                            2002153260

Printed in the United States of America.

10 9 8 7 6 5 4 3 2 1

For Elyse, who's loved me through
summer wind and winter wind . . .

Acknowledgments

The motto on the Haggerty family crest (Hegarty in Ireland) reads *"Nec flectitur nec mutant,"* which translated from the Gaelic means: "They neither bend nor change." Anyone who has worked with me (or, for that matter, lived with me) over the years knows just how true that can be. So I have many people to thank.

I start with my wife, Elyse DeMayo Haggerty, my partner in the truest sense of the word. Among other things, she has to live with me . . . and deserves special acknowledgment just for that. Not only has she supported this book from the beginning, but during the development she's been pregnant, given birth, and cared for our young son Liam (in addition to her fulltime job). Propped up on the couch in the final days of pregnancy, listening to me blather on about publishers and proposals and writer's block—well, you can imagine the extent to which her contribution goes above and beyond the call of duty.

Next, I thank Robert Shepard, in my opinion the best nonfiction agent in publishing. He did far more than just bring this book to the right publisher—he nursed the project from conception to completion, and was instrumental in helping a shaky, first-time book author through a process that can be quite daunting (even for someone like me who, over the years, has written numerous articles, speeches, press materials—even fiction on occasion).

I must also thank my parents (corny though that might sound): my mother, who grew up in rural northwest Ireland in a two-room house with seven cousins and two grandparents, then worked nights for 20 years so that we would have a better life; and my father, who handles life with such grace, humanity, and outright courage that he is nothing less than my hero. Together, they taught me that no matter how modest your circumstances, if you work hard and believe, you can succeed—so long as you understand what success really is.

Professionally, there are more people to thank than I could ever fit in one book. First among them is Alan (Max) Metrick, to my mind the most skilled consigliere in the public relations business, currently the director of communications at the Natural Resources Defense Council (NRDC). Max has, at various times, been a mentor, employee, business partner, and client—but has, at all times, been a great friend. Then there's Jeffrey Sandman (who appears at various points in this book), CEO of Hyde Park Communications, another of my closest friends, who works in partnership with me and is the perfect complement to my sometimes-scatterbrained (I would call it "creative") methods. Richard Schrader, among the most respected minds in New York City politics, is a senior consultant to The PR Consulting Group and a great friend. Rich reads a book or two each week, and has been enormously helpful in making sure that this book is something he would read. Bruce Berman, a senior counselor to our firm and fellow Wiley author, gave me great advice on the publishing business and how to effectively manage the process.

Other political, public relations, and public affairs professionals have influenced me enormously through the years—taught me most of what I know—and I'm sure I've forgotten some, but I especially thank John C. Carns, David P. Warner, Lee Silberstein, John Softness, John F. (Jack) Drum, Paul DelPonte, Howard Teich, and Richard Aborn. In the legal world, I thank C. Bryant Boydston of the St. Petersburg, Florida, law firm of Boydston, Dabroski & Lyle, who gave me my start. Also thanks to George P. Sape, managing partner of Epstein, Becker & Green, who has been a client, friend, and mentor through the years. Speaking of clients, I should particularly thank Ronald M. Green and all the attorneys at Epstein Becker & Green, a longtime client, along with Pat Martone, Kevin Culligan, Ed Bailey, Jesse Jenner, and all their colleagues at Fish & Neave, another law firm that I have worked with closely. I thank all of the lawyers and clients who have worked with me through the years. Without them, I'd just be "playing office."

I must also give special acknowledgment to the many talented people who've worked with me and for me over the years, and played a role in many of the examples in this book. There are too many to mention here, but I thank them all. I also acknowledge those who—over the course of several years—helped with the research and writing of this book, including Carol McKoy, Liz Hall,

Matthew Kramer, Kristen Ruckdeschel, Daphne Kaye, and John Pappas.

Finally, I must thank all the editors at John Wiley & Sons, and particularly Debra Englander, who saw the promise of this book from the beginning—that it would be both a treatise (in the best sense of the word) *and* a good read. Here's hoping I've come close to this original vision.

Contents

Preface

This is the first book of its kind. It presents a commonsense but, in some circles, radical notion: that public relations during lawsuits should be handled with the same seriousness and care as any other aspect of the case. Whether you're a business executive, corporate counsel, a lawyer at an outside law firm, or a senior communications professional, you need a *system* for managing communications during litigation, to ensure that you "win" this critical battle—and perhaps, in the process, the war.

Put this way, I'm sure this doesn't seem like a radical idea at all. Yet you'd be surprised at the extent to which communications and other public relations considerations are shunted aside during litigation—sometimes even ignored. "We won't try this case in the media," is often the knee-jerk reaction of lawyers and clients alike.

Consider the e-mail I received just last week from a prominent litigator on the West Coast:

> We have something I'm working on that may need your services.
> I'll give you a call if it blows up.

As you'll see throughout this book, waiting until a case "blows up" is probably the worst time to begin communications planning during litigation, although in reality that is when the first phone call usually comes. Yet smart clients and their advisors are beginning to realize that *litigation public relations* (or *litigation communications,* as it's also known) is, at its core, a *litigation management* function—as important to the case as any other element of modern litigation practice: legal research, expert opinion, investigations, document management, jury consulting, you name it.

Moreover, while not every case will wind up on the front page of the *New York Times,* lawyers and their clients should routinely ask the following questions of *all* their legal matters:

- Will this case be subject to public scrutiny?
- If so, what procedures can be put in place to manage the public aspects of the matter?

In the Court of Public Opinion will show you how to put your legal issues to this test—and if indeed your case might be subject to public scrutiny—show you how to use media coverage to your advantage when litigating your side of the case.

Who should buy this book? Well, I've written it for the following audiences:

- You are a **CEO, CFO, or other business executive**—or a small business owner—and you'd like to know how to harness the power of the media when dealing with lawsuits, government investigations, or other legal proceedings that come your way.
- You are an **attorney in the legal department** of a corporation whose job includes offering advice on those areas where legal and public perception issues collide.
- You are an **attorney at an outside law firm** who realizes that your clients are frequently finding themselves in the glare of the public spotlight—and they're turning to you (as always) for wise counsel.
- You are a **plaintiff** looking to even up the odds in a battle against a defendant with far greater resources.
- You are a **senior communications professional**—or a public relations firm executive—looking to refine your skills in an increasingly litigious business environment.
- You are a **student**—either in law school or in a communications program—wanting to learn the ropes in a practice that is a true synthesis of the legal and public relations professions.

Every company, every nonprofit or governmental organization, every high-profile individual—to save time, let's just say *everyone* who interacts with the public—will likely find themselves at one point or another immersed in legal issues or crises—and, increasingly, in situations where those legal matters place the client under the glare of the public spotlight.

Thus, this is a book for *both* legal and nonlegal audiences. Properly handling the media aspects of litigation requires the involvement of inside and outside lawyers *as well as* the company's top executives, senior internal communications professionals, and outside public relations firms. To ignore one of these audiences in the creation of this book would have been . . . well, it would have been *negligent.*

One of the advantages I have, by the way, in aiming this book to both legal and nonlegal audiences is the fact that, as you'll see, the practice of litigation public relations is relatively new and very little has been written to explain its basic principles over the course of its two-decade existence. In other words, lawyers and nonlawyers alike are all starting at the same base level of knowledge. This is also true of professionals in the public relations field, many of whom have only a vague knowledge about the particular public relations challenges that face them when confronting high-profile legal action.

Although much of the book will be focused on the media, they are not the only audience relevant to our discussion. Especially when dealing with the complex issues and myriad ramifications of legal disputes, there will likely be a variety of audiences, in addition to the media, that you'll need to reach, including:

- Customers or clients.
- Shareholders and investors.
- Employees.
- Government regulators.
- Federal, state, and local elected officials.

I've occasionally included some basic information about the law or legal processes essential to a nonlawyer's understanding of what's going on. These areas are few and far between, but lawyers should feel free to skip these particularly elementary sections. Similarly, for the public relations professional, a section such as "Ten Tips for Interviews" is specifically related to the problems of litigation and other legal disputes. It should be of interest to even experienced communications practitioners looking to apply their considerable repertoire of skills to the legal context.

Hopefully, you'll find this book readable—even enjoyable—and useful whether you are a seasoned litigator, business executive, public relations professional, or neophyte with no particular communications or legal training. With lists of *how-to's* (and, as importantly, *how-not-to's*), *Action Point* summaries for each chapter, and checklists on various topics, this book should be a valuable resource for business executives, lawyers, and communicators as they confront these complex issues. I've also mixed in some interesting case studies, a few good stories, some personal opinion—even some humor where appropriate.

It's a challenging undertaking, but again, I am helped considerably by the newness of the field—which means that, no matter our prior training or experience, we're all starting out at pretty much the same place. It is my hope that this book also brings us to the same place: a basic understanding of the intersection of media, public opinion, and legal process, and how lawyers and clients can use this understanding to operate successfully in this new environment—where all the world is your courtroom, and public opinion, more often than not, your judge and jury.

BUT I'M NOT A COMPANY!

The primary focus of *In the Court of Public Opinion* is business— more specifically, companies whose lawsuits and other legal matters are subject to the increasingly probing eye of the media and other audiences. These might be publicly traded companies, privately owned conglomerates, small entrepreneurial enterprises, professional service practices, mom-and-pop shops, and so on. In addition, there are nonprofit organizations, including associations, labor unions, environmental groups, and other enterprises that don't necessarily serve the bottom line, but have considerable constituencies nonetheless.

But, there is also a certain class of high-profile individuals who find themselves immersed in legal issues that bring them into the public spotlight, and this book is for them and their attorneys as well. Many have chosen to be high-profile, while others have had it thrust upon them. What is clear in my years of working with these types of matters is that an individual's needs when dealing with the media in litigation are no less important than an organization's—and individuals will find there's plenty of useful information in this book about handling the communications aspect of litigation. In other words, whether you're General William Westmoreland or General Motors, Tropicana O. J., or O. J. Simpson, this book is for you.

About "winning"

I was initially a bit uncomfortable with the subtitle of this book: "Winning Your Case with Public Relations." My concern was based on the fact that there's no way you can actually *win* a case solely using public relations techniques.

But it is important to remember that, in the context of litigation and other legal disputes, "winning" can mean many things:

- It can mean convincing a plaintiff (or prosecutor, or government regulator) not to file a lawsuit in the first place.

- It can mean convincing a defendant that you mean business, and that despite the defendant's outsized resources, this case is just not going to go away.

- It can mean getting the other side to realize that the damage to their reputation will be great, and therefore, settlement ought to be top-of-mind (or, alternately, that the damage that will be inflicted can be contained).

- It can mean preventing copycat lawsuits from other parties looking to capitalize on a company's travails.

- It can mean millions of dollars at the settlement table, depending on how weakened a party is by the damage to business and reputation.

- It can mean tailoring a settlement in ways that limit the public relations or public opinion damage.

- It can mean outright victory in the courthouse.

Can public relations be instrumental in bringing about the resolutions described here? You bet. In fact, on many occasions, effective communications techniques can be the *deciding* factor.

In the end, I decided to do just what I advise clients: Tell it like it is. If you believe in what you're saying—and it's an accurate statement—don't qualify, differentiate, or otherwise window dress the message you are trying to get across. And it is my fervent belief that while you can have a victory in the court of public opinion without a victory in the courtroom, your legal victory doesn't amount to much if, in the process, you sacrifice reputation, corporate character, and all of the other elements that make up an organization's goodwill in the marketplace.

ALL ABOUT ME . . .

I've always felt that many otherwise good public relations books have suffered by spending too much time recounting the author's biographical details and resume, his or her personal history and reputation in the field. I hope to do little of that here, but in the interest of satisfying your curiosity: I'm a New Yorker who started out wanting to be a journalist, wound up working in politics and government and then became a lawyer. In that role, I increasingly began to use my combination of legal and communications skills to help other lawyers with the particular needs of their profession: first, helping them promote themselves and thereby develop new business, then, increasingly, getting involved with their cases and clients, and the particular communication conundrums that were critical to the resolution of their legal disputes.

Over the years, I have worked with hundreds of attorneys and have been involved in some very interesting—at times utterly sensational—cases. I've included many of these cases in this book. Where the litigation and the parties have been extremely well known and no confidential information is at stake, I have used real names—otherwise, names and certain fact patterns have been changed to protect client confidentiality. Some of the cases have been the largest of their kind in history, while others were small matters that were resolved with a little strategy and proper execution. And while I'm not by any means the most famous public relations practitioner in the country, I think it is fair to say that I'm among a handful of lawyer/PR pros who have established a niche practice and national reputation in this area. It is this experience that serves as the foundation for the insights and practical tools presented in this book.

A TOOL FOR THE RESOLUTION OF LEGAL DISPUTES

"Discourage litigation," Abraham Lincoln once said. "Persuade your neighbors to compromise whenever you can. Point out to them how the nominal winner is often the real loser—in fees, expenses, and waste of time."[1]

This, more than anything, is the guiding principle of the work I do—and what I hope to impart as the central benefit of effectively using communications during litigation: It helps clients and their lawyers resolve their legal disputes in a more favorable manner. Depending on your particular legal strategy, this can mean many things, but for plaintiffs and defendants alike it ultimately means just one thing: Getting the legal dispute over with (and with it, as Lincoln said, all of its fees, expenses, and waste of time) and getting back to more important things—matters that are at the core of our business, professional, and personal lives.

Introduction

Why would a lawyer or client need this book? Aren't public relations matters peripheral (at best) to most litigation? Doesn't the media just cover "celebrity" cases? Aren't public relations strategies during litigation best left to the lawyers handling the case?

The answers to the latter questions provide a pretty good idea about the answer to the first. Now more than ever, public relations is an integral part of litigation. And it's not just sensational cases that are garnering press. In a world full of business and financial media, all manner of legal disputes are subject to public scrutiny. Ultimately, this public attention can mean the difference between success or failure—not just for the lawsuit itself, but for the company's reputation and its future.

In my line of work, there are three statements that send a chill down my spine. They are:

1. The best response to the media during a lawsuit is "No comment."

2. We'll fight this case in the courtroom, where it really matters.

3. Don't worry, my attorney will handle the press.

If business executives, communicators, and lawyers learn anything from this book, I hope it's this: Throw those statements out the window. Lawyers and their clients have been falling back on clichés like this since at least the mid-1970s. But the world has changed immeasurably since then—a quick glance at CNBC or the array of business magazines at your local newsstand will show you that. If these statements ever worked, they certainly don't anymore.

They're as outdated as eight-track tapes; about as useful as the Be-tamax machine my father keeps in his garage.

In this media age, old approaches don't work. Communication is now central to the management of modern litigation. It can mean communicating to external audiences such as the media, or to internal audiences like employees, investors, shareholders, and others with a vested interest in the organization.

The camera-shy shouldn't fear, however. As you'll see throughout this book, I'm not talking about holding a press conference on the courthouse steps for every small claims suit that comes your way. Far from it. Sometimes, effective litigation communications requires the feather-light touch of a well-placed phone call to the right reporter, sometimes the sledgehammer of a satellite press conference or fifty-market media blitz. But it always requires thought. It always requires strategy. And it always requires careful execution.

The fact is that most businesses will be sued more than once during their existence. Now more than ever, such lawsuits will likely land a company in the media spotlight. This book is designed to show business executives—everyone from CEOs, to chief com-municators, to general counsel, to outside lawyers and PR pros—just why the three statements I mentioned are so wrong, and how an understanding of ways to properly handle the media during litiga-tion can help your case immensely.

LITIGATION AND THE MEDIA: NOW PART OF DOING BUSINESS

Everyone knows that lawsuits are now a part of the American busi-ness landscape. There are several million companies across the United States—from the largest of the *Fortune 500* to the smallest privately held corporation—and many will be subject to newswor-thy litigation at some point in their existence. Statistics from the 600,000-member National Federation of Independent Business (NFIB) indicate that nearly a quarter of businesses across the country are sued *each year*. A Gallup Organization survey released in 2000 by NFIB found that 56 percent of business owners with more than 50 employees believed their odds of getting sued in the next five years were "abundant."

At the same time, business lawsuits have increasingly become the fodder of news coverage. The rise of the business magazine, 24-hour cable coverage, the Internet and emerging technologies—all of this has meant that business litigation is big news, in a way that would have been hard to imagine 20, or even 10, years ago.

Consider the following: According to Lexis-Nexis, in the grueling 15 years of the IBM antitrust lawsuit (1970–1985), the *New York Times* wrote approximately 500 stories on the case. Another well-known case, Polaroid's 14-year patent case against Kodak (which ended in the early 1990s), was the subject of 104 *New York Times* articles.

By contrast, the recent Microsoft antitrust case generated more than 1,000 *New York Times* stories between 1998 and 2001—just three years! Clearly, the past 20 years have witnessed an explosion of interest in business and business-related litigation.

What is also clear is that companies are more and more finding themselves using the techniques of public relations in managing litigation. A survey recently completed by my company of the top 200 corporate law departments in the United States revealed that nearly 50 percent regularly use public relations techniques when involved in litigation—and 22.9 percent use public relations either "often" or "always."

All Lawsuits Are Public

Our research also shows that more than 500 stories are written *each day* by U.S. newspapers and other media outlets on various lawsuits around the country—most involving businesses or other organizations. These include lawsuits of every kind, in every local community, and on every conceivable subject.

What types of cases are covered by the American media? Let's take a date picked at random: May 8, 2001. There were 562 stories in American media on lawsuits that day, articles and other news reports in every major U.S. city, on subjects as diverse and varied as the cities themselves. Besides the "marquee" cases underway at the time—including the Microsoft antitrust case, the tobacco cases, the Napster copyright case, and so on—a sampling of the types of lawsuits covered by American media on May 8, 2001, includes the following:

- In Albuquerque, a lawsuit was underway against a dental practice that allegedly fired a receptionist because she was pregnant.
- In Indianapolis, a maker of magnets used in many computer disk drives and other home electronic components sued two major computer manufacturers asserting they infringed patents.
- In Davenport, a tire retread company sued a major tire manufacturer over franchise contracts with a competitor.
- In Houston, a lawsuit was filed by a computer company against a competitor for allegedly stealing key employees.
- In Las Vegas, a former casino worker was awarded $75,000 for being falsely accused of sexual harassment.
- In Detroit, an auto parts manufacturer was sued for allegedly selling faulty auto parts online.
- In Los Angeles, a patients' rights group sued a chain of nursing homes alleging substandard care in a string of California-based homes.
- In Ft. Lauderdale, a trash hauling company sued a major financial firm over Broward County's $326.4 million resource recovery bond issue.
- In Boston, drug makers threatened to sue HMOs over nonprescription access to allergy drugs.
- In Los Angeles, an invasion of privacy lawsuit by a software company over the placement of "cookies" on computer users' hard drives was allowed to proceed.
- In New York, a shareholder in a speech products company filed a lawsuit against an investment bank and its auditor alleging fraud.
- In Grand Forks, a major chemical company sued a local farmer for planting genetically modified soybeans without paying the relevant technology fees.

- In Durham, an Internet company faced several lawsuits from suppliers alleging the company owed them almost $790,000.

- In Omaha, wrongful termination lawsuits were filed against car rental agencies on behalf of 33 Somali refugees that were working at their establishments.

- In Tampa, cabdrivers filed suit against a cab company that failed to pay minimum wage.

- In Chicago, a major retailer was negotiating to end a long-standing lawsuit filed by retirees over the reduction of company-paid life insurance benefits.

- In Columbus, a bank sued a competitor over a "business practices" patent relating to a check clearing system.

This is just a sampling—on a single day in 2001. Clearly, it's not just the O. J. Simpsons and Bill Gates that are being covered by the American media. All businesses, in every region of the country, are susceptible to the type of lawsuit that will put them in the glare of the media spotlight.

WHY CAN'T MY LAWYER HANDLE THIS?

It is a source of endless amazement to me that litigators who otherwise seek every possible advantage when facing the other side would be so neglectful when it comes to handling media strategy in litigation. But it happens more often than you think.

On the subject of seeking advantage, some lawyers are legendary. When I first started working in this field, for example, I visited a particularly hardnosed financial litigator in his Tampa, Florida, office—as usual, with my leather briefcase slung over my shoulder by its strap. The lawyer was very skeptical on the subject of why my services were needed and it showed. The first words out of his mouth when he met me were: "That's a very nice briefcase . . . my *wife* has one just like it." As I pondered whether this was a compliment or an insult to my manhood, he led me to a plush chair by his desk—where I sank in to the point that my knees were practically hitting my chin. He then proceeded to his massive desk, where he glowered down at me from on high like a judge looking down at a guilty party. Needless to say, the meeting didn't go well, as he picked apart my strategy and my purported "contacts" in the financial world.

The next time we met was about six weeks later. By this time, the case and his client had taken a savage beating in the press, and the litigator's client insisted I become involved. It was clear his case was on the ropes—not in the court of law, but in the court of public opinion. This time, we met in the litigator's conference room, and the chairs were remarkably equal in both height and size.

Here's my point: Litigators who are otherwise minutely attuned to issues of perception—before a judge, before a witness, before the other side—seem to develop a bit of a tin ear when it comes to *public* perceptions of the litigation. They'll do anything to gain an advantage over the other side, but they fail to consider managing the communications aspects of their client's case for that purpose. Business executives—or anyone involved in litigation—should be wary of this and take steps to ensure that their attorney is making communications strategy an overall component of litigation strategy.

To be fair, there are some lawyers who consider the media when planning legal strategy, and they do it to great effect. I'm not talking about flashy types like F. Lee Bailey—who, as the story goes, in the 1960s installed television lights above his desk so he could be interviewed at a moment's notice. A litigator like David Boies is more the example I'm thinking of. In the Microsoft antitrust case, for example, he opened the trial with the videotaped deposition of Microsoft Chairman Bill Gates (where the billionaire seemed distracted, argumentative, and obtuse, often arguing over the meaning of such words as "competition"), knowing well that for all its probative value in the courtroom, its resonance to a wider audience—the media and general public—would be far greater. The Microsoft case is one of the seminal cases in the growing field of litigation communications, one that we'll look at in greater detail in Chapter Seven of this book. But, suffice to say, despite subsequent appellate victories by Microsoft, neither the company nor its leader ever fully recovered from the initial bungling of the communications aspects of the lawsuit.

But lawyers like Boies are an exception. That's why it is incumbent upon clients to ensure that lawyers are making communications issues part of their legal strategy *before* a lawsuit commences.

Why are lawyers, on the whole, so bad at this? After all, they have years of training in the ability to research a problem, frame it properly, and come up with a solution. Isn't dealing with the media just another argument?

We'll look more at this issue in Chapter Six, but here's one theory I have: lawyers thrive on *precedent*—that is, what has gone before. It's the way they are taught. They want to see the "case law" before proceeding on any issue: be it a litigation issue, a business issue, or a communications issue. Because litigation public relations is so new, there just hasn't been a whole lot written on this topic—not much precedent on which to rely.

This is the niche that *In the Court of Public Opinion* is designed to address. Throughout this book, we'll examine how companies have succeeded in handling the media and other communications issues in litigation, and how they've failed. How business executives can work with lawyers and public relations professionals to ensure that the public relations aspects of a case or investigation are properly handled. And how businesses of all sizes need to be prepared for the day when there's a news crew knocking at your door along with the process server.

ACTION POINTS

✔ The old excuses for ignoring public audiences during litigation just don't work in the media-saturated public opinion environment of the twenty-first century.

✔ For better or worse, as business and trade publications, 24-hour television news, the Internet, and other technologies have proliferated, the media has now become an integral part of modern litigation—and more and more companies are making public relations a part of litigation planning.

✔ It's not just huge, scandalous, or celebrity cases that make headlines—everyday lawsuits of all sizes and types are big news in business, trade, and general interest media across the country.

✔ Litigators skilled at controlling every other aspect of the case can sometimes turn a blind eye to the media aspects of litigation—but more and more litigators are learning that *public relations* and *public opinion* skills need to be a central part of their repertoire.

CHAPTER ONE

Welcome to the Hotseat: This Is Litigation PR

"Oh sure, litigation PR. That's an interesting niche you've carved out for yourself." This from a technology reporter at the New York Times *as we poured over some legal documents relating to an Internet lawsuit I was working on.*

It seems litigation communications is on many lips these days—but there's a great deal of misunderstanding among businesspeople and their lawyers as to what the term really means. In this chapter, we'll consider the use (and misuse) of communications as a means of advancing your position in legal disputes. Along the way, we'll look at the difference between litigation PR and other forms of crisis communications. We'll also look at the birth of the discipline, less than 20 years ago. Finally, we'll examine why some of the usual rules of public relations don't apply, using one of 2001's top tabloid stories—the divorce case of former New York City Mayor Rudy Giuliani—as an example.

W hat is *litigation public relations* or *litigation communications*, as it's also known? To some, it's a press conference on the courthouse steps, or Alan Dershowitz arguing with Geraldo Rivera on late-night cable over the guilt or innocence of O. J. Simpson, or Microsoft's daily briefings at its recent antitrust trial.

In truth, it is usually none of these things. Each scenario occasionally comes up in the practice of litigation communications, but only in isolated instances. The late night shoutfests in front of Chris Matthews or Sean Hannity, the impromptu courthouse press conference, the mass-produced and distributed press release announcing the commencement of a lawsuit—these are only a part of what we do, and a small part at that, especially for the classic "business" lawsuit, which is more often fought in the pages of the relevant business and trade magazines than on *Nightline*. In fact, for reasons that will become clear in the course of this book, press conferences and other "in-your-face" approaches are precisely the types of tactics I *don't* recommend in most circumstances.

Which brings me back to my original question—What is litigation PR? Well here's the textbook definition:

> **Litigation PR can best be defined as managing the communications process during the course of any legal dispute or adjudicatory proceeding so as to affect the outcome or its impact on the client's overall reputation.**

Now that's a bit dry. So to illustrate the power of public relations in influencing the course of litigation, let's consider the following example, *not* from my work as a consultant to lawyers and their clients in high-profile court cases, but from my experience as an attorney. It is a "small" case, which further illustrates that using the media to influence the course of legal proceedings is not necessarily the domain of the Microsofts or O. J. Simpsons of the world, but anyone whose case has the potential to bring them into the public eye.

AN APPEAL TO REPUTATION

Let me be clear: Although I am an attorney licensed in New York and Florida, I've rarely practiced law. For about six months after law school, I did some legal work in an insurance defense firm in Florida, writing briefs and motions relating to auto accidents. Anyone who knows me and knows this type of work will understand why I'm in the communications field today. The usual case went like this: Car A hits Car B. Whose insurance covers first? Whose insurance covers second? I lasted about six months before I had to give it up. (I don't mean, by the way, to offend all of the very talented insurance defense attorneys out there. It just wasn't for me.)

These days, I tell clients that law is my hobby, and I generally only get involved in cases as a *lawyer* if it involves an issue of particular interest to me.

This was one of those cases. John* was a five-year-old boy who walked with a brace on his left leg. In late August, just before the beginning of John's first day in kindergarten, his mother called me. John needed a new leg brace to begin school. The old one, affixed to a heavy brown shoe, was worn, even rusted at points, and had a noticeable squeak when John walked. It was barely functioning and clearly unacceptable for a child just beginning the educational process. Kindergarten, as we all know, is the first great leap into socialization for a boy John's age, and his mother was worried that if he went to school with a rickety leg brace—or even worse, with no leg brace at all—it would exacerbate what was already an anxious situation for the child. John's mother had already been to the orthopedist: The new leg brace was measured, fitted, and ready to go.

But here's the problem: John's father had recently switched jobs and his health insurance was refusing to cover the cost of the new leg brace. He'd been at the job for too short a time, they told him; thus, coverage for special services hadn't kicked in yet (a questionable reading of the health insurance contract, by the way). Come back in six months, they said. It was days until school was to begin, and John's parents didn't have the money to buy the leg brace outright.

In my capacity as attorney, I spoke to the claims representative. "Sorry," he said, "rules are rules." If John and his family didn't like it, they could appeal the decision, and if they didn't like the results of the appeal, they could go to court. I figured John would be a college graduate before we ever saw a final decision.

I next wrote a letter to the General Counsel of the insurance company, explaining the situation and asking for his intercession to waive the appeal requirement—I was relatively sure insurance companies could do this under the right circumstances. I mentioned in the letter that it probably wouldn't look good for the company to be denying a child's claim on a technicality just before he

---

* Not his real name.

started school. No response. It was Wednesday at that point, and kindergarten was set to begin the following Tuesday.

On Thursday morning, I finally was able to get the General Counsel for the insurance company on the phone. I described the situation and how unseemly it was that this child should be starting school in a few days without the leg brace that the insurance company would approve under any other circumstance. Wasn't there anything he could do?

It turned out there was a procedure for overriding the decision on coverage without going through the normal appeals process. He just wasn't going to do it.

"Why?" I asked.

He said something along the lines of: "Because I don't think it's warranted in this situation." I can't remember exactly, because at this point, I was getting pretty angry.

We argued back and forth a while longer, and then—just before hanging up—I pulled my trump card. I said, "Well let me tell you this: That child is going to start kindergarten on Tuesday, and he's going to be accompanied by a new leg brace or a television crew." I hung up.

John's mother called me again on Friday morning—this time to let me know that the insurance company had reconsidered her claim, approved it, and that the leg brace would be delivered later that afternoon.

This is the power of litigation PR.

Interestingly, I was watching *60 Minutes* recently and saw a similar scenario play out in a segment on experimental brain tumor treatment pioneered by Duke University doctor Henry Friedman. The insurance company refused to cover the experimental treatment— and did so, unfortunately for them, with Ed Bradley of *60 Minutes* in the room:

> BRADLEY: [Voiceover] Thirteen-year-old Daniel Glancey has a fast-growing brain tumor, and Dr. Friedman believes that experimental therapy is the only chance he has to survive. So Dr. Friedman calls the family's insurance companies and threatens them with negative media exposure if they don't give in.

FRIEDMAN: [On telephone] Everybody has to understand what you're saying, basically, means you won't treat cancer—treatable cancer on your policies. I think this is something that people who purchase insurance from your group really must be aware of.

UNIDENTIFIED MAN: [On telephone] We're not going to participate in an argument through the press.

FRIEDMAN: [On telephone] Well, belatedly, I'll tell you that you're already involved with the press as we speak.

[Later that day] The question was posed, and I posed it: "Who would like to receive the call from Mr. Ed Bradley to discuss this for a forthcoming segment of *60 Minutes*?" I don't think they liked you, because they didn't want to talk to you. But yet that night, they called back and said it's been approved.

BRADLEY: You enjoy this, don't you?

FRIEDMAN: I enjoy helping my patients. I'm not afraid to mix it up with anybody to help my patients. I won't break federal or state laws. I'm not about to commit a crime. But I believe that showing people the right way to do things and the consequences to their business of not doing the right things is very appropriate. Yeah, I enjoy this.[1]

MEDIA'S INFLUENCE ON THE COURSE OF LEGAL DISPUTES

These examples are not earth-shattering cases, not cases with the national or worldwide ramifications of a Microsoft antitrust case or Ronald Perelman divorce. But they highlight the enormous power of the media to influence the course of legal disputes—and how effective that power can be if attorneys and clients know exactly which buttons to push.

These examples also illustrate why communicating during litigation is not all press conferences on the courthouse steps and end-of-day summaries of court proceedings on *Nightline*. The simple fact is this: Most cases settle. According to R. Lawrence Dessem in his book *Pretrial Litigation: Law, Policy & Practice*, less than 10 percent of lawsuits filed in this country ever see the inside of a courtroom.[2] That's not counting the untold millions of *administrative* *cases* (cases that are not in a courtroom but before an administrative body such as the Social Security Administration) and *regulatory investigations* (where government regulators—such as those that deal with Medicare fraud among doctors—begin investigating a client in anticipation of litigation). Not to mention the many cases that are settled before a formal action is even filed. Clearly, the bulk of the legal activity in this country goes on *outside* the courtroom, long before a lawsuit ever goes to trial—and the overwhelming majority of communications counseling in litigation occurs outside the courtroom as well.*

Thus, litigation PR more often than not involves managing the communications aspects of litigation well before a case is ever adjudicated. And while its impact can be enormous, admittedly, sometimes there's precious little you can do. Several years ago, for example, we were approached by a major national restaurant chain that was being threatened with a lawsuit by several employees for racial discrimination. Leading the plaintiffs in the case was the popular pastor of a major Southern church. The client had clearly done some things wrong, so we worked with them to admit publicly that mistakes had been made, that the company was doing its best to resolve the issues, but that they would not allow themselves to be the victim of frivolous lawsuits. They were able to settle the matter quickly and amicably, and their reputation survived relatively intact.

About a year later, they called again. There was another case about to be filed on similar racial discrimination grounds in another Southern city. The case itself was highly questionable, but in reviewing the new facts, it became clear that the company's message of change hadn't been entirely sincere. Little had been done to rectify some of the real problems with the company's behavior. The language that accompanied the prior settlement seemed nothing more than "lip-service," designed to put the episode behind them so that they could get back to business as usual.

---

*Some other statistics, also from Professor Dessem's book: For the 12 months ending June 30, 2000, only 2.3 percent of civil actions in U.S. federal court ever made it to trial. Moreover, a 1991 study of 2,000 contract and tort cases in federal and state courts showed that all but 2.9 percent of contract cases and 3.7 percent of tort cases were settled before trial.

What is the best way, we were asked, to resolve the matter without creating a media firestorm that would quickly spread nationally and damage the restaurant's reputation forever?

My answer was this: Get the correct spelling of the plaintiff's name for the check.

Sometimes the best solution for a company, from a reputation standpoint, is to settle the matter quickly and quietly well before it ever reaches the courthouse *or* the media. Particularly when it becomes obvious that, from a public opinion standpoint, the case is a sure-fire loser.

BIRTH OF A NEW DISCIPLINE

I want an article as soon as possible in the *Globe*—"St. Cat's, neighborhood giant, serving the community, etcetera"—they've got it in the files. And I want something in the *Herald* Monday morning—"Our gallant doctors . . ." eh? Be inventive!

And television . . . we've got to have television. Friedman, since you're still with us, why don't you have a word with, ah your friend at GBH, hmmm?

　　　　　　　　—James Mason in the 1982 movie *The Verdict,* playing an
　　　　　　　　unscrupulous defense lawyer fending off a medical
　　　　malpractice lawsuit against a prestigious Boston hospital.

Ah, if only life were this easy—I could take more vacations.

Obviously, this is not the way things work, and in an otherwise wonderful movie you get a bit of a skewed perspective of how easy it is to influence the media in the course of a lawsuit—in this mythical case, a personal injury suit by a brain-damaged former patient of the venerable old-line hospital St. Catherine's. But even if James Mason is your lawyer, things are never that easy—not in 1982, and certainly not now.

What is interesting about the quote is this: It is no coincidence that this quote was from a movie made in the early 1980s. It was just about that time that public relations techniques first started being used in major litigation, and many of the techniques that are now considered *de rigueur* were just then in the process of being born.

Think about that for a moment. Twenty years. That's how new communications in the legal context actually is, while the law itself dates back at least to the time of Hammurabi. Thus, among most business executives, lawyers—and even public relations professionals themselves—there's only the vaguest notion of how the process of using communications works, how it fits into the overall practice of law, and what parties are really trying to achieve when they use public relations techniques to manage the course of litigation. It is too new a practice to have been subject to much critical scrutiny thus far. It's true, of course, that the media has always covered certain court cases, and parties have always attempted to influence public opinion during lawsuits—informally for the most part. But as a formalized discipline, litigation communications is still in its infancy—and most observers believe it had its birth with the famous libel lawsuit of the early 1980s by William Westmoreland against CBS News. And its father, most agree, was the Runyonesque, sometimes scurrilous public relations man John Scanlon.

I got to know Scanlon a bit before his death in 2001—but then again, everyone in New York, it seemed, knew him to one extent or another. We had been on opposite sides in a few battles. Like myself, he was the son of Irish immigrants who started out his career working on economic development projects for the City of New York. Perhaps that's the basis of my grudging admiration for Scanlon, despite the sometimes nasty nature of the clients he represented and ethical byways he chose.

Named by *PR Week* magazine as one of the most influential public relations professionals of the twentieth century, Scanlon was a remarkable figure in many respects—not the least of which was the way the media loved him. I mean they *loved* him. So much so that Pete Hamill wrote a full column in New York's *Daily News* after Scanlon's death entitled "No Sad Songs for Scanlon: Our 35-Year Friendship Lasted Through Thick and Thin." The story detailed his friendships with leading media figures like Peter Jennings, his ability to quote Yeats and Shakespeare, his tendency to launch into an Irish ballad on a whim. "In his presence," Hamill wrote, "I always felt as if I were talking to one of those Irishmen from New York's nineteenth century. Many were rogues, absolutely capable of ruthlessness, driven by a belief that after decades of hunger and bigotry, their time had come. They rose out of the squalor of the Five Points and built Tammany Hall and their own fortunes and the modern City of New York. I can hear Scanlon, at his table in Delmonico's, trying to convince me that Boss Tweed was framed (he was) or that Jim Fisk and Jay Gould were innocent (they weren't). Life is tragedy, says the Irish fatalist, so pass the butter."[3]

Again, this was the ethical divide that puzzled many who knew Scanlon and admired his work. He could represent anyone, and over the years, he did: at various times, Corazon Aquino, Monica Lewinsky, Bruce Ritter (the famed priest and founder of Covenant House, who was accused of having sexual relations with some of the runaways he took in), Jesse Jackson, Ronald Perelman, Bob Kerrey. All in highly contentious legal matters that thrust his clients into the public spotlight. In the process, a new practice of public relations was born.

It began with the case of *William Westmoreland v. CBS,* a real barn-burner of a lawsuit over one of the most controversial U.S. activities of the past half-century: Vietnam.

Westmoreland: A Media Case Launches a New Media Strategy

The gist of the Westmoreland libel trial against CBS News was as follows: CBS had broadcast a segment by Mike Wallace on its *60 Minutes* program that alleged that Westmoreland, while in charge of U.S. forces in Vietnam, knowingly exaggerated enemy casualty figures to convince the Johnson administration—and the American public—that we were winning the war. Westmoreland sued CBS, charging that he had been libeled by the report, and a media circus seldom seen in noncriminal court cases ensued. Every step of the way, from shortly after the filing of the complaint until the case actually reached the courthouse, there was John Scanlon, cleverly working to manage the coverage of the case on CBS's behalf.

How new was what Scanlon was doing? Consider the wonder with which his performance was documented at the time of the Westmoreland trial—not by any public relations trade publication, but instead by the venerable *New York Times:*

Public Relations a Facet of Westmoreland Trial

(October 23, 1984)—Almost every day, a 49-year-old barrel-shaped man with a ruddy face and a gray curly beard shows up in the courtroom where General William C. Westmoreland is suing CBS for libel. He sits with the press. He knows each reporter by first name. He laughs with them, and when the day's session is over he is very often standing outside the courtroom handing out documents.

Sometimes the documents are the evidence that had been discussed in court that day and sometimes they are materials that have *not* been used in court, but relate to the day's evidence. The man, John Scanlon, is not a member of the press, and he is not a lawyer. He is on CBS's side, but he is not a CBS employee: He is new scenery on the landscape of legal procedure. He represents one of two public relations companies working for the opposing sides, and while the legal battle is being fought according to the principles of law, Mr. Scanlon and General Westmoreland's representative, David Henderson of Washington, are fighting with the uncodified art of public relations.

The presence of two public relations companies at this trial has raised questions: Should the opposing sides in a trial be seeking the outside world's approval when the ostensible goal of litigation is to attain justice inside the courtroom? And what is the propriety of the press possibly taking its cues from a paid information officer during a trial?

When the press needs transcripts of the day's testimony, Mr. Scanlon, a senior executive vice president of the Chicago-based public relations company Daniel J. Edelman Inc., provides them. When the press asks for documentary evidence submitted from either side, he, or an associate, James Noonan, checks with the CBS attorneys and does his best to produce it. Reporters turn to him for material, and he gives it to them, along with a passionate discourse about the trial. Sometimes when he thinks they have described CBS's case clearly, he congratulates them the next day.

"It's pretty unusual," said Professor Arthur R. Miller of the Harvard Law School. "I've noticed other instances of it in the last couple of years. You sort of get the feeling that you want to get your point across in the newspapers, or the broadcast media. When you're dealing with the integrity of a broadcast organization, you want to get CBS's message out so there's no ripple effect in the public—that unless you get your side of the story communicated, people lose their faith in CBS News.

"For the Westmoreland side, there may be a feeling that there's a certain symbiotic relationship between the media and CBS."

"Both sides," said Professor Geoffrey Hazard of the Yale Law School, "are seeking a public opinion verdict as well as a jury verdict."

Neither professor found anything wrong or improper in the presence of public relations men at the trial.

Source: Peter W. Kaplan, *New York Times,* October 23, 1984.

The first thing you'll notice about this article is how far we've come in such a short time (or, perhaps, traditionalists in the legal community might say, how far we've fallen). As you'll see throughout this book, in most major pieces of litigation today—and certainly in those of the high-profile variety—it is expected that both sides will have spokespeople reaching out to the media on a daily basis. Indeed, a party to a lawsuit that attracts media attention might be considered remiss if they did not have a point of contact for the case.

Of course, it's important to note that the Westmoreland case is atypical in certain respects—including the fact that it actually went to trial, which, as we've already noted, is a rare occurrence in the American legal system. But a closer look at the *Times* description of Scanlon's work reveals that, even in 1984, he was using many of the tactics that have become the basis of the practice of influencing the media during court cases, many of which we'll discuss through the course of this book. Consider:

- "He sits with the press. He knows each reporter by first name. He laughs with them, and when the day's session is over he is very often standing outside the courtroom handing out documents." Scanlon is working here to develop the type of relationship with the media that will establish credibility, and therefore make reporters more predisposed to his client's point of view.
- "When the press needs transcripts of the day's testimony, Mr. Scanlon . . . provides them." Scanlon is working to make the media's job easier—and showing a willingness to work

with the media to get reporters the kind of information they need to cover the story.

- "Sometimes the documents are the evidence that had been discussed in court that day and sometimes they are materials that have not been used in court, but relate to the day's evidence." Scanlon is choosing his message carefully, and working to adapt that message to the events of the day in a way that brings reporters, however subtly, back to the "theme" that CBS is looking to advance.

In the Westmoreland libel trial, Scanlon's tactics seemed to work. Just at the height of the contentious court proceedings, the case was settled, in a manner highly positive for Scanlon's client, CBS—and of high interest in our discussions:

> General William C. Westmoreland dropped his $120 million libel suit against CBS last night, the network announced.
> Under the terms of the settlement, CBS will not disavow the 1982 documentary on the Vietnam War that is the basis of the suit, and will not pay any money to General Westmoreland.
> The parties, according to legal sources on both sides of the case, will issue a joint statement today saying *they now agree that the court of public opinion, rather than a court of law, is the appropriate forum for deciding who was right in the case* [emphasis added].[4]

In this case, not only was the media used decisively by CBS in fending off General Westmoreland's advances, it was ultimately decided that the public arena was where the case should be decided. The use of public relations techniques in litigation had arrived.

A sad postscript to the Scanlon story is that John was also involved in one of the biggest litigation communications blunders of the past 20 years—The Brown & Williamson/Jeffrey Wigand imbroglio that served as the basis for the movie *The Insider*, starring Al Pacino and Russell Crowe (and Rip Torn in a small role as John Scanlon).

In the Wigand case, former Brown & Williamson employee Jeffrey Wigand had gone public and with certain allegations about the tobacco giant and its research. In response, the Brown

& Williamson team did a background investigation of Wigand and produced a report titled "The Misconduct of Jeffrey S. Wigand Available on the Public Record." The report was compiled by a private investigative firm, Investigative Group Inc., whose New York office was headed at the time by Raymond Kelly, now New York City's police commissioner (in an odd coincidence, in 2002, Kelly's boss, New York City Mayor Michael Bloomberg, publicly embraced Jeffrey Wigand at a hearing related to Bloomberg's proposed anti-smoking regulations. Small world!)

The fact of the matter is that this type of investigation goes on all the time in litigation. It is as routine to see what dirt exists on a plaintiff in litigation as it is in a political campaign. But if you handle the dissemination of such information in a reckless or ham-fisted manner—or if your information is misleading or factually inaccurate—such research can blow up in your face. And that's exactly what happened in the Wigand/Brown & Williamson mess.

Someone—maybe Scanlon, maybe the lawyers—decided to supply the entire investigative report to the *Wall Street Journal*. The entire thing, without winnowing the good facts from the bad, without removing the irrelevant claims and unproven allegations—without even a good editing job, as I understand it. The report included such subheadings as "Wigand's Lies about His Residence," "Wigand's Lies under Oath," and "Other Lies by Wigand." But many of the allegations were unproven, others were so small and strange as to seem silly. As revealed in a comprehensive article on the case in *Vanity Fair*, the report detailed, for example, that "On November 10, 1991, Wigand wrote to Coastal Cutlery Company and returned an allegedly damaged knife for repair," and "On March 18, 1992, Wigand wrote Coach for Business requesting credit to his American Express card for two returned items."[5] There were more serious allegations as well, but the effect of leaking all of this information created a public relations firestorm—with John Scanlon firmly at its center. The *Wall Street Journal* published a highly skeptical account of the report under the headline "Getting Personal: Brown & Williamson Has 500-Page Dossier Attacking Chief Critic";[6] and, in a bizarre coincidence, a *60 Minutes* news crew chased John Scanlon down a snowy Manhattan street for a story they were doing on the investigation and its aftermath—the same *60 Minutes* Scanlon had so skillfully defended years before.*

Rather than discrediting Mr. Wigand and his assertions, Brown & Williamson wound up doing exactly the opposite, feeding every conspiratorial notion about big tobacco companies as Soviet-style monoliths, complete with secret police and a ministry of propaganda. It was a stunning public relations disaster, and while it doesn't take away from Scanlon's reputation as the father of litigation communications, it certainly shows that toward the end of his career, he might have been forgetting many of the very lessons he put forth in cases like *William Westmoreland v. CBS,* when the practice of litigation communications was being born.

LITIGATION IS NOT JUST ANOTHER PR ASSIGNMENT

In my surlier moments, I curse the perception of public relations, the training offered at many schools (and, indeed, on the job at many PR firms), and the general public's sense of what works and what doesn't, especially in the litigation context. I roam the halls of my office, decrying (to anyone who will listen) the perils of thinking that all public relations is handled in the following manner:

1. Write the press release.
2. Prepare the media list.
3. Send the press release to the media.
4. Repeat steps one through three.

This is the "lather, rinse, repeat" method of public relations. Unfortunately, unless you're publicizing a simple product like shampoo, it usually doesn't work. In fact, it often does more harm than good by sending the wrong message to the wrong audience at

---

*There was, of course, another big issue in the Brown & Williamson saga: *60 Minutes* initially killing its own interview with Jeffrey Wigand under a threatened lawsuit from Brown & Williamson—events at the center of *The Insider,* but less germane to our discussion here.

the wrong time. Then everyone sits around and tries to blame everyone else for why they didn't get the particular story they wanted.

Why don't these tactics work? They fail primarily because they reinforce the perception that public relations is "mindless" work, that it is just about "connections" and the logistics of getting information "out there," a sense that with the proper writing skills, the right list of media, and an operable fax machine, anyone can do the job. This can be a particular mindset of attorneys, by the way, who seem at times to believe they could do everything themselves—if only they had the time.

I usually tell clients this: It may look easy, but Willie Mays made centerfield look easy, too. There's a huge difference between doing this job and doing it well. (Being a lawyer myself, another thing I often say to lawyers is: "And I could try your next case, couldn't I?" They tend to cringe at the suggestion, thus further driving home my point.)

This premise is particularly important when dealing with communication in litigation—because the stakes are so high, the issues so complex, and because, in my estimation, litigation PR is unlike any other kind of public relations out there.

Invariably, lawyers and their clients come to my firm with the following preconceived notions about the procedure for promoting their case:

- If you want to announce something important, write a *press release.*
- If you want to make an even bigger impression, hold a *press conference.*
- The best way to get a story in the media is to speak to *a reporter you know.*
- Litigation is just like any other *crisis*—you need to get out all the information you can, as quickly as you can, to the widest possible target audience.

Moreover, it is *exactly* because these methods are so procedural that lawyers fall prey to thinking that this is how you handle public relations in the litigation context. Litigators eat, sleep, and drink procedure: Rules of Civil Procedure, Rules of Evidence, local court rules. When they need to know *how* to do something, they go to the library and find the proper procedural guide. It is natural, therefore, that they translate this thinking to communications in legal actions, and fall prey to thinking the tactics listed above are the procedural rules of the game.

The last point, by the way, regarding crisis communications may be the most important one. Therefore, I feel it's important to spend a little time discussing how litigation differs from traditional crisis communications.

LITIGATION PUBLIC RELATIONS VERSUS CRISIS COMMUNICATIONS

Think crisis: the Coca Cola recall in Europe; the syringe-in-the-Pepsi-can incident; the Union Carbide explosion in Bhopal, India; and the seminal case in the field—the cynanide in the Tylenol incident. These are all classic examples from the discipline known as *crisis communications*. Crisis communications is a high-pressure, high-stakes specialty in public relations, a specialty that many firms excel at. But it is often confused with communication during litigation, and that confusion can cause unintended—even disastrous—consequences.

How does communication during a lawsuit differ from crisis communications? At its essence, crisis communication is about *immediate* response—response that allows a client, usually a corporation, to limit the damage from a story about an incident or event that will affect the reputation of the client. Some of the major elements of effective crisis communications include the following:

- Having a crisis plan and a crisis team in place well before a crisis ever occurs. This is called *crisis communications planning,* it is an activity many corporations have undertaken in recent years to prepare for the sudden, immediate crisis that can damage their company forever.
- Alerting the crisis team at the earliest possible moment, so that the crisis plan can be put into effect at the outset of the event.

- Securing the site or crisis location (if there is one) to limit access and prevent unwanted leaks or other dissemination of information.

- Assembling all the facts, to ensure that accurate information is flowing to the media.

- Having a spokesperson ready to communicate to the media—the higher up in the organization the better (and in the best-case scenario, never, never, never the company's lawyer or PR representative).

Virtually all of this activity happens within the first 24 to 48 hours after a crisis has occurred. Companies and consultants skilled at crisis communications are usually ready to respond to any crisis, anywhere, at a moment's notice.

While all of this *may* be necessary when the crisis in question is a lawsuit, litigation PR is much more than this—and strict reliance on classic crisis communications techniques can at times do more harm than good.

Why is communications during litigation so different? Consider the following:

- *Litigation unfolds over weeks and months (and sometimes years), not days.* Therefore, the 24- to 48-hour crisis response model usually doesn't work. As we'll see throughout this book, communications during the litigation process needs to follow the ebb and flow of the litigation itself. This requires a constant exertion of pressure—building relationships, telling a party's story, explaining complex legal ideas and maneuverings, building trust with your target audiences (including media, regulators, and the public at-large). Absent this foundation, other efforts tend to crumble. Wise lawyers, clients, and communications consultants need to know when and how to apply the pressure—and how to cut through any interference to focus on activity that will help the client prevail in the long run.

- *Litigation is less event-driven than traditional crisis communications.* More often that not, the big event—the rally, the press conference, the petition drive—is less effective here, where the story is stretched out over months, if not years. Usually, an event strategy falls flat on its face with the media, who see it as a less-than-subtle attempt to influence the outcome of litigation. The one time that I can think of where an event strategy worked was in the Hooter's EEOC case several years back, where they dressed up a big, hairy guy in a Hooter's outfit at a press conference to show the absurdity of an EEOC suit alleging men were being discriminated against for waitress positions. It worked. But how often in lawsuits do you get the opportunity to dress up a big, hairy guy like a woman?

- *In litigation, the issues involved are usually considerably more complex.* I like to tell clients—especially lawyers—that even the most complex issue can be summed up in the proverbial 10 words or less. But I am being a bit facetious, because unlike other areas of public relations—including most forms of crisis communications—litigation often revolves around issues that are stupefying in their complexity. As we'll see, even the best reporters only "skim the cream off the top" of any issue. Distilling the complexities of a particular court case into a format reporters can easily digest is an art form most communications counselors don't routinely have to master.

- *In litigation, the client may not be the most appropriate spokesperson.* This flies in the face of one of the central tenets of crisis communications, but it's true. Sometimes positioning the client— whether it be a CEO, an organization head, or a high-profile individual—as spokesperson for the case is inappropriate and even damaging. In fact, litigation PR is one of the few areas where you can hand off the spokesperson's role to one of the attorneys on the case without fear of repercussions. These are, after all, legal issues we are dealing with. The press and the public want to hear from the real "experts" on the case— in this case, the litigators handling the matter (assuming they are well-trained in media response—a matter that we'll get to in subsequent chapters).

These are just some of the differences. Thus, classic PR techniques—even crisis communications techniques—can fall far short of what is needed to properly do the job in litigation PR. A widely disseminated press release, a press conference, or a rally of supporters may be far less useful than the highly targeted story that reaches the *right* audience with the *right* message.

Here's a perfect example of how the "issue-the-press-release" approach can sometimes backfire, from an intellectual property case between two pre-IPO dot-coms. The plaintiff in the case requested a continuance for additional discovery—in layman's terms, another week to collect relevant documents. The judge granted the continuance, a routine event in any litigation. This is where the fun began.

The plaintiff, used to issuing laudatory press releases for every milestone—a new round of financing, new product, new advisory board member—issued a press release with a headline along the lines of the following: "Judge Rules in Plaintiff's Favor in Intellectual Property Case." The press release described in considerable detail the plaintiff's "victory" and what a positive sign it was for the future of the company. It went out over one of the business wires, reaching media, analysts, and all sorts of financial-types. This was standard operating procedure at the time for dot-coms and their public relations firms looking to create the kind of buzz that attracted interest, and investors, to their company.

But in the lawsuit, the results were disastrous. The defendant in the case (with our help, of course) launched a publicity attack of its own—more sophisticated and, ultimately, more successful. Furthermore, the plaintiff lost credibility with the legal media who knew just how routine a continuance is in major litigation. And—perhaps most importantly—the judge in the case was not amused, and this was reflected in his future rulings on the case.

This is an extreme example, but it highlights the important differences between public relations in litigation and public relations in other contexts. Not every piece of information needs to be broadcast to the widest possible audience. And not every legal ruling in your favor is a "victory."

UNFEATHERING RUDY'S LOVE NEST

Finally, one more example of why the press release/press conference approach can be less than effective in certain situations. It is a good example, because it was not a long, drawn-out dispute with myriad twists and turns (like many of the cases in this book), but instead involved an intense *day* of activity where we were able to use the threat of imminent litigation to achieve the client's desired result. It is also an example I love to use not just because of the high-profile story or the good result, but because there were probably a dozen ways we could have overplayed our hand and blown the resulting coverage.

One of the top legal stories in New York in late 2000 and early 2001 was New York City Mayor Rudy Giuliani's rather acrimonious divorce proceedings against his wife, television personality Donna Hanover. This was a battle primarily waged in the months preceding Giuliani's dramatic and inspiring efforts in the aftermath of September 11, back before the heroism that earned him *Time* magazine's Man of the Year honors (deservedly, I believe), back when he was just Rudy!—the controversial lame-duck mayor and cancer survivor with an in-your-face style and a very tangled private life.

I won't go over all of the sordid details of the Giuliani divorce saga and its tabloid headlines, but suffice to say this was *the* New York City tabloid story of early 2001. Our part of the case dealt with only one aspect of the Giuliani/Hanover divorce: the infamous *New York Post* "Rudy's Love Nest" story:

The original story appeared on the front page of the *New York Post* on Tuesday, June 5, 2001, under a *Post* front-page banner headline "Rudy's Love Nest":

RUDY AND JUDY "INN" LOVE—POSH ST. REGIS HOTEL IS THEIR SECRET HIDEAWAY

Mayor Giuliani and his "good friend" Judi Nathan have a romantic hideaway at one of the city's priciest hotels, the *Post* has learned.

Although the city's spurned first lady, Donna Hanover, convinced a court last month to keep the "other woman" from Gracie Mansion, nothing is standing in the way of the sweethearts staying at a suite at the posh St. Regis hotel, sources said.

One source said the mayor and his girlfriend spent several nights at the hotel, on East 55th Street off Fifth Avenue, last week. The source said the pair also shared a room or suite there on previous occasions—including on New Year's Eve.

A room at the St. Regis can go for anywhere from $590 to $750 a night. A normal suite rents for $1,100 a night. The Presidential Suite rents for up to $11,000 a night. It's not clear what kind of deal Giuliani and Nathan made for a mayoral suite.

Another source said when Giuliani and Nathan stay at the hotel, they usually keep a low profile and rarely come out of their room.

A butler is sent up to deliver fresh flowers and fruit, this source says.

Giuliani usually has the hotel press his suits, and the couple always has coffee delivered with their early-morning wake-up calls.

A spokesman for the mayor could not be reached for comment.

Source: Larry Celona, David Seifman, Paula Freelich, and Cathy Burke, *New York Post,* June 5, 2001, page 1.

Now as it turns out, the story was dead wrong. Giuliani had indeed been in the hotel—for meetings and receptions and the like. His aides had booked a room for him to use to make phone calls, which is standard procedure for politicians at public events. But he never spent the night. The "Love Nest" angle was apparently hatched by some enterprising account executives at a New York public relations firm. They were looking for ways to get their client, the St. Regis Hotel, in the news. They found it!

Giuliani immediately threatened to sue for defamation, but the next day, the *Post* was back on the story again:

SUITE-HEARTS, INDEED!
SOURCES BACK *POST* DESPITE RUDY DENIAL

They were there!

Five sources confirmed to the *Post* yesterday Mayor Giuliani and gal pal Judith Nathan have stayed together at the St. Regis Hotel within the past 10 days—despite the mayor's angry denial.

Giuliani disputed a *Post* report that the couple has been spending nights at the swank hotel. "It is entirely and categorically untrue," the mayor said at a news conference in Washington Heights.

"I think the *New York Post* is shameless in what they did . . . And I can prove [the story is untrue] in court if I have to, not just beyond a doubt, but beyond any doubt."

The mayor's lawyer Kenneth Caruso demanded a retraction and apology.

Source: Larry Celona, Kirsten Davis, Daneh Gregorian, John Lehmann, and Cathy Burke, *New York Post,* June 6, 2001, page 3.

On Thursday morning of that same week, my partner in Washington, Jeffrey Sandman, received a call from Bart Schwartz, president of Decision Strategies/Fairfax International, one of the largest private investigative firms in the world. Jeff's firm, Hyde Park Communications, is one of the fastest growing independent public relations/public affairs firms in Washington, and Jeff is considered one of the best strategic minds in the field. But equally important for my purposes is the fact that Jeff is an attorney who practiced at such stellar firms as Loeb & Loeb in Los Angeles and Baker & Hostetler in Washington, DC. Moreover, over the years, he had been involved in a communications capacity in some of the most high-profile cases in history, including breast implant litigation, asbestos class actions, and the historic tobacco litigation of the late 1990s. Given this background and experience, our firms formed a true partnership—most of the time we work together as if we were one and the same.

Bart Schwartz and Rudolph Giuliani are old friends—Schwartz was one of Giuliani's top aides when Giuliani was a crusading U.S. attorney in the 1980s. Decision Strategies had been retained to investigate the *New York Post* report, and Bart had already begun working on the case. He and Giuliani's private attorney, Kenneth Caruso, visited hotel officials the day before to interview them about the story and its origin. Rumors of these visits to the hotel by "detectives" were already making the rounds, there was concern that the tabloids might come to the conclusion that Rudy was using New York Police Department detectives to investigate, or even intimidate, employees at the hotel.

Bart wanted to know if we could publicize his investigation so that (1) after seeing the seriousness of Giuliani's intent to sue for libel, the public would be convinced the "Love Nest" story was false; (2) the *New York Post* would realize just how wrong they were and drop any further coverage of the story; and (3) any rumors of detectives visiting the hotel—who they were and why they were there—would be effectively squashed before they did further damage to the mayor.

Our answer was a guarded "yes," but we would have to work quickly—it was already 10 A.M., and if we wanted to get something going for the next day's paper, we'd have to get things rolling right away.

A press conference was initially considered, but given the sensitive nature of the case, we ruled it out, along with any sort of a press release, for fear that the potential defamation suit would be drawn into all the other sensational aspects of the case.

There's another reason why we ultimately decided not to pursue a press conference—or even write a press release for that matter—and it dealt with the probable defendant in this part of the case: the *New York Post*. Who would want to really stick it to the *Post?* Why the *Daily News,* of course.

As most people know, the *Daily News* is the *Post*'s vicious rival, and each paper loves beating the other to the exclusive—and beating the other up when they get the story wrong. We reasoned that we could likely get as much coverage through a well-placed exclusive with the *Daily News* as we could get with any news release or press conference.

So working with Jeff Sandman and my colleague, Liz Hall, here's what we did:

1. We reviewed all prior *Daily News* articles related to the Giuliani divorce and determined that Mike Blood, City Hall editor for the *News,* was the reporter to go after.

2. I called Mike Blood and left a voicemail saying that I had some important information regarding the "Love Nest" story that we'd like to give exclusively to the *News*.

3. An hour later I called back and left another voicemail saying, provocatively: "You may have heard rumors of visits to the hotel by two detectives. I have some information about the rumors that we can give exclusively to the *News*."

4. Mike Blood called back about 20 minutes later, a little confused but interested in what we had. I briefed him on Decision Strategies' retention by Giuliani's lawyer—leading off with the fact that it was Giuliani's lawyer and Bart Schwartz,

not two NYPD detectives, who had visited the hotel executives the day before.

5. We emphasized that we were giving this to the *News* exclusively. I must have also said the following five times: (a) that
this is another indication as to how false the "Love Nest"
story was, (b) that Giuliani was investigating the story because he intended to sue for defamation, and (c) that Bart
was one of New York's preeminent private investigators and
Decision Strategies one of the largest investigative firms in
the world. We then offered to set him up on the phone with
Bart Schwartz, again with the caveat that Bart would—initially, at least—be speaking to him for "background" purposes only.

6. We tracked Bart down about an hour and a half later, then
contacted the reporter on his cellphone, and set up the
call for about an hour after that, or around 3 P.M. In the
meantime, I told the reporter I would send over a biography
of Bart for his use.

It took a lot of hustle to put the story together, but the results
were better than we could have expected. The news of Decision
Strategies' investigation made the front page of the first edition of
the *Daily News,* under the full-page, banner headline "Hide and
Seek." The resulting story was a complete victory for Giuliani and
his assertion that the *New York Post* "Love Nest" story was false and
probably libelous:

RUDY PROBING HOTEL STORY:
HIRES INVESTIGATORS TO FIND SOURCE OF
ST. REGIS "LOVE NEST" TALE

Mayor Giuliani has unleashed private investigators—including one
of his top guns from his days as a U.S. attorney—to probe a report
that he and girlfriend Judith Nathan overnighted at the St. Regis
Hotel several times last week.

Executives of Starwood Hotels & Resorts Worldwide, which
owns the St. Regis, were grilled Wednesday in Manhattan by investigators from Decision Strategies, a company headed by Bart

Schwartz, who was Giuliani's criminal division chief when the mayor was Manhattan U.S. attorney.

"Our goal here is to figure out how this false story was concocted and disseminated," Schwartz said. The broadening investigation follows Giuliani's threat to slap a libel lawsuit on the *New York Post,* which reported Tuesday that the mayor and Nathan used the luxury hotel as a "love nest," where they "spent several nights . . . last week."

Decision Strategies, one of the world's largest investigation and security firms, was hired by Giuliani lawyer Kenneth Caruso.

"We are investigating the facts," Caruso said. "You talk to people, you look at documents."

This isn't the first time Schwartz has helped Giuliani deal with a crisis.

Earlier in his career, Schwartz served as chief of the public integrity section of the U.S. attorney's office; last year, Giuliani chose him to head a city task force on the long-troubled Buildings Department.

Source: Michael Blood, *New York Daily News,* L.P., June 7, 2001, page 3.

It was the story of the day, the lead on local radio and the local all-news cable channel, New York 1, every half-hour or so. It was also picked up by the Associated Press, *Newsday,* several New Jersey newspapers—and even some national news outlets like the *National Journal's Hotline.*

The most important result was this: After that day, the "Love Nest" story disappeared from the pages of the *New York Post.* Coincidentally, on the very same day, the *Post* also fired a slew of its reporters and editors in a housecleaning the likes of which New York City newspapers had rarely seen over the years. The stated reason was that the paper's new publisher, Australian Col Allan, wanted to start fresh. I would never suggest that the two events were somehow related. Still the timing does seem curious . . .

News Is News?

This is an important example because there is a habit in the public relations business of thinking that a particular event either is a story, or it isn't. That in addition to getting the information out there, there isn't much we can do to influence whether a story is written, or how big the story will be. "We lead them to water," the saying goes, "it's up to them to drink."

As I will emphasize throughout this book, particularly in regard to legal cases, nothing could be further from the truth. The investigation into the "Rudy's Love Nest" case was not the biggest news in the world—particularly considering all the other stories surrounding Giuliani's rather strange and scandalous divorce proceedings. It was reported on that very same day, for example, that Giuliani's girlfriend, Judy Nathan, was ducking process servers at a Manhattan restaurant—in a story headlined "Court Papers Await Judy, Who's in Dodge City" (hence the front page headline "Hide and Seek"). The article, which was directly below our article on the "Love Nest" story, started off like this:

> Where's Judy?
> Mayor Giuliani's girlfriend, Judy Nathan, is playing a cat-and-mouse game with her ex-husband's private investigators, who are trying to serve her with court papers . . .

As an aside, why parties ever think it's wise from a public opinion standpoint to duck service of court papers is beyond me. But we weren't working that aspect of the case. My point is this: This single story alone had the ability to knock us off the front page, to bury our message deep within another story as part of a routine round-up of the day's events in this sensational case. I can imagine where the story might have wound up, deep in the text of an article regarding Ms. Nathan ducking service, a little tidbit something like this: "Giuliani's forces also announced today that they hired private investigators . . ." And that would be it. Our story would have withered and died on the vine, and the "Rudy's Love Nest" tale probably would have gone on in the pages of the *New York Post* for another week or more.

In other words, it only became a story because we *exactly* followed the procedures outlined earlier. We could have blown the story in any of the following ways:

- We could have written a press release, prepared a media list, sent it out to the relevant media—all of the "lather, rinse, repeat" methods described earlier.
- We could have taken hours to formulate the message, or wait to bring together the entire crisis team—thus blowing our chance to meet the reporter's deadline.
- We could have thought to ourselves "what reporters do we know?" rather than "what reporter is most likely to do the story?"—and wound up going after the wrong person.
- We could have arranged a massive press conference—and then the *Daily News* would not have considered it an exclusive, and the *New York Post* would have had time to respond.
- We could have waited for Mike Blood to eventually get back to us, rather than staying on top of him and "teasing" him with the various elements of the story.
- We could have simply given him the facts—"We want to announce that Mayor Giuliani's lawyer has hired a private investigator, blah, blah, blah . . . . (snore!)"—rather than piquing his interest by offering an exclusive on the rumors about the detectives who visited the hotel the previous day.
- We could have been less aggressive about putting Bart Schwartz on the phone with the reporter to discuss the case in a timely fashion.

Again, lawyers and clients should think about this the next time they think that handling the public relations aspects of a case involves writing a press release, holding a press conference, or figuring out what reporters they "know." And they should immediately dismiss any notion that handling the communications aspects of litigation is "easy."

ACTION POINTS

✓ Litigation PR is not simply press conferences on the courthouse steps, mass-produced and distributed press releases, and late night shoutfests on *Hardball* or other public affairs programs.

✓ The vast majority of lawsuits settle before trial—thus, much of litigation PR takes place well before the case ever makes it to the courthouse.

✓ The media exert an enormous amount of influence over the course of legal disputes—in everything from noteworthy but small-scale cases to the most tabloid-driven slugfests.

✓ Litigation PR differs from virtually any other type of public relations—especially crisis communications, its distant relative.

✓ The "lather, rinse, repeat" tactics that most people associate with public relations—write the press release, create the media list, arrange the press conference—usually don't work effectively when managing a litigation story.

CHAPTER TWO

All Cases Are Public: Why Communication Is Now Essential to Most Legal Disputes

"My case is none of the media's business. Let them draw their own conclusions."

I hear things like this all time. But what's interesting in this case is that I was hearing it from the head of a media company: a publicly traded, New York-based operation that owned a string of radio stations across the country. Even he failed to grasp the impact of the media on his lawsuit—until the negative stories started appearing and his company's stock went down the toilet.

There is no way around this simple fact: In the information age, lawsuits and other legal disputes are fair game for media coverage. This coverage can make or break a case and, ultimately, a business or organization's reputation. In this chapter, we'll examine how plaintiffs and defendants can—and should—use the media to influence the course of litigation. We'll also look at what the media needs, and how to give them what they want. Then we'll take a look at an important tool we have created for summarizing your legal dispute for a media audience: the Media Brief.

Paul Newman thought I should be fired.

A hard thing to do, of course, since I'm the owner of my company. But he was clearly unhappy. You might even say that what we had was a failure to communicate.

Now, I don't routinely work with the famous—at least not on the level of Mr. Newman. But I think this anecdote helps illustrate an important point that runs throughout this book: The difference between what we *want* to give reporters, and what they *need*.

In August 2000, my company was called into the Screen Actors Guild (SAG) strike against the commercial advertising industry, working closely with my partner firm in Washington, Hyde Park Communications (a firm you met in Chapter One), and an affiliate in San Francisco, Staton/Hughes Communications. By this time, the strike was more than five months old, and it was floundering. After an initial media splurge announcing the strike in May 2000, things had quieted down considerably—so much so that I was unaware a strike was still going on. That was precisely the problem.

A labor dispute is a peculiar kind of legal fight, with its own rhythm and "feel," particularly because you've got thousands of "plaintiffs" involved in the dispute—the union members themselves. Moreover, unlike other forms of legal disputes, there's a great history of use (and misuse) of public opinion and media in labor disputes, going back at least as far as the Pennsylvania coal strikes at the turn of the 20th century, where President Theodore Roosevelt famously brought John Mitchell of the United Mine Workers (UMW) and the rather vicious coal tycoon George Baer to the table using only the power of public opinion (since he had no other legal authority to intervene). Thus, the "Bully Pulpit," as it came to be known, was born. Teddy Roosevelt, by the way, also once said: "The first essential in determining how to deal with the great industrial corporation is the facts—publicity,"[1] an endorsement of the techniques of public relations in legal matters if I ever heard one.

So, yes, a labor dispute is somewhat different from the typical piece of litigation, but in many ways, it is the classic legal confrontation, and the communications elements of such a fight are quite similar to other legal actions. The goal is the same: To use the media and other forms of communication to convince your target audiences—including the other side—that the law is on your side, the facts are on your side, and that you're going to win.

Back to Paul Newman. Once we were hired by the Screen Actors, I dispatched a colleague of mine, Fred Winters, to be the man on the scene at strike headquarters and help coordinate the activities of the New York strike leaders. Our first goal was to let the world know that there was, indeed, a strike still going on and that the so-called "high-profile" members of the union (they disliked the term "celebrities") were solidly behind the rank-and-file. As the strike dragged on, a key problem was that, since that first burst of publicity, the high-profile members had all but disappeared. But that was about to change, and the credit belongs in large measure to Paul Newman himself.

Working with strike leaders in New York, Newman arranged for a group of some of the most important actors in the New York area to get together for an evening strategy meeting to discuss ways they might get involved in the strike. The one caveat: No press could attend, for fear of scaring off the high-profile actors.

Fred and I arrived at the meeting and, again, although I'm no stargazer, it was heady stuff. Paul Newman, to his credit, was a key force in getting high-profile SAG members like Tim Robbins, Kevin Bacon, Bebe Neuwirth, Sam Waterston, Ashley and Naomi Judd, Marisa Tomei, Robert Klein, and others excited at the prospect of fighting alongside rank-and-file actors to preserve the "residual" system and other key elements of the way they are paid for appearing in commercials. While I stayed in the background for most of the meeting, at one point, as the crowd was breaking up, Paul Newman, Harry Belafonte, and I became sequestered in a corner as Mr. Newman discussed ways to get the media to cover upcoming meetings between the two sides that were scheduled for early September. Newman even offered to sit in on the negotiating sessions himself. He was filled with energy and ideas, and he impressed me with his enthusiasm and still-sharp intellect. In many ways, he reminded me of my father.

The next day, I confronted the immediate strategic concern: How to let the world know that the meeting had occurred and that the high-profile members were revving up to support the strike and its goals. I quickly drafted a short press release, which Fred Winters then sent to the strike leaders and Mr. Newman for approval. I really had only one goal, however—I wanted the story in the "Boldface Names," section of the *New York Times*. I spoke briefly with James Barron, the editor of the column and let him know we were working on a press announcement, but that he could have the story first if he liked. Perhaps we could even get Paul Newman on the phone to speak with him about it. Needless to say, he was interested.

An hour later, still no press release. It was moot, at this point—we'd given James Barron just about everything he needed to write the piece, and he'd interviewed actor James Naughton—well-known for his work on Broadway and in movies—along with Bebe Neuwirth and Sam Waterston.

Suddenly, Fred burst into my office.

"I have Paul Newman on the line. Can I take it in here?" he asked.

It turns out Mr. Newman didn't like the way I'd written the press release. I could hear him say so right through the phone receiver at Fred's ear.

"Who wrote this?" Mr. Newman asked.

"Jim Haggerty."

"Well, he should be fired," Mr. Newman said.

Now I have no doubt that Paul Newman probably didn't know exactly who I was, and still has no idea, and in no way do I mean to take away from the enormous contributions he made to the striking actors' cause. Moreover, Fred is more than a decade older than I, and it turns out that most of the striking actors thought I worked for him and not the other way around. In any event, Mr. Newman had many, many objections to what I'd written—language, word choice, sentence construction, etcetera, etcetera. It was obvious he was a man used to final script approval, and he felt mine had some major holes in it.

A sample concern: I wrote that the advertisers had refused to negotiate with the union. At another point, I implored the advertisers to deal with the actors fairly when they next sat down at the negotiating table.

"How can it be a negotiating table if the other side is refusing to negotiate?" Newman asked Fred. A fair point, I guess, in the literal sense—but splitting hairs to me, especially when we had an important *Times'* reporter on deadline.

Again, I mean absolutely no disrespect. Mr. Newman is a great man who has devoted a large portion of his life to charitable causes. But it turns out Paul Newman was more like my father than I imagined. I felt like I was setting up a VCR and he was standing over my shoulder shouting: "Don't you think you should use the Phillips-head screwdriver?"

In the end, I did what any good boss would do. I told Fred to work it out anyway he could with Newman, and went back to work on making sure James Barron had all the information he needed to write the story. The *Times* piece that appeared the next day really got the ball rolling, letting the public know that some serious celebrities were about to throw their weight behind the strikers' cause:

Public Lives: Rank and File Get Star Support

Robert De Niro's TriBeCa Grill was filled Tuesday night with stars invited by Paul Newman, who called them together for a briefing on the three-month-old strike against the advertising industry.

The main issue in the strike, which involves 135,000 members of the Screen Actors Guild and the American Federation of Television and Radio Artists, is how to pay actors for appearing in commercials. Negotiators for the advertising industry have said that they want to do away with longstanding rules governing residuals. "I gather that we're kind of at an impasse," said James Naughton, who attended the session. "It means a lot to what they call the rank and file in the union, to know there are guys like Paul who are involved and willing to assume some kind of leadership role."

"I don't know what it means to the other side. I suspect it can't be good news. We're told they're asking for rollbacks, which doesn't make a lot of sense to those of us in this business at a time when everybody seems to be making more."

Among the 40 performers who attended were F. Murray Abraham, Harry Belafonte, Ashley and Naomi Judd, Tony Lo Bianco, Bebe Neuwirth, Kyra Sedgwick, Marisa Tomei, Kathleen Turner, Sam Waterston, and Mr. Newman's wife, Joanne Woodward.

They watched a video that showed Olympia Dukakis, Blair Brown, Jerry Orbach, and Mr. Lo Bianco talking about the importance of the union. "Even though I don't think there were too many people in the room whose immediate livelihoods would have been affected by the outcome of this strike," Mr. Waterston said, "the people who were in the room have a memory, and they know what it was like getting started."

Ms. Neuwirth, who said she used to do commercials for household cleaning products, made a similar point. "The union has helped to protect us now and always through our career," she said, "and we stand with the rank and file."

Ira M. Shepard, who has represented the advertising industry, said that the goal in changing the way residuals are computed was not to take away residuals altogether.

"I'm hopeful that when we meet again," he said, "the parties will be able to hammer out an agreement. The only thing we have to have is a modernization of the system."

Source: James Barron, The *New York Times,* August 17, 2000, page B2.

Which highlights the key point: When communicating with the media about your dispute, *it is vitally important to work backward from what the media really needs, rather than forward from what you want to give them.*

FOCUSING ON MEDIA NEEDS

In any story, but particularly in a legal story, there is an enormous amount of information—some of which may be relevant to you, but not to the media you're attempting to influence. Conversely, you'll find many reporters are more interested in elements of a legal case that you find mundane or off-point. This is particularly true in legal disputes, where you are usually dealing with reams of facts and legal theories that need to be "distilled" for a reporter who has, say, 500 to 1,000 words to write his story, or—if we're talking television—three and a half minutes for the evening news segment. In the Screen Actors example, the story wasn't the most complex I'd ever worked on, but if we'd gotten bogged down in the definition of "negotiating table," we never would have gotten the story in before the deadline. It was certainly important to Paul Newman, but not important at all to James Barron, who just wanted to write an interesting 300- to 500-word piece for the next day's *Times.*

The key point is this: Give reporters what they want, not what you think they should want. Often a hard point to get across to parties to a legal dispute, who are usually immersed, hip deep, in the intricate details of their lawsuit and believe zealously in the rightness of their claim. In most cases, the parties—and their lawyers, for that matter—want not only to give reporters what is needed to write the story, but they want to *convert* them to their cause. I can't tell you how many times I've spoken to the legal team or to the parties and have heard something like: "If I just lay out all the case documents in front of the reporter, I'm sure they'll see how right we are in this dispute."

Wrong!

Reporters don't care. They don't care about your lawsuit, about how your rights have been violated, or about the way the other side has been acting.

Okay, that may be a little harsh. They do care on a certain level. Particularly if you have been wronged, as many parties—both plaintiffs and defendants—have been. But reporters are also professionals. As professionals, they maintain a certain distance from most of the stories they cover. The idea of the crusading reporter, the ardent pursuer of right who is going to take your case and run with it until justice is served . . . well, let's just say that that sort of ideal probably never existed, and it certainly doesn't exist today, in the era of 24-hour news and Web editions of every major newspaper.

In fact, I've been re-reading *All the President's Men* recently (which is, sadly, what media junkies like myself do in their spare time), and I think it's fair to note that the caricature of Woodward and Bernstein as crusading reporters hell-bent on getting the truth probably didn't even exist then—although the truth about Watergate and Richard Nixon was certainly a by-product of their efforts. If you read the story closely, you begin to realize that Woodward and Bernstein weren't necessarily looking for the truth as much as they were looking for a good story—and, not incidentally, looking to do a good enough job to hang on to the story and thereby buttress their nascent careers (they were both Metro reporters afraid the national guys were going to steal the story away).

This is a more important point than you would think when dealing with the media—a point we come back to later in this chapter.

The Influence Game

Of all of the silly things I hear attorneys and their clients say during the litigation process, this is the silliest:

> "Look, the media is going to write what they're going to write. We can't influence the process. Just send over the pleadings . . ."

How misguided is this attitude? Consider how you'd react if your attorney said the following:

> "There's no reason to try to be persuasive in that brief—the judge is going to decide what the judge is going to decide."

Or:

> "Research is research. Just throw together whatever cases you have available and send them to the judge—he'll get the idea."

Odds are you'd fire that attorney on the spot. But when discussing the media, it is somehow all right. Why?

One reason is the times in which we live, and how the world has changed since many of the leading lawyers out there went to law school and were trained to practice. We'll talk more about attorneys and their particular worldview in Chapter Six, but it is important to note that most of the top litigators out there were educated in the early 1970s—a period when:

- There was no *New York Times* Business Day section.
- The entire *Wall Street Journal* was one section long.
- There was no *USA Today*.
- There were exactly three general business magazines of note—*Forbes, Fortune,* and *BusinessWeek.*
- Most cities didn't have a weekly business publication.
- Most courtroom reporters were covering grisly murder trials, not business cases.
- Most Americans still didn't have cable television—so there was no CNN, CNNfn, CNBC, MSNBC, FOX News, Bloomberg television, and so on.

- The Internet was still a twinkle in the eye of a handful of geeky computer scientists.

Then there are the hundreds of regional and local newspapers that have expanded their coverage of business issues—including legal disputes—and the thousands of trade publications that have cropped up across the country (and around the world) in the past 20 years, whose audience is highly segmented, but who can have an enormous effect on your company and its future.

You want names and numbers? Consider:

- *Advertising Age* (circulation 85,000).
- *Architectural Record* (circulation 94,000).
- *Business Vehicle Management* (circulation 250,000).
- *American Trucker* (circulation 515,000).
- *Air Line Pilot* (circulation 73,000).
- *Bank Director* (circulation 45,000).
- *FutureBanker* (circulation 150,000).
- *CFO* (circulation 367,000).
- *Bartender* (circulation 147,000).
- *Chemical and Engineering News* (circulation 152,000).
- *Javaworld* (the computer code, not the coffee) (circulation 130,000).
- *ADA (American Dental Association) News* (circulation 141,000).
- *American Druggist* (circulation 101,000).
- *Variety* (circulation 35,000).
- *Electrical Engineering Times* (circulation 150,000).
- *Government Executive* (circulation 60,000).
- *Modern Health Care* (circulation 90,000).
- *AV Video Multimedia Producer* (circulation 100,000).
- *Business Facilities* (circulation 41,000).
- *Restaurant Business* (circulation 130,000).

Even when compared to the nation's newspapers, the circulation figures for these publications are significant. True, the average regional newspaper has a circulation of approximately

300,000—more than most of these trade publications. But remember that these individual trade publications are also targeted to the audience that buys your products and services. In other words, if you are the typical business enterprise, an article in your local newspaper may reach 300,000 people—but odds are only a small percentage of these people are interested in your particular story. But if you are, say, in the semiconductor business and being sued, you can bet *Electrical Engineering Times* will be as important to your company and its future as the *New York Times*. Moreover, few of these magazines even existed 20-plus years ago—when most of the lawyers handling major litigation were in their formative years. Hence, the disconnect.

No doubt about it, the world has changed—and the practice of law has changed with it. In fact, let me make a bold statement: *The rise of business and legal media is among the greatest changes in the practice of law in the past 100 years.* Even bigger, I would wager, than computers and technology, which have streamlined the creation of the tools of legal practice, but left the substance relatively unchanged. Legal research, document management—they're the same, just handled more efficiently now through computers and related technology (although perhaps even that point is debatable).

By contrast, the rise of *media coverage* of court cases is a real sea change. The lawyers who were educated in law in the 1970s—and trained by litigators who came of age in the 1950s and 1960s—just weren't given the tools to handle the media as it exists now.

There's no denying the impact of this phenomenon on the way lawsuits are handled, yet most litigators are notoriously blind to its effects. As we've discussed, lawyers at their core are control freaks—they want to feel in control of every situation in which they operate. They like to leave nothing to chance. But to be effective in the court of public opinion, this type of control needs to be extended to the communications process.

Consider another example of lawyers' need to control events outside the courtroom: I know a female lawyer who designed her firm's offices to have unisex bathrooms off the conference room where most settlement negotiations and transactional closings take place. As opposed to the traditional "Men's" and "Ladies" rooms. Why? Because she most often faced groups of men during settlement—men who would trot off to the bathroom during breaks and conduct their own negotiations, *ex parte,* as lawyers like to say, over the urinals and wash basins (not unlike, I suppose, the movie *Patton,* where Field Marshall Montgomery and one of General Eisenhower's assistants plan the invasion of Sicily on a Men's room mirror). The female litigator was being left out of this key facet of negotiations, and it was affecting her ability to control the course of the proceedings. So she eliminated the problem altogether by putting unisex bathrooms in the firm's offices. Lesson to be learned: Good litigators are control freaks—and the best of them are learning, albeit slowly, that media and public communications elements of their cases need to be handled in the same manner, with the same seriousness and care as every other aspect of the case.*

Moreover, because the business media have risen so quickly and so dramatically, there's been little instruction and training as to how to handle this critical new component of legal disputes. When confronted with the prospect of media influence, litigators often fall back on lawyers' traditional defense mechanisms when their case is weak: bluster, endless differentiation, even rhetorical derision. This, too, is part of a lawyer's training. When you're presented with a "dog" of an argument, you argue your point anyway, as forcefully as you can, factual or logical consistency be damned. Thus:

There's no controlling the media. They write what they write.

Absolutely untrue: Just because you don't have absolute control doesn't mean you can't influence the way your case is presented to the public. After all, you have no absolute control over the judge or jury either.

We'll fight our battle where it really counts, in the courtroom.

Again, a statement that's stunning in its disregard of reality. If a $200 million publicly traded company loses half its value because of the negative publicity generated by a $10 million case . . . well, just ask Martha Stewart how damaging that can be.

---

*I understand that this unisex bathroom concept was also a major element in the television program *Ally McBeal,* but I hadn't watched the program that closely enough over the years to tell if it was done for the purposes of negotiation—or just enough to add another layer of interpersonal relationship to the mix.

> Here's our media strategy: We will not comment on matters that
> are currently in litigation.

Not a strategy at all, but rather turning a blind eye to a huge
element of modern litigation—one that can have as big an impact
on the case as anything that happens inside the courtroom.

Maybe I exaggerate a bit. Not all lawyers are this bad at it. Some
see the reality, and are arming themselves to deal with it. They
understand that media will have a huge impact on their case—
whether it's a contract dispute in Tucson or a product liability case
with plaintiffs spread across the country. They realize that you can
influence the development of the reporting on the case and how
the media, the public, and the other side perceives your argument
and its effect on your company's reputation, stock price, and, ultimately, future.

What Reporters Want

Given the enormous influence of the media on court cases, a
threshold issue (to use lawyers' terminology) is knowing what a reporter wants—and needs. Understanding this is essential to working with the media, particularly on legal matters—which by their
very nature run counter to the immediacy and brevity of modern
media.* In other words, if you are going to fit this square peg in the
round hole, you'd better know the round hole pretty well.

So what do reporters want? Well, here are my "threshold" guidelines—the three most important things you need to know—based
on what I've observed of reporters from all manner of media, at all
levels, for more than 15 years:

1. Reporters want the *truth*.

2. They want it *now*.

3. They want it in a form that's *useful* to them and their readers.

Seems simple, doesn't it? But it is deceptively difficult. In the
next chapter, we'll go a little more in-depth and look closer at what

---

*When I say "reporter," by the way, I mean all media-types creating the story,
whether it be reporter or editor, television producer or on-air broadcast or
radio correspondent.

motivates a reporter, which becomes critical when deciding how to develop the proper *message* for communicating your case. For now let's take a closer look at these threshold elements, so that we can see more closely how they apply in the context of litigation and other legal disputes.

REPORTERS WANT THE TRUTH

Again, this seems simple to the point of being simpleminded, I know. I can see the reviews of this book now: "Reporters want the truth? How earth-shattering!" But I'm telling you, in this world of high-priced spin-doctors and focused-grouped media messages, it is a point often forgotten. All reporters want the truth—which is to say: They want to get the story right, and they don't want to be misled.

As you describe your case or legal matter to a reporter, you can usually hear what they're thinking in the tone of their questions. They're thinking: "Is this guy leveling with me? What isn't he telling me? Is this the truth, or just his version of the truth?" Every reporter's greatest fear is to be duped, to be taken in, convinced of something that turns out not to be the truth. So virtually everything they do is informed by this interest in getting the story right.

Okay, so we've established that reporters want the truth. But what is the truth? Let's face it: Truth is like light through a prism—the same light can be reflected as very different colors depending on where you're standing.* But while there are shades of *meaning* that can be assigned to facts when presenting the "truth" of a story, facts are facts, and if you start playing too loosely with the facts—and this includes *omission* of factual elements of your case that are perhaps unfavorable—you risk damaging your entire relationship with the reporter.

---

* I owe this metaphor to two-time Pulitzer Prize columnist for the *New York Times,* Thomas Friedman, who said about truth in the Middle East: "I once described to someone what it is like to be a reporter in Beirut. It's as if you are standing there watching this white light of truth coming at you. But before it hits you it is refracted through this prism of Lebanese factions and fiefs and religious groups, so that before it reaches your eyes it is splayed out in fifteen different directions. Your challenge as a reporter is to grab a little bit of the blue band, and a little bit of the red band, and a little bit of the green band, and try to paint as close a picture of reality as you possibly can." Thomas L. Friedman, "From Beirut to Jerusalem to Washington," *The Writing Life: A Collection of Essays and Interviews* (New York: Random House, 1995), p. 142.

So, let me say this quite forcefully, unequivocally, and without ambiguity: Give the reporters the truth, or you're dead. Nothing kills your credibility with the media more than a lie, or even a half-truth. Nothing.

Okay, how can I reinforce this point further? Let me repeat: *Give reporters the truth.* And make sure *you know what the truth is* before speaking to reporters. Particularly in lawsuits, where layer upon layer of fact—and subtle nuances in interpretation of law—are between you and the "story." In these cases, the credibility of your information is paramount. If you begin to show cracks in that foundation, the legitimacy of your side of the case is going to start to crumble.

I'll give you an example from a case I was working on involving a major health care corporation being investigated by the U.S. Department of Justice. It was our belief that the investigation was prompted by another powerful corporation that my client was suing.

On a Monday afternoon, I was scheduled to call a *New York Times* reporter to brief him on the case. It was a reporter I'd worked with before on various matters, so our credibility was good. That morning, I received a call from my client's attorney.

"Jim, I have more evidence that it was the other side behind the Justice Department investigation," the attorney said. "Henry Adams is the lead attorney for the other side. John Adams, his brother, is a senior attorney at the Justice Department and on the team investigating this case."

This was a bombshell, supporting our theory that the Justice Department investigation was a straw dog, that there was nothing to the charges, that they were designed to distract and embarrass my client, which would soften their position on the lawsuit against the competitor. The fact that the lead attorney's brother was involved in the Justice Department investigation—that was big. I carefully relayed the information to the *New York Times* reporter in a manner designed to reinforce our main theme.

Two hours later, the reporter e-mailed me:

Hi Jim. I'm making good headway with the story (as you know, it's complex) and hope to be done in a few days. I'll keep you posted about exactly when it's expected to run. Thanks again. By the way, the two Adams are apparently not related.

The two Adams weren't related? I was livid. I immediately called the attorney.

"They're not?" he said, "But they have the same last name. Seems like an awfully big coincidence to me."

In the end, it didn't hurt the resulting story (which got in all the points we wanted to make), but it could have killed us. Luckily, we had already established a certain level of trust with the *Times* reporter. But it is mistakes like this that keep me up at night. They undermine credibility and the coverage of your case is almost certainly going to suffer. Particularly in the context of litigation and other legal matters, since you're likely to be working with the same reporter over and over again throughout the course of the proceedings. Therefore, what the reporter thinks of you vis-à-vis the credibility of the information you are providing is key. Mistakes—even inadvertent—will chisel away at your ability to convince the reporter of the validity of your story, which affects your ability to "frame" the story in a manner that gets your side heard.

Here is what really bugged me about this case. The litigator, who would *never, ever* introduce a fact in court proceedings without determining its accuracy, thought nothing of passing along information about the two attorneys supposed kinship based on nothing more than a hunch. As if two people had never had the same names and not been related before. As if "Adams" weren't a common name.

This reinforces my earlier point. When dealing with the media, sometimes attorneys will do things they never do in other aspects of their legal practice. More on that later.

REPORTERS WANT IT *NOW*

The reporter called my office around 10:15 A.M. on a Friday morning, and I was on the phone with the client and her attorney by 10:30.

The reporter was from *Legal Times,* the leading legal publications in the Washington, DC, area. She was writing on a case involving sexual harassment at a Virginia-based insurance company. We provided the reporter with all the necessary information regarding our side of the story, and it seemed as if the resulting article—which would appear the following Monday—would be highly favorable. The reporter called because she wanted the attorney to comment personally, just to add a little flavor to the piece, perhaps add a little something "off-script." A good comment from the attorney would put us over the top, I wagered. *Legal Times* goes to press on Friday afternoon, and therefore the reporter was facing a tight deadline. Hence my haste.

By the way, this happens fairly often, even on the most mundane stories. Reporters will usually always try to speak directly with the interview subject, even if they have all the information they need, including direct quotes. This is part of their training: Go directly to the source; don't be spoon-fed information from the PR flack. In most cases, the interview subject will just reiterate what's been given to the reporter in background materials anyway, but it makes no difference. Indulge the media in their interest in getting right to the source. It is part of the process and the resulting article will be better for it (but first read Chapter Seven on "Message" to ensure the attorney or client is trained sufficiently to stay on point during the interview).

Back to my story: On the phone with the client and her attorney, we quickly went over the main message points we wanted to get into the resulting article: How complaints of sexual harassment had been dealt with promptly, how managers were reassigned and sent for additional training, and about the company's stellar history in equal opportunity employment.

I gave the attorney the reporter's number.

"So you'll call her."

"I'll call her right now."

At 3:30 P.M., one of my colleagues came into my office to tell me the *Legal Times* reporter had called to say she hadn't heard from our attorney.

Five hours later.

Here's the point: Reporters work on a very different schedule than you or me—and especially different from attorneys. In this context, calling the reporter right back means . . . well, it means *right back*. Lawyers often work on a far different timetable—responses to pleadings, for example, are usually due in days or weeks. And we all forget—anyone who's worked with me knows that I can, at times, be the chief culprit (in fact, everyone in my office is under strict orders to remind me of things incessantly to ensure that they get done). In the rush of the daily grind, it's often difficult to return all the calls that pass through an office. But attorneys are notoriously bad at returning phone calls. So bad, in fact, that some law firms pledge to their clients that "all calls will be returned within 24 hours."

Within 24 hours? Well, don't knock yourself out, there, counselor.

Reporters have deadlines. Reporters for daily newspapers usually have a deadline of about 4 P.M. the day before; reporters at a weekly paper like *Legal Times,* generally have early afternoon deadlines a day or two before the publication appears. Yes, I know you have deadlines, too—but if you're aiming for an important article that will greatly enhance your position in a legal dispute, the reporter's deadline is far more important than yours. These deadlines are inviolate—so get back to your reporter by deadline or suffer the consequences.

This brings us to a broader concept. Think for a moment about the job reporters have to do, particularly when reporting on complex legal matters. They have to take information contained in a 50- or 100-page complaint (or some other legal filing or document), find the areas of relevance, get to the heart of the issues at hand—and then condense that information to the 500 or 1,000 words (on average) that will convey the story to their usually nonlegal audience. And they have to do it before four o'clock. Not an easy job. I sometimes think that if clients and their attorneys would just view the situation from this perspective, there would be much more respect for the time constraints reporters work under—and many more phone calls would be returned promptly.

REPORTERS WANT IT IN A FORM THAT'S USEFUL

I can't tell you how many times I've heard something like this:

> "A reporter from *Fortune* magazine called me about the case."
> "So what did you do?"
> "I sent over the pleadings. And all the depositions."

Usually, this is the type of thing I hear about a week or so after the fact. And I break into a cold sweat when I think about a pile of documents—sometimes 12 inches thick or more—arriving on a reporter's already cluttered desk. Usually with a terse cover note that says something like: "Per our discussion, enclosed are the

documents you requested regarding *Smith v. ABC Corporation.*
Please let me know if you have any questions."

Clients and their attorneys do this without telling me all
the time, by the way, and for a decade or so I've been trying to
figure out why. Sometimes I think it's a passive-aggressive thing—
it's a client's way of saying: "See, I know how to deal with reporters, too."

In most cases, though, they don't. Or they wouldn't have tried
to send out thousands of pages of documents to a reporter with a
deadline that evening, with no further hint of an explanation.

Again, it flows from the two faulty premises that underlie dealing
with a reporter during a court case or other legal matter: (1) they're
going to write what they're going to write, there's no use persuading
them; and (2) once they read through my 10,000 pages of documents,
they'll understand the rightness of my cause.

Make no mistake: Reporters need things in a format they can
use. That means not 10,000 pages, but 10 words or less. Okay,
maybe not ten, but the point is too important not to dramatize.
Do not rely on a reporter digesting all of the relevant documents
surrounding a case. It's not that they're not intelligent, interested
people capable of accurately analyzing you case. It's just that they
don't have the time.

This is not in any way suggesting that clients and their attorneys
should *hide* the actual case documents from the reporter—far from
it. I believe in total openness when dealing with the media on legal
matters, and there is no reason why a reporter shouldn't see everything (and they will—if you're not going to provide it, the other
side most certainly will). But I am suggesting that clients and their
attorneys *should not* rely solely on the pleadings and other documents to give reporters information regarding the case. It's just too
much detail, too much information—there has to be a distillation
of the information so that the reporter can easily come to terms
with the key question: "What's the story here?"

What do you do instead? In most cases, I recommend that well
before the first reporter ever calls, a party to a legal dispute should
prepare a 1 to 2 page summary of the case, highlighting the parties, the issues in dispute in the legal matter, and your side's legal
argument. I call this a *Media Brief* based on the "case briefs" we used
to prepare in law school.

For those who have not trudged through three years of law school, a case brief is a simple summary of a case—highlighting the case name, who the plaintiff and defendant are, the issues in dispute, and the "holding"—otherwise known as the decision of the court.

Here, for example, is the case brief for one of the most important cases in Supreme Court history: *Brown v. Board Education:*

BROWN v. BOARD OF EDUCATION
347 U.S. 483 (1954)

DATE OF ARGUMENT:	Argued December 9, 1952. Reargued December 8, 1953. Decided May 17, 1954.
QUESTION PRESENTED:	Does legal segregation of schoolchildren based on race deny African American children the equal protection of the Fourteenth Amendment of the Constitution even though the physical and other "tangible" facilities may be equal?
HOLDING:	Yes—the doctrine of "separate but equal" as described in *Plessy v. Ferguson,* 163 U.S. 537 (1896) has no place in the public education system. The effects of the doctrine act in such a way as to violate the protections of the Fourteenth Amendment.
PROCEDURAL HISTORY:	This was a consolidated suit, comprised of cases from Kansas (the title case, *Brown v. Board*), South Carolina, Virginia, and Delaware. The court accepted the cases together not because of similar facts or local conditions, but based upon common legal questions. All cases involved the plaintiffs being denied relief based on the application of the "separate but equal" doctrine from *Plessy v. Ferguson.*
	This decision comes from a reargument. The original hearing was held in 1952, and then this hearing was announced to address concerns related to the Fourteenth Amendment as laid out by the court to the parties involved.
REASONING:	Opinion by Chief Justice Earl Warren. Reexamining the doctrine of separate but equal in the context of the modern U.S. public education system, it becomes clear that reasoning apparently appropriate

at the time of *Plessy v. Ferguson*—1896—and the Fourteenth Amendment—1868—is no longer valid. In those eras, there was no public education system in the sense we know it now, and as a result there was never an effort made by Congress or the Supreme Court to apply Fourteenth Amendment Education was viewed as secondary to life as an American citizen. It was perfectly possible to be successful and fulfill the requirements of citizenship without a formal education in the past.

Both our modern understanding of the effects of segregation on the hearts and minds of the African American population and the essential nature of education today require the discontinuation of the current system of segregation. To continue would be to place African American children at a distinct disadvantage to other children. Because of the history and social conditions that accompany segregation, it is difficult to maintain equal conditions (although that concern has been addressed somewhat recently). Pay for teachers and physical conditions at many African American schools have been improving.

But more importantly, because this segregation is based solely on race, by keeping the children separate, the system is denying the African Americans the ability to interact with children from other races, and this causes feelings of inferiority. As Chief Justice Warren writes in the opinion, "the policy of segregating the races is usually interpreted as denoting the inferiority of the Negro group. A sense of inferiority affects the motivation of the child to learn. Segregation with the sanction of law . . . has a tendency to [retard] the educational and mental development . . . and to deprive them of some of the benefits," of an education.

A law that harms someone based solely on his or her race is in violation of the Fourteenth Amendment and cannot stand.

Many thanks to Matthew Kramer, a lawyer from my firm, for this brief of *Brown v. Board of Education*.

This becomes, in many cases, the most useful document a reporter will receive in the course of a case—and, in many situations, I've had reporters retain the *Media Brief* for the entire litigation as a key reference tool when reporting on a case.

But in order for the Media Brief to become this indispensable tool for reporters to use, it must be objective in its treatment of the facts and issues in the case. This doesn't mean that it needs to be totally *unbiased* as to your legal argument. As discussed, reporters expect the conclusions you draw based on the facts of a particular case to be somewhat biased. Whether you are the attorney or the actual client (or the public relations contact), you are expected to be an *advocate* for your side's position. But your factual information should be as objective as possible, so that the reporter has confidence in using your summary in his or her reporting on a case.

The best way to illustrate a Media Brief is to show you one—this taken from a very complicated case involving an electronics manufacturer sued for patent infringement. The complexity of the legal action (as in a lot of litigation, this was actually a combination of suits and countersuits) lent itself especially well to this sort of summary.

Here are the facts: The electronics company (let's call them ABC Technologies) was sued for patent infringement—*not* for anything they had produced themselves, but for using equipment sold to them by another supplier (let's call them Supply Co.) that infringed the plaintiff's patent (let's call the plaintiff T Corp.). This was a proper application of patent law,* but one seldom used—usually T Corp. would just sue Supply Co. directly, since they are the so-called "bad guys" in the case. Moreover, ABC Technologies had an indemnification agreement with Supply Co., which Supply Co. was refusing to honor (indemnification is where you agree to defend someone else and pay damages if they are sued). So ABC Technologies decided to sue Supply Co. to force them to indemnify. Thus, two separate lawsuits on the same issue.

A very complicated set of facts. The question: How do you explain this case to reporters and convince them that the story merits coverage? We felt that the Media Brief method was the best way to do this. The Media Brief we created for the litigation follows:

---

* Technically, anyone who is in the "stream of commerce" can be a violator of a patent if they use an infringing product.

MEDIA BRIEF

ABC Technologies Sued by T Corporation over Patents; ABC Countersues Supply Co. for Indemnity

Case is unusual in that no ABC products or processes are involved. Patents relate to technology of equipment purchased from Supply Co., ABC's supplier.

CASES: *T Corporation v. ABC Technologies,* Civil Action No. 2:01–0000 (U.S. District court); *ABC Technologies v. Supply Co.,* Civil Action No. 2:01–0001 (U.S. District court).

SUMMARY: In a case with ramifications for the entire semiconductor industry, ABC Technologies has been sued by T Corporation in connection with three patents relating to the equipment and processes of ABC's supplier, Supply Co. The patents relate to the operation of the equipment sold to ABC Technologies by Supply Co. for the manufacture of circuits.

No ABC equipment or processes are at issue, and ABC denies the allegations contained in the suits. It is highly unusual for a major electronics company like T Corp. to sue the company that is not creating equipment or processes that violate patents. It is common industry practice to sue the manufacturers of such equipment directly.

The lawsuit relates to two patents issued to T Corporation. ABC has indemnity provisions in all its contracts and purchase orders with Supply Co. These agreements require Supply Co. to defend ABC in the event a lawsuit brought over any equipment sold or leased to ABC by the Supply Co.

The lawsuits were filed January X, and February XX, XXXX. Copies of the lawsuits and relevant public background materials are available.

PATENTS: U.S. Patent No X,XXX,XXX ("the 'XXX patent"); U.S. Patent No. Y,YYY,YYY ("the 'YYY patent).

ATTORNEYS: John Smith of Smith, Jones and Hernandez, for Defendant ABC Technologies.

As you can see, this Media Brief is even easier to read than my earlier description of events. Rather than straight narrative that has to be read in a linear manner, the reporter can scan and pick through the relative facts and legal theories as needed—and bounce back and forth between sections when putting together an article on the case. In the present example, this provided a neat package for the reporter, who—as all reporters do in these cases— was struggling with the highly complex set of facts that needed to be put together on a tight deadline.

The Media Brief lists all the relevant information the reporter would need—including case title (what lawyers call the "style"), the attorneys, the court, and even the patents at issue in the case. There's also a summary of the key issues in the case. Less than two pages of material provided the reporter with all the basic information he needed to know.

Also, notice how, while definitely holding to our opinion of things—particularly in the headline and the summary—the Media Brief provides objective information to the reporter, information that the reporter will use as he organizes his own thinking to report effectively and fairly on a case. In other words, we provide a *factually accurate* account of the case, one reporters can rely on— but one that is *framed* in terms of our arguments and theories.

It's a delicate balance, to be sure—and again let me emphasize that nothing will hurt your credibility more than a document that reeks of bias and attack (see "The Misconduct of Jeffrey S. Wigand" in the Brown & Williamson whistleblower case that we looked at in Chapter One). But the value of providing an accurate, concise, succinct description of a complex legal action is worth its weight in gold, and will influence the reporting throughout the course of the proceedings. Again, it's a *credible* presentation of the facts, not a fluff piece that seems like a cheap advertisement for your side of the story—obscuring facts, blurring timelines, misquoting the law or experts, and otherwise doing all those things that ultimately scream, "Don't believe this document" and, in the long term, "Don't believe this side of the case."

How did this story turn out? Well, our plan was to launch a trade story that would be the first "shot across the bow" to the plaintiff—designed to get them to back down on what the industry would view as "dirty pool." We also wanted to alert the

supplier—who was supposed to indemnify ABC Technologies—
that the company was going to battle this case aggressively. That's
exactly what we achieved, with a story in a major electronics trade
publication:

ABC Sues Equipment Makers for Alleged Failure to Indemnify

ABC Technologies has lifted its veil of silence regarding patent-infringement litigation because, it says, it believes a disturbing trend
is afoot.

In January, rival T Corporation, Inc. filed suit against ABC on two
patent-infringement claims. But ABC said it believes the claims
have nothing to do with its technology and has everything to do
with equipment ABC purchased from a major vendor.

In response to the T Corp. lawsuit, ABC sued Supply Co. for fail-
ing to protect ABC from the patent claims brought against it by T
Corp. An ABC spokesman said that the purchase agreements the
company signed with all the three equipment vendors have clauses
that would indemnify ABC from patent-infringement claims. In
other words, ABC claims that Supply Co. should defend it from T
Corp.'s claims. ABC's suit includes charges of failure to indemnify,
breach of contract and fraud.

ABC is taking issue with the T Corp. complaint because it refers
to technology that comes bundled with the capital equipment it
purchased from Supply Co.

"The fraud claims are based on a highly unusual set of circumstances," said Jim Haggerty, ABC's spokesman. "ABC alleges that
Supply Co. sold equipment to ABC with full knowledge that the
use of such equipment had been held to infringe a T Corp. patent."

"ABC views this as dirty pool," Haggerty said. "T Corp. is going
after ABC instead of the real culprits."

ABC also is claiming that none of its own process technology
for making chips or its equipment is at issue. All of the allegations
of infringement relate to the operation of the equipment as designed and manufactured by the three suppliers, ABC said.

A T Corp. spokesman said that ABC's manufacturing processes allegedly violate T Corp.'s patents and that the equipment claim is not an issue in its intellectual property (IP) fight.

Representatives from Supplier Co. did not return calls requesting comment by press time.

Note how closely the information in the article tracks the information we provided the reporter in the Media Brief. Again, this is primarily because we provided the reporter with a fair, objective summary of the litigation—not without advocacy, but fair nonetheless. This allowed him to understand the underlying issues at a quick glance (which is what reporters need to do). Ultimately, it also allowed us to "frame" the story in our favor—but to do so in a fair, objective and credible manner.

ACTION POINTS

✔ It is important to work *backward* from what the reporter really needs, rather than *forward* from what you want to give him.

✔ Reporters have a extraordinarily difficult job to do: They need to review the thousands of pages of documents related to your case and understand them sufficiently to get the "story"—then they need to communicate the essence of your case to their readers, usually in 1,000 words or less.

✔ You can't absolutely control what reporters write, but you can frame the issue sufficiently to influence the coverage of your legal dispute.

✔ Reporters' needs are deceptively simple: They want the *truth,* they want it *now,* and they want it in a form they can use.

✔ A key tool for giving reporters information they can use is the *Media Brief*—a specialized tool that, if prepared properly, can serve as a resource reporters use throughout the case.

CHAPTER THREE

The Rules of Media Procedure— And How to Use Them

"Where are the rules? I don't understand the rules." This is a familiar refrain from lawyers when dealing with media during litigation. Lawyers, remember, live their lives by rules: Rules of Civil Procedure, Rules of Evidence, local court rules, appellate court rules, and so on. But in dealing with the media, lawyers are in a court of a different kind— the court of public opinion—where the rules are shifting, amorphous, difficult to understand, and even more difficult to enforce.

In this chapter, we look at some of the rules that govern reporters during interviews, and some of the reasons why the media behaves the way it does. We give lawyers and their clients a host of tips and techniques for handling the media during litigation, and then take a moment to return to a central issue in working with the media: understanding what reporters want.

A few years ago, I was at lunch with an attorney and an editor of *BusinessWeek*. It was an off-the-record discussion of a case the law firm was working on that we expected would be big news in the coming months. This particular lawyer—one of the most prominent litigators in New York, in fact—prided himself on his no-nonsense, tough-guy demeanor. On the walk over to the restaurant, we discussed the importance of not going into detail about his client's case, for reasons of strategy and to avoid revealing any information that might be considered confidential. Instead, the lawyer was to speak generally about the issues involved in the case and what they might mean for the future of this area of the law. If something came up that was confidential, I made sure the litigator knew to say something like "that's a confidential part of the case that I can't get into" and move on.

It started off a cordial affair with the *BusinessWeek* editor and the attorney hitting it off famously. But then something went horribly awry. There I was, halfway through my salad, listening as my lawyer friend began to reveal intricate details of the case and his client's position. He made one revelation after another and seemed to have no idea what he was disclosing. Confidential details, the kind of inside information he wouldn't normally divulge to anyone unconnected with the litigation, never mind an editor at a national magazine.

I shot him a glance, but he ignored me and continued.

Finally, I choked on some lettuce, cleared my throat, and interrupted: "We're all agreed that this conversation is strictly off-the-record, right?" The editor smiled and agreed—she knew the lawyer had crossed the line, but also remembered the ground rules we had set for the interview. But my insistence stopped the litigator dead in his tracks. He suddenly realized what he had done. An awkward silence ensued. His face turned as red as the cherry tomato on my plate.

After a moment more, he shakily rose from the table and excused himself to use the men's room. It was some 15 minutes before he returned.

It was a surprise to see so stalwart a legal lion shaken, but I know what was going through his mind as he wobbled away from the table. This was *BusinessWeek*, after all. He realized that he had not only revealed some very compromising information about his client and his case, but that he'd done it to a person who (as the saying goes) buys ink by the gallon.*

Why did he do this? Part of the reason, no doubt, was the sheer rush of it all—the feeling of power that comes with breaking bread with an editor who reaches almost a million readers

---

*The old saying I'm talking about is, "Never get into an argument with someone who buys ink by the gallon."

each week. This can have a powerful, inebriating effect on a lawyer's ego.

I believe there's more to it than this, however. There's something particular to the lawyer's mindset, something that makes lawyers prone to getting into all sorts of confidential areas when speaking with reporters.

Lawyers, you see, are trained to win. Not just cases, but opinion. Lawyers want the weight of their argument to carry every encounter (if you don't believe this, just ask my wife). It is a tribute to a lawyer's persuasive ability, intellect, the sharpness of his or her mind. It's a matter of professional pride. The higher the court, the harder they try.

And is there a more vaunted forum than the major media? Particularly in this age? To convince *BusinessWeek,* the *New Yorker,* the *Wall Street Journal,* or the *Washington Post* of the rightness of your argument is truly to win in the highest court in the land.

But here's the problem: The court of public opinion is like no other court these attorneys have ever been in. Down at their local courthouse, there are written rules of procedure, rules of evidence, rules for the particular court and judge hearing the case. Not so when dealing with the media. The forum is constantly changing, the rules are amorphous, and there is far more opportunity to be conversational, chatty—to let your hair down, to let your guard down.

With that in mind, one of the first things we teach lawyers when answering questions from the media is to *answer the question asked, then stop.* Wait for the next question. Reporters, whether by training or temperament, will often pause after an interview subject is finished answering and wait a second or two, to see if there's anything else they'd like to add. An awkward silence ensues—dead air, they call it in radio. The attorney, thinking he has not yet persuaded the reporter of the validity of his or her position, will continue—often heading off on a dangerous tangent, or revealing information that is confidential, or strategy that is better revealed in the course of the litigation—not in the pages of the *New York Times* or *Fortune.* Filling the dead air may make the conversation more comfortable—and it certainly makes the resulting story more interesting—but it is almost always not in the best interests of the lawyer, the client, or the case.

This is a simple rule, but how would anyone, especially an attorney, know this, having never been told? There are few books on giving interviews, and none, to my knowledge, on speaking with the media during a court case. No "Rules of Media Procedure" that an attorney or client can keep on the desk and refer to when a reporter calls about a case or other legal dispute.

Until now. In this chapter, we'll look at some of the guidelines that both lawyers and their clients can follow when dealing with reporters during the course of litigation. Some of these are elementary, and lawyers and clients may have come across some of these rules before—but never particularly adapted to the litigation context. Combined with our discussion of "What Reporters Want" from Chapter Two, these tips and techniques should give anyone involved in litigation an idea as to what motivates a reporter following your case—and how you can properly manage the interview relationship to ensure the essence of your "story" is presented properly in the media context.

THE RULES OF MEDIA PROCEDURE

The case has been filed and you are back at your desk. If you are the client, perhaps you're back at headquarters plowing through the reports that have piled up while you were attending to the final lawsuit details with your in-house or outside counsel. If you are the company's lawyer, perhaps you've gotten back to your office and turned your attention to one of your other clients. The phone rings and it is an Associated Press reporter who has discovered the lawsuit (or, more likely, been tipped off about it by the other side's litigation communications team) and he would like to ask you a few questions. What do you do?

Would you believe: Hang-up?

Not literally, of course, but true. With the enormously complex issues involving lawsuits and other legal matters, we have a standard guideline when dealing with the unanticipated media call: *Clients and their lawyers should always take the reporter's name and number, find out what his deadline is, then call him back.*

The reason is simple: You need a moment to take a breath, to think about what you're going to say before responding. Whether it's five minutes or five hours, every interview subject needs some time to think about the message and how to convey it properly to the reporter covering the case (and, as we'll discuss in later chapters, hopefully the core of the message has already been prepared well before the first reporter calls).

The usual scenario is as follows. Even if an attorney or client is working on the lawsuit at issue at that particular moment, she is immersed deep in the complexities of some element of the legal or factual argument—perhaps a draft of the complaint or answer, perhaps for a motion or a brief that she is preparing on the case. Perhaps on some element of discovery. The phone rings and it's a reporter asking about the case. If that attorney or client doesn't take a step back and think about what she's going to say—what her message really is—she's likely to start speaking in the same "voice" as in the brief she was just preparing. In other words, it will be laden with complexity and great specificity, with detailed legal arguments on particular issues that are foremost in her mind, discussing precedent and the application of precedent to the facts of this particular aspect of the case before the court.

Any core message that the legal and communications team has considered regarding the case is out the window, and the attorney is responding as she might before the other side and before a judge.

Why is this so bad? Information about the case is information about the case, and that's what's important, right?

Not quite. As we learned from Chapter Two, reporters need information in a form they can use and, given the complexity of most legal actions, if you're not prepared with your message before the interview begins, you're doing a grave disservice to the case. We'll learn more about developing the core message in Chapter Seven, but suffice to say, if an attorney or client is speaking to a reporter the way they speak to a judge or to the other side, the message is likely not getting across. The focus is all wrong.

Hence, the need to take a short breather, to coordinate your thoughts, and refocus your attention before responding to the reporter's call.

THE VALUE OF PROPER FOCUS

Try this experiment. Hold a piece of blank white paper up to your eyes—about two inches or so away—and stare at it for a full minute. Now lower the paper and stare out across the room.

See how looking at something that closely screws up your focus?

It's the same thing with lawsuits. Whether you are the attorney or the client, you are, figuratively speaking, two inches away from the details of your case all day. It's natural that you need a little *decompression*—even if it's just a few minutes—before you begin looking at the case from another perspective: that of the media and the general audience the media is writing for.

Here is another example of how being too close to a matter skews perception and therefore the way you communicate. In giving seminars on communications issues across the country, I often pull an unsuspecting volunteer from the audience and ask him or her to stand facing the wall—again, about an inch or two away—and tell me what they see.

Depending on the wall, I usually get a response like the following:

"I see paint . . . I see a few cracks . . . there appears to be a pen mark . . ."

Then, standing on the other side of the room, I ask: "Now . . . ask me what I see."

"What do you see?"

"I see a wall."

That's the point. Lawyers and their clients are looking at the cracks, the pen marks, and the paint chips. Reporters want to hear about the wall.

Hence, the importance of telling the reporter you'll call him or her back. I usually say: "Look, I'm in the middle of something right now. Let me put it aside and call you back. What's your deadline?" This is no lie, by the way—I'm always in the middle of something. Whether you are attorney or client, I'm sure you are as well.

I'll even go further to say that, in more than 15 years doing this type of work, I can count on one hand the number of times I've answered a reporter's questions on the first call (except those that are routine, i.e., What time is the press conference? Where are we meeting for lunch?). There's nothing devious about this. You just need a moment to put aside what you're doing and focus on the reporter and his or her questions. So long as you are cognizant of the reporter's ultimate deadline, he will respect this response and work with you.

In addition to deadline, here are some other questions you might ask:

- What type of information are you looking for?
- Would you like some background information on the case (such as the Media Brief from Chapter Two)?
- Who else have you spoken to about the story?

The last two questions are somewhat extraneous, but the answers are useful if you can get them. But by far, the most important question to ask is about the reporter's deadline. The reporter has to understand that you know and respect the constraints he is working under and you are going to do everything you can to ensure you are helping him in this effort.

TEN TIPS FOR A SUCCESSFUL INTERVIEW

So you've told the reporter that you're calling him back and now you've had a chance to consider the message—the key points of your case, which you have committed to memory. *Now* you're ready to answer the reporter's questions.

There are many books and articles on the proper way to answer media questions, so I won't go into too much detail here on the basics. Instead, I offer my "Ten Tips" for answering interview questions and relate these to the particular nuances of a lawsuit or other legal proceedings. Some of these may seem obvious to the more experienced business executive and public relations professionals— not to mention to the lawyers who often serve as the spokespersons in a particular case. But you wouldn't believe how many times, in the heat of the legal proceedings, these rules are disregarded. Interview subjects should remind themselves of these important elements *before every interview*. If I could, I would tattoo it on my clients' foreheads so they would see it when looking in the mirror in the morning—but in lieu of this, I have created a one-page handout for the attorney or client to review before he or she step in front of the microphones. It works almost as well.

Here are the Ten Tips:

1. *Relax.* This is an extraordinarily important point, especially in interviews on court cases or other legal matters, since these tend to get pretty contentious—at times combative—in tone. Moreover, as you will see, a good interview is not necessarily a comfortable experience, particularly when dealing with layer upon layer of law and fact and interpretation.

On occasion, I've had colleagues in the public relations field scare the daylights out of interview subjects with a long list of details to remember regarding style and manner of answering questions:

"Don't say 'Uh.'"

"Look at the interviewer's forehead."

"Pull your hair back."

"Sit on your suit jacket tail."

But it is far more important to feel relaxed about the process, so that an attorney or litigant doesn't appear nervous—what my father would call "shifty." In any interview, this is important; when dealing with legal matters, it can be critical. But even as you are relaxing, it is important to remember the next tip.

2. *Never let your guard down.* In a legal sense, it is critical to bear in mind that even the most amicable interview is *adversarial* in nature. That is to say that there is a great difference between your goals and the reporter's—and if you forget about this important fact, you may find the interview going off in a direction you never expected, or wanted.

As I discuss in the opening of this chapter, attorneys in particular are vulnerable to forgetting this. Over the years, I have seen more than one hard-nosed litigator—lawyers who would never give an inch in front of the other side or before a judge—just gush when in front of a reporter, many times giving away confidential and strategic information they would never otherwise impart. You've already heard one of my theories as to why this is so: The attorney's predisposition to convince, to persuade. I have others: The ego rush of being in front of a reporter from a major publication ("I've arrived!" The reporter thinks . . . "Just wait until I send the *Time* magazine clip to my father!"); the fact that the attorney is free from the confines of the courtroom and its stifling guardedness. But whatever the cause, attorneys have to be particularly cognizant of this fact and work to remember what they always seem to remember in other aspects of the case—that while a relationship with a reporter can be amicable, even friendly, it is *always adversarial*.

3. *Every interview has a theme.* I often hear the following from lawyers and business executives when discussing a case, "Well, it was just a background interview. I explained the issues to the reporter and the legal principles surrounding the case—just so she would understand. We'll get to our message when there's some 'hard news' happening in the case." Mistake. Every interview has a theme. This theme can been "framed" in several different ways: by the reporter herself (or her editor); by the other side; or by you.

But the key point is this: *Every interview is a chance for your side to establish the theme in the reporter's mind by sticking to the case's overall message.* In that regard, there is no real difference between the "background" or educational interview and other interviews. You should be reinforcing your core message at every step in the interview process. The more you are working to "frame" the theme of an interview, the more your side of the case is going to get out. This is all about upping the percentages—the more you are working on your "theme," the higher the chance it is going to influence the final story a reporter writes.

4. *If you don't have complete information on a topic, say so.* This is standard advice when giving media interviews, but it's often forgotten in the legal context, where lawyers and the parties themselves want to seem like they have a handle on *all* aspects of the case. Very often, the interview subject will try to speculate based on the best knowledge he has. This is, again, a mistake. It is far better to dispense with the question quickly—"Well, I don't have that particular information in front of me . . ."—and then go right back into one of the aspects of your message that you want to get across—"but the central issue of this case is whether Ms. Jones traded her stock based on inside information, and we can tell you unequivocally she did not."

5. *Never say "No comment."* Nothing creates an impression of guilt, a "hand-over-the-camera-lens" evasiveness, more than a terse "No comment." Even when you are not going to comment, don't say "No comment." We train our spokespeople to say something akin to the following: "Well, I'm not going to discuss that aspect of the case, but I can tell you that ABC Corp. has a 30-year commitment to equal employment opportunity." See how much better that is?

6. *Always assume you are on-the-record, and play the attribution game wisely.* Some interview subjects—particularly those who have begun gaining experience with the media—tend to go on- and off-the-record with such regularity that it makes your head spin.

Off-the-record, on-the-record, off-the-record again. They bounce around more than my eight-month-old son in his exersaucer. But here's the problem: Reporters' notes can get jumbled—and if you're not playing the attribution game wisely, before you know it the comments you thought were off-the-record wind up on the front page of the *Washington Post*.

This is not to say that there aren't situations where you wouldn't go off-the-record or "on background" with the reporter. It is an excellent way to provide the reporter with the information he or she needs to complete the story, information you may not want to have attributed to your name. And, by and large, reporters tend to respect the rules of attribution, although I will say that there are numerous instances of interview subjects who were burned because the reporter did not. Besides complaining to the reporter's editor (which sometimes works, because if the editor gets enough complaints over attribution rule violations, they'll tend to watch the reporter more closely), there's no real recourse.

Thus, when preparing lawyers and their clients, we advise them *never* to say anything that you wouldn't mind seeing in print. We also suggest that, while there may be times when you absolutely want to go off-the-record, on background, or not for attribution, do it very wisely. In other words, don't make the decision when you're on the phone with the reporter and the interview has started. Better to decide before the call, in consultation with the legal team—and, hopefully, your public relations advisors. (The rules of attribution are important, so we spend some additional time with them later in this chapter.)

7. *If caught off-guard, take a moment to compose yourself.* Yes, even on television. There is a tendency to want to hop in immediately, to jump right on a question, as if to say to the reporter and the audience, "See, I'm so confident in the validity of my position that I'm not even waiting a heartbeat before responding." Stop. Take a deep breath. Again, even on television, you can think for a moment about what you want to accomplish with your answer before proceeding. If you're practiced and comfortable, it will seem natural. One of the purposes of training for media interviews (as we'll discuss in Chapter Seven) is to ensure that you are comfortable answering the questions, so that it doesn't seem like you are fumbling around searching for a response. Experience has taught me that most interview subjects come off quite naturally if they just take a deep breath, think about what they are going to say and how it is going to move their message forward, and then respond. An exception to this rule: the so-called debate-style interview—the shout-fests that now populate the cable news channels every evening. In these circumstances, you may have to jump in—or else the other side will.

8. *You don't have to answer the question asked.* Ah . . . the greatest cliché in all interviewing, one that has been spouted so often that it has lost all meaning, one that has been mangled by presidential candidates and Sunday morning talk show guests since time immemorial. You know what happens: The presidential candidate is asked a question about defense, and he responds by giving his policy on education. The audience groans, and everyone wonders why the moderator doesn't jump in and say: "But that's not the question I asked you . . ." This is not what I'm talking about.

Here is what I mean: You have to *respond* to the question, but you don't necessarily have to *answer* it. The difficulty lies in the fact that this behavior goes against the grain of how intelligent people have learned to answer questions. We are taught to answer the exact question asked. Attorneys in particular are taught to answer questions definitively, with specificity, anticipating opposing arguments and dispensing with them categorically. Which is fine . . . but if you do that during an interview, you'll never get to your core message, which should be the "theme" of your interview, the "story" of your case. To avoid this problem, you should always *address* the questions asked, but you shouldn't necessarily feel that you have to answer a question *definitively*—beyond a shadow of a doubt, as they say in criminal law. The key is to *respond to* the question, then bring the discussion back to the issues that are at the core of your message.

9. *If asked the same question several times, give the same answer.* Reporters are not trained to trick you; rather, they are trained to work to get the most information they can out of their interview subjects. My reporter friends will excuse me if I say that sometimes to the interview subject, it appears like the same thing.

One tactic reporters use is to ask the same question several times, perhaps in several different ways. This might be because you haven't given anywhere near a complete answer, but often it's because you didn't give them the answer they were looking for. So they'll ask you again. Then again. They may change the subject for a moment, then ask again.

There is a natural inclination to think to yourself, "Wow, this person is just not getting it. I'd better go into more detail to make sure he understands." Before you know it, you've meandered off the well-thought-out path of your message into the thicket of details and complexities of your case. In some cases, you may say something wrong—that is, something damaging to your case. But more likely, it's not that you'll say something bad (since you'll be looking to avoid this at all costs), more that the message that you want to present will be buried under a morass of facts and legalities. Your resulting response will be lukewarm, fuzzy, packed with nuance and qualification. In other words, it will do nothing to *effectively* communicate your message to the target audience.

Thus, our advice: *Give the same answer each time.* Not verbatim, but if you feel you responded to the question sufficiently and that there's nothing to add, give the same answer. Do not be afraid of repetition. Intelligent people hate feeling that they're repeating themselves, and it's going to feel a bit awkward, stilted, unusual. You, naturally, want to add something new and original to the reporter's story, something that will further the discussion. But that's not your job— by which I mean two different things: (1) it's not your responsibility; and (2) it's not what you set out to do by agreeing to have the interview. While you want to give the reporter everything he or she needs to do the story (and you should), you shouldn't be doing it to the extent that it gets in the way of getting your message across. Compiling information for a story is the reporter's job, not yours.

Remember, you had a goal when you sat down for the interview (or took the phone call, or whatever); so did the reporter. Your goals, to a certain extent, may be similar, but they are not the same. You have a message to get across, and before you consider the effectiveness of any interview, you should ask yourself: Did I fulfill my goals in this interview? Or—either out of nervousness or a desire to please—did I fulfill the reporter's goals?

10. *Don't fear "dead air."* This is the rule we opened this chapter with. Dead air is a radio term for when no sounds are going out over the airwaves—and I can think back to my days as a college radio disc jockey, running through the hallways with an LP in my hands, desperately cuing it up before too much silence had elapsed (for younger readers: An LP is a flat, black thing with a hole in the middle that worked similar to a CD, just not as well). Ten seconds of dead air can seem like an hour. So, too, in an interview.

When being interviewed by a reporter, dead air occurs after the reporter has finished his or her question and you've answered it. Many times, the reporter will just sit there, staring at you, or perhaps look down quickly at his or her notes. An awkward silence ensues. There is a natural human tendency to want to fill that uncomfortable void, to add more information, to relieve the tension. Resist this. Reporters are taught to sit and wait for a moment after you've answered, to see if there's anything else you want to say—again, not malevolently, but in the interest of getting all the information they can. But if you feel you've given the answer you want to give and have correctly responded to the question . . . stop. Sit there. Wait for the next question. It may feel a bit awkward and unusual, but it's not your job to relieve that tension. Wait for the reporter's next question. After sitting there in silence for a few uncomfortable moments, it'll come.

KNOWING THE RULES OF ATTRIBUTION

In Tip 6, the various rules of attribution were mentioned, along with the dangerous game of using those rules willy-nilly when speaking with reporters. But what are these *rules of attribution* and how can they be used? Generally speaking, they are as follows:

• *Off-the-record.* This means that the reporter cannot use the information you have given at all. This causes confusion, because many people think the information can be used as long as it's not attributed to the interviewee (that's not-for-attribution, see below). Another point: Although he can't use the information you have given him, that doesn't stop the reporter from going to some other party and getting the same information from them in a manner that can be used in the story. For example, if you tell a reporter: "Off-the-record, the real problem with this case is that the judge is a drunk, and that's why he's ruling for the other side," the reporter cannot, under any circumstances, include this in his or her story. *But,* the reporter can go to the lawyers for the other side and say, "So . . . Why does your side keep winning on the these motions?" and get confirmation that way. It's still not attributable to you, but it's in the article—which will not be a good thing for your side, since it's likely to anger the judge (particularly if he reads it after an all-night bender). He'll naturally think it came from your side, even if a lawyer for the other side is quoted. Lesson to be learned: *If you don't want to see it in print, don't say it.*

• *Not-for-attribution.* This is a statement that can appear in the article, but cannot be attributed to you. It can be attributed, however, and generally reporters will choose something innocuous, such as "someone close to the situation said" or "a source close to the plaintiff said" or perhaps even "someone with knowledge of the settlement negotiations said." Sometimes, the reporter and the interview subject will agree beforehand how the information will be attributed, as in "a source from the defendant's legal team." But again, although your name will not be attached to the comment, interview subjects play a dangerous game if the quote is something they otherwise wouldn't want to see in print—such as something that can be damaging to the case by annoying the judge, emboldening the other side, or harming the litigant's overall reputation. This is particularly true in the context of a lawsuit or other legal dispute where there are only *two* sides: if it hurts the plaintiff and helps the defendant, it's probably the defendant's side who said it; if it helps the plaintiff and hurts the defendant, it's probably the plaintiff's side. This is in contrast to, say, politics—the Mecca of background conversations—where there are usually numerous sides with varying agendas all spouting off at the mouth about this issue or that. It's a lot harder in this arena to tell who said what.

• *On background.* This is where the information cannot be quoted at all, but can be used in the article to fill in the gaps for the reader. Sometimes in court-related stories, this can be information on the fine points of the law: "A Title VII discrimination claim only applies to those areas that are protected classifications under the Civil Rights Act, such as race, gender, religion, or natural origin." It can also be background information on the factual information of a case—"Storm water runoff is a major source of water pollution in Southern California"—or on the people involved in a case—"Texas Instruments has a history of aggressively defending its patents." Again, the key point here is that the information cannot be attributed to anyone, even anonymously.

These are the three major classifications of the rules of attribution. There are other variants, but they generally just tend to confuse—deep background, deep-deep background, super-secret deep background (okay, I made that one up)—but, again, these tend to be used in the attribution hot-bed of Washington, DC, where it is considered an art form. Generally, the three categories listed are the only ones that you need to effectively conduct an interview. Finally, if you don't know what the particular ground rules are for the interview you are giving . . . *ask!* Set the rules beforehand to help limit misunderstanding.

USING THE ATTRIBUTION
RULES TO YOUR ADVANTAGE

By now I hope I've made my point: Use the rules of attribution carefully. A natural follow-up question is: How can you use the rules of attribution to help your case? How best do you use the rules to really get your message out? Here is an example of one way of using the rules of attribution to explain a complex topic to a reporter while also ensuring the theme of your case—as encapsulated by your message points—gets through.

In July 1999, we were called in by the plaintiff in a contract dispute relating to a joint venture for software development on a new type of accounting software. This was not the type of accounting software you'd use for home checking accounts. Rather, this software was to be a high-ticket item, specifically targeted to Internet companies, and the program was supposed to have all sorts of bells and whistles. My client was in charge of the sales and marketing of the software after it was created by their joint venture partner, a software development firm. The agreement: The software developer would come up with the software by March 1999, and the sales and marketing partner would launch in the fall. This being the dotcom world, the joint venture itself and the development of the software were both announced in the trade media and even mentioned briefly in the general business press.

March rolled around and the software developers couldn't deliver. The software they developed was clearly not ready for prime time—and particularly not for the rather cynical and technologically advanced dot-com audience. After a week of delays, the software partner suggested that they instead create "vapor ware"—software that really didn't work as intended, but instead simulated the way the software was supposed to work (and presumably someday would). The marketing and sales partner objected. Among other reasons, delays such as this would push the rollout of the new product into the New Year. This would have a disastrous effect on their business projections, which their venture capital backers were watching closely.

But here's why my client sued so quickly: They suspected there was a reason why the software was late, and it had nothing to do with the software developer's inability to complete the task. Our client and their lawyers suspected the developers had grown weary of this particular joint venture and had decided to move on to another—a fairly common occurrence during the height of the go-go 1990s, when small companies were flipping partners faster than Roller Girl in *Boogie Nights*. My client wanted the software developer to honor its original commitment—and they suspected the publicity surrounding a breach of contract lawsuit for failure to deliver might be the leverage needed to get the software developer to fulfill what they had originally promised.

Thus, our strategy was as follows: We wanted one or two articles in the trade media offering the defendant a hint of what was to come—that the publicity was going to get harsher as the case progressed, and that the ultimate damage to the software developer would be considerable.

Working with the client, we analyzed the case and came up with a core message consisting of three main points:

1. Our joint venture partner promised *radically* new accounting software by the end of March 1999.
2. This new system was supposed to include technological firsts such as "Internet-based auditing" and "one-touch customization."
3. The joint venture partner delivered a product with *none* of this—what they created wasn't anything better that what you can buy at your local computer store.

This last point was an important one because we knew it would resonate with the Internet and technological community—the main audience of the software developer—a group they couldn't afford to be embarrassed in front of.

But, as with most legal issues, this was a pretty complex set of facts and issues, and the worry was that if we got into all sorts of detail about the software and its potential applications, there wouldn't be enough focus on our core message—and thus the effect of our effort in using the media to get the defendant to honor his contract would be dulled, perhaps to the point of being ineffectual.

Here's what we did: We contacted a reporter from the local business press in the community where both companies made their home and offered to bring together the client and the lawyers to sit down with the reporter and—on background—explain in detail all of the technology involved, the business decisions behind the new software, and the legal aspects of the case. Then we'd go on-the-record to answer a question or two regarding what the case was really all about.

Voilà. The reporter got all the background he needed to write the story and do it well—and we got a direct quote from the client that held pretty closely to our message points. If we had made the entire interview on-the-record, the direct quote might have been something totally peripheral to the main theme of the case, and therefore the entire thrust of our story. Remember: Every reporter needs a direct quote for his or her story. It's more often than not going to go high up in the story, and there's a high likelihood it's going to set the tone for the entire piece. By carefully controlling what was said on-the-record, we were able to better control the entire tone of the resulting article. From the reporter's standpoint, he was able to collect all the information he needed to do the story well.

It takes a certain level of strategy and sophistication to do the job right. Clear planning and direction is essential. If we had made a spur-of-the-moment decision to go on-background—without any clear idea as to the type of story we were driving for—who knows what type of article would have resulted. Again, playing the attribution game well can get your core message out no matter how complex and difficult your case is, *but* you've got to be sure you have a clear strategic goal, lest you wind up with less than you were aiming for or—worse—an article that sets your case back instead of moving it in the right direction.

WHAT MAKES A GOOD INTERVIEW

Anyone who has been interviewed has had a conversation like this:

"How did the interview go?"
"I think it went well. But we'll see . . ."

The next day (or week, or later that afternoon, depending on the medium): BOOM. You get creamed. The reporter either trashes you or—more likely—misses your point entirely. You wind up with a half-baked quote only tangentially related to what you thought you were sitting down to talk about. Or, worse, rather than advancing the themes of your message, the story actually hurts your case.

Why does this happen? You thought everything really went well, that you and the reporter really connected—that the reporter really understood the background of your case and the reasons why your client is right.

This just proves, you think to yourself, that it's impossible to exert any sort of control over the course of an interview and/or the news story that results. So why bother?

I can tell you right now what happened: You had a good conversation, but you didn't have a good interview. Which leads me to the main point to be taken away from this section:

A good conversation is not the same as a *good* interview.

In fact, let me go even further:

A good conversation is usually a *bad* interview.

Here's why: If you are doing all the things we discussed in prior sections—hitting your message points, not attempting to answer every question "within a shadow of a doubt," bringing each question back to the theme of your interview, waiting for the next question when you feel you've answered a question sufficiently, not falling for the "dead air" game—the interview is going to feel a bit awkward, a bit stilted, a bit repetitive. In other words, it is going to feel like a bad conversation. Like a conversation you might have with a third cousin who you've never met before, or the spouse of one of your wife's friends that you've been forced to talk to at a party (or your husband's friend, or significant other . . . you get the point). Put another way, a good interview is, of necessity, not going to feel as "good" as a good conversation. Hence, a fair amount of confusion.

Why do clients prefer good conversations to good interviews? There are at least four reasons, including:

1. *Intelligent people enjoy good conversation.* This is particularly true of lawyers, but it's also true of most of us. We all like a good conversation. Thus, despite our interest in hitting our message points, in getting our theme across . . . deep down a good conversation is what we aim for. It's simply more enjoyable—and in an otherwise uncomfortable situation like an interview, it's natural to gravitate to things that are more enjoyable.

2. *We* want *the reporter to understand.* To understand our side of things, that is. Remember, in almost every case, a litigant in a lawsuit is in the midst of one of the more emotional, even traumatic, experiences of his or her life. Moreover, in the heat of battle, even most lawyers become emotionally invested in the client and the cause. Thus, there is an urge to convince, to explain, to persuade. Never mind the message, the interview subject thinks, if I just engage the reporter in sufficient detail, she'll see the rightness of my cause.

3. *Intelligent people don't like to be scripted.* They don't want to seem forced or canned; and most of all, they don't want to feel awkward. If they follow the rules of a good interview, they're going to feel that way.

4. *A substantive conversation is our comfort zone.* For most of us, no matter the business we're in, no matter the field of expertise, we have substantive conversations all day. It's what we do; it's

what we're good at. In uncomfortable situations, we always retreat to our comfort zone. It's just easier.

This final point is an important one: It's easier to have a good conversation with a reporter than to give a good interview. It is easier to be substantive than sharp, particularly when the issues are complex and there are two sides to the story. A good interview takes hard work and practice to get right.

That's the good news. It can be done. But the first step to doing it right is to believe. If you believe that there's no way you can get your message across in the media, that they're going to report what they're going to report no matter what you say—well, then you've created a self-fulfilling prophesy.

MORE ON WHAT REPORTERS WANT

Finally, let's bring the discussion back to a topic we touched on in Chapter Two: what the media want. To refresh: In Chapter Two, we learned that all reporters want the truth, they want it now, and they want it in a form they can use. But that begs the question: What makes a reporter interested in your story at all? Over all of the other stories out there? Over the other side's version of the facts and themes of the case?

This is a very difficult question to answer, whether you're a client or a lawyer. After all, much of the time reporters can seem like such a different breed. They're not businesspeople. Journalism, to many, is a calling. Or at least it starts out that way.

So what motivates the media? Yes, reporters are all professionals—probably the most ethical professionals you're every going to meet (especially when compared to public relations professionals and lawyers, I suppose). But at their core, they're just human beings, just like you and I. They have the same motivations, the same hopes and dreams, the same egos. If you prick them . . . well you get the idea.

This is not a book about how the media works, what they think, or how they do their job. But here, in a nutshell, are some thoughts on what makes reporters tick:

• *Reporters are not just working on your story, they're working on their careers.* My great fear is that no reporter will ever speak to me again after reading this. But it's true: Most reporters are looking to report stories in a manner that furthers their career. And there's nothing wrong with this.

This doesn't, by the way, mean that reporters will step on you to advance their career (although, like in any business or profession, there are those that will—but, honestly, they tend to be few and far between). Again, hold reporters ethically against any other professional out there and they look pretty good. But let's face it; reporters want to advance, and their reporting on your case is part of that process.

Consider: Most daily newspaper reporters follow a career path that goes something like this: They start out at a small newspaper, trade publication, or weekly. They eventually get hired by a major daily. Initially, they're assigned to writing small, un-bylined articles, perhaps for the "Metro Briefs" section or something like that. Soon, they get a small story with their own byline, or maybe a joint byline with another reporter. Then a bigger story where they hold the byline alone. Then the front page story. Then, perhaps, the front page story that other media starts talking about. Then the book deal.

Or whatever. My point is this: Your story is in the continuum of reporting that the reporter is doing in order to advance his career and reach the types of goals he's had in mind since he applied to journalism school. These goals can differ, depending on the personal interests and temperament of the reporter in question. Some want the Pulitzer Prize; some want the coveted seat on the evening or weekend interview programs; some want the lucrative speaking circuit; some want to report on interesting topics that appeal to their intellectual curiosity and allow them the freedom to pursue the types of stories they find of greatest interest. But all are reporters working on this goal at the same time that they're working on your story. In all cases, they want to impress their editors, their agents or book publishers, their parents, and they want to satisfy themselves and their own high standards for excellence.

Naturally, they *want* to get the story right, and none of this, I should add, is wrong, or bad, or unethical. But it's good to know.

Because the more you and your lawyer know about the motivation of the reporter, the more you'll be able to give the reporter what he or she wants to do the story better.

• *Reporters are under an enormous amount of pressure.* I've mentioned this before. A reporter's job is not easy. He or she needs to get the story, get it right, and get it told in, say, 500 words. And he needs to do it before 6 P.M. This is an incredible challenge.

It's even more of a challenge today than it was in years past. A strange paradox of the world in which we live is this: As the number of media outlets have grown tremendously in the past three decades, the amount of space given to each story has shrunk. Take the network evening news, for example. In the early 1970s, the average evening news story was over three minutes in length. In 1988, it was down to little more than two minutes. Today, an average evening news report is 80 seconds, and the average sound bite has dropped from an astounding 43.1 seconds in 1968 to five seconds or less today. That's a measure of the kind of challenge we're facing in this channel-surfing, multitasking, post-MTV environment in which we live.

We're not just talking about television news here. Consider for a moment how little space the reporter actually has in which to get the job done. Even the most "substantive" of the news media have a tiny space to tell the most important story. For example, recently we had a major—and I mean major—story for a client in the *New York Times*. Front page, color photos . . . it seemed the entire world saw it. It reframed the entire debate in the lawsuit and led the other side to serious settlement negotiations.

In my office, we were thrilled. I excitedly pulled up the story online and did a word count:

1,247 words.

That's it. For a major article in the *New York Times*.

Why is this relevant? Because if you understand the limited amount of space that even the most high-level media are working with, you begin to understand the importance of *honing* your message to ensure it gets across in the story. Given the complex nature of most lawsuits, this is hard to do. But you must. Knowing this is the first step to doing it well.

• *The "news hole" will determine how much space your story gets.* It may sound crass, but news, at its most basic level, is what gets put between the advertisements in a newspaper or other media outlet. Whether television, radio, or print, there's only so much space, and the amount of space devoted to each story is entirely dependent on how much other news happens that day. Even if your case seems to be the most important lawsuit to come down the pike in some time, if it comes on a busy newsday, there just isn't going to be a big enough "news hole" to cover your story. End of discussion.

Consider this example: I have a colleague in the public relations field who in the mid-1990s scheduled a major media event in Chicago on behalf of a client. Although a bit far afield from my area of expertise, watching the action at a distance, it seemed everything was done well. It was exquisitely prepared and enormous media coverage seemed guaranteed.

Then, on the day before the event, Joseph Cardinal Bernadin of Chicago died.

Absent a second Chicago fire—or the Cubs winning the World Series—I can think of no bigger story in Chicago than this and, needless to say, it dominated the news coverage for a week. Despite all of my friend's good work, his Chicago event received little coverage. Despite the fact that there was nothing my friend could have done about it, his client was not happy, and it eventually led to an awkward end to the relationship. Which is a shame, but as Hyman Roth said in *Godfather II:* "This (snort) is the business we chose (snort)!"

• *Even the best reporters just "skim the cream."* This is a constant source of frustration when working with the media: The sense that they just aren't getting the "complete" story—that things are missing from the final product, that the reporter missed the "essence" of the tale. Nowhere is this more true than in a story covering a court case, since even the simplest of court actions involved layers of facts and intricacies. How do you sum this up in 1,000 or maybe 2,000 words?

The answer is: "Very carefully." I know that lawyers and their clients will think this means "very superficially," but there's a difference. There is a way to tell a story succinctly, in short, measured sentences, to the point, without losing any of the meaning or any of the complexity. But it requires certain things of lawyers and their clients—all of whom are wrapped up, day in, day out, in the complexity of what they do. It requires that you:

—Shed the layers of complexity that often envelop your particular legal issue.
—Refrain from qualifying, differentiating, or otherwise anticipating and refuting opposing arguments.
—Lead with your conclusion, not with your factual argument.

We'll take a closer look at developing your message in Chapter Seven, but for now it's important to note that this last point is key, because attorneys are taught to lay out their argument in sufficient detail to prove the conclusion they are going to reach. This is also fairly common in those trained in the sciences: doctors, engineers, researchers, and so on. All build their arguments to a crescendo before reaching an unrefutable conclusion. But in a 500-word newspaper article, you just don't have time to build up the argument to the conclusion, nor the ability to lay out all the myriad levels of evidence that support your conclusion. Better to state the conclusion first—affirmatively, without qualification—and then provide the evidence to back it up. Otherwise you and the reporter may never get there.

• *Reporters are, first and foremost, writers, with a writer's love of words and language.* I've tested this theory on more than one occasion. Sitting around with current and former reporters (both print and television, by the way) I'll make the following point: "Most reporters started out in life wanting to be novelists . . ." I've never gotten an argument—the most I've gotten on occasion is a qualification like, "Well, I didn't start out that way . . . but in my ideal world, I'd be a novelist now."

Here's the point: Reporters, almost without exception, love words. They love language and, in one form or another, aspire to the literary. A particularly effective use of language will catch a reporter's attention and, inevitably, make it into the coverage of your case or legal issue.

I first learned this many years ago when working for the city of New York in the Koch and Dinkins administrations. I was a young political aide in what was then called the Public Development Corporation (now called the Economic Development Corporation), and my job was to write news releases on the latest city-sponsored real estate projects. Sometimes these were big projects like the re-development of Times Square or the MetroTech development in downtown Brooklyn. But more often they were smaller projects scattered throughout the five boroughs. On these smaller projects, I would write a news release—complete with a quote from the mayor—send it to City Hall for review, get it back virtually unedited (in truth, I don't think anyone ever read the press releases I sent over), then send it out to the local newspapers. We'd usually receive pretty good coverage from the local weekly newspaper covering the borough, perhaps also an article in *Crain's New York Business* (the weekly business newspaper) *and,* if we were lucky, maybe a small article in one of the major dailies covering the city: the *New York Times,* the *Daily News,* the *New York Post,* or *Newsday.*

On one of these projects—I think it was a small development in Queens—I was writing about the effort to keep businesses in New York City, and wrote the following quote for the mayor at the time (I believe it was Mayor Dinkins): "Dollar for dollar, doing business in New York makes great economic sense."

Get it? "Sense." A play on "dollars and cents."

Well, I thought nothing of it—and neither did the mayor's office, since it came back to me unedited—and off it went to the media, like any other low-level press announcement.

The next day I opened one of the major newspapers, and, not only was the story one of the lead stories in the Metro Section, the "call-out" (which is the boxed sentence or two you see in many newspaper articles that highlights a key point of the story) was the quote that I had written for the mayor. The play on words had attracted the attention of the editor, who decided to make it a far bigger part of the day's news than it otherwise would have been.

If you think I was surprised, imagine how surprised the mayor's office must have been, since I have no doubt that this was the first time many of them, the mayor included, had ever seen the quote.

Media love language. This doesn't mean you have to be cutesy or coy or silly in what you say—but it does mean that if you can find ways to use language *effectively* to get your point across to reporters, do it! You're likely to get your message across—and may even get more coverage of your story that you originally expected.

ACTION POINTS

✔ Lawyers and their clients often complain about the lack of identifiable rules governing relations with the media—and sometimes this lack of rules can lead even the most hardboiled litigator to make mistakes that can jeopardize client confidences, or the case as a whole.

✔ When a reporter calls, it is usually best not to answer questions right there, but instead to take the reporter's contact information, find out his or her deadline and call back—after you've had time to "refocus" on getting your message to the reporter in an effective manner.

✔ Our "Ten Tips" for interviews are simple rules that all attorneys and their clients can use during litigation to ensure that their communication's message is getting through to the media in the manner intended.

✔ Knowing the rules of attribution can help a party to a lawsuit isolate the communications message, while still offering sufficient background to allow the reporter to understand the case more fully.

✔ Knowing the media's motivation can help a party to a lawsuit to deliver a message that a reporter both *wants* and *needs*—since it is these types of messages that will ultimately find their way into the reporter's next story.

CHAPTER FOUR

Stepping into High-Profile Litigation

As we emphasize throughout this book, communications strategy for litigation or other legal matters should be securely in place well before the lawsuit actually begins.

But it almost never works that way.

In most cases, the first thought as to communications strategy occurs only after the first reporter has called. Unfortunately, up until that point, the focus has usually been solely on the legal aspects of the case, with barely a thought given to the court of public opinion.

In this chapter, we'll look at what to do when a business executive, lawyer, or communications professional is thrust into the center of the media storm. Central to this effort is a response discipline I call "Control, Information, Response," or CIR. Then we'll look at another high-profile case that made headlines—the Ronald Perelman/Patricia Duff child custody battle—to see how we used the CIR system to begin to turn the tide.

My brother is a plumber, and we often joke that much of the time it seems we're in the same business: We can be called at any moment, it's usually an emergency, and we both often find ourselves knee-deep in "it" before too long.

In October 1999, I faced just such a situation. I returned from a lunch meeting with my lawyer to a somewhat curious voicemail message. In heavily accented English, a man was asking me to call him . . . I think. In fact, in the relatively long message, that was about all I understood. While I was listening to that message, two more voicemails appeared. One of them was from a lawyer who is a continuing client of mine.

"Jim, you should be getting a call from one of the firm's clients, a large foreign company, about a touchy legal matter they have on the West Coast. Give me a call when you get the chance to discuss it."

The next message, just as my client predicted, was from the general counsel of the foreign company, which was based in New York. He introduced himself, said he had been referred by my lawyer client, and asked that I return his call.

No sooner had I listened to that message than the phone rang again. It was another executive of the foreign company, calling from the West Coast.

"Mr. Haggerty, uh, this is Mr. Agnello." (This is not his real name.) His English was far better than the man who left the original message.

"Mr. Agnello," I said, "Your general counsel in New York just left me a message. He was referred . . ."

Mr. Agnello interrupted me.

"Mr. Haggerty, uh, we have a difficult legal problem here. And a news crew wants to interview me about it."

"They called you?"

"No, they're here."

"Where are they?"

"They are standing right next to me."

Now I have been called very late in the action in many cases, but this took the cake! I'd like to say I was full of confidence as I instructed Mr. Agnello about what to do, but, again, this was a pretty unprecedented moment. Among other things, at this point I knew nothing about the company, nothing about the issue they faced, or exactly what the news crew was looking for.

Clearly, the first thing we needed was time.

"Mr. Agnello," I said, "here's what I want you to do. Put me on hold, escort the camera crew to the nearest conference room, ask them if they'd like anything to drink—coffee or water or something—and tell them you'll be right with them. Then come back and tell me what this is all about."

I clearly remember Mr. Agnello hesitating for a moment, as if mulling it over, then thanking me very quickly before putting me on hold.

It would have been very easy to make the wrong move in this situation. I might have instructed Mr. Agnello to politely ask the camera crew to leave, and if they refused, call security to escort the crew from the building. That is the usual response when a trespasser refuses to leave—even one with a video camera and a daily news slot. But let's face it, this was exactly what the news crew wanted! It would have turned the entire proceeding into a circus—and these things never look good on television. Many of us probably have seen this before—I'm always reminded of the incident where, after NBC was bought by General Electric, David Letterman showed up at the General Electric headquarters with a basket of fruit, camera crew in tow. He was met at the door by security guards who rudely told him to leave (even though he was technically a General Electric employee at that point). The head security guard then refused to shake Letterman's hand and threw his hands over the television camera lens before throwing the camera crew, and Letterman, out. That must have been 15 years ago, but they're still showing it on highlight reels.

Lesson to be learned: Hand-over-the-camera lens never works. So don't try it—unless every other attempt to deal with the camera crew showing up at your offices or facilities has failed.

The case that opens this chapter is a perfect illustration. Instead of throwing the camera crew out, we decided to politely escort them to a comfortable, secure area of the building while we planned our next move.

While I was on hold with Mr. Agnello and he was escorting the news crew to the conference room, I quickly did online research to see if there was anything written in the past day or so that would give me an idea as to what this was all about. I found the following in a small local newspaper:

MAN COMMITS SUICIDE AFTER SETTLING DISCRIMINATION CLAIM

A local man hung himself in his garage last night, three days after settling a racial discrimination lawsuit with his employer . . .

That's about as far as I got before Mr. Agnello came back on the phone.

"Mr. Haggerty, uh, this is Agnello again. They are now in the conference room." Mr. Agnello let me know that the camera crew had put up no resistance and were happy to wait. For now.

"Mr. Agnello," I said, "does this have to do with Mr. Bartow's suicide?"

"Yes."

"What does the news crew say they want?"

"They say they want to interview me."

This was obviously a very difficult situation. Though an intelligent, well-spoken man, Mr. Agnello was in no way ready to speak to the media on this issue.

"Okay, Mr. Agnello, here's what we do next," I said, "go back to the news crew and tell them politely that you won't appear on camera, but you will have a written statement for them in about 10 minutes."

"Okay," he said. "But Mr. Haggerty, what will you tell them?"

"I don't know. But I have 10 minutes to figure that out."

Technically, I was skating on thin ice here. At this point, I hadn't even spoken to the lawyers—either the company's in-house lawyer or their outside counsel—and here I was making promises on their behalf. But I knew there needed to be some sort of response and the outside lawyer was already a client of my company. So I decided to take the chance.

My next call was to my lawyer client, who conferenced in the company's general counsel. I explained the latest developments.

The initial reaction from the lawyers was typical—even with a camera crew impatiently sitting in their conference room 3,000 miles away.

"We have no comment on this case," the general counsel said, "and that's all any sort of statement should say. We need to get them to leave."

He paused for a moment, then added: "Of course, we feel bad about Mr. Bartow's death." A moment more of thought. "But we never comment on matters related to employment."

"I believe it's illegal to do so in California," my lawyer client chimed in.

I thought for a moment.

"Well, can you say that?" I asked

"Say what?"

"Offer your condolences, but say that you won't comment on the specifics of his employment because it's against the law."

I could hear the proverbial wheels grinding as both lawyers considered my suggestion. Finally, my lawyer client spoke up.

"I think Jim's right," he said, "there's certainly no reason why we can't offer our condolences."

I know an opportunity when I hear one, so I said, "Why don't I draft something simple, get it to you for review, and then fax it to L.A. At the very least, it should get the camera crew out of your conference room." And our plan was in place.

About five minutes later (after confirming the name of the company!), I faxed off the following:

FROM: FORCO, INC.
               Los Angeles, California

CONTACT: THE PR CONSULTING GROUP
             (212) 683–8100
             Jim Haggerty, ext. 224
             Elizabeth Hall, ext. 230

STATEMENT OF FORCO, INC.

We are shocked and saddened at the news of Mr. Bartow's death. It is a true tragedy, and we offer our deepest condolences to his family and friends.

At this time, we have very little information as to the circumstances of his death, and thus feel it would be inappropriate to comment further.

Moreover, it is our policy not to comment on matters relating to the employment of any person by ForCo.

Again, our sympathies go out to Mr. Bartow's family and friends during this difficult time.

And that was it. The company had said nothing in the statement that they would feel uncomfortable about seeing in print. They managed to seem compassionate and concerned, and—most importantly—avoided the dreaded "no comment," which without a doubt would have made them seem guilty. Of something.

As an aside, even the way I've phrased that last thought would set off alarm bells in a lawyer's head. "Guilty?" the lawyer would ask, "How can we seem guilty in these circumstances? At most, this is a case of discrimination, which is civil law. 'Guilty' is a criminal law term—in civil law, the most you can be is 'liable.'"

True enough—but it is exactly that kind of legalistic thinking that trips lawyers up when thinking about how a client looks to a wider audience. Yes, a client in a civil action for employment discrimination can never technically be "guilty." But they can sure as hell look guilty—and if we had issued a terse "no comment" to the news crew, or had the camera crew thrown out of their offices, the company certainly would have looked guilty in this instance.

Instead, I faxed the statement to Mr. Agnello in Los Angeles— about five minutes late, if I recall correctly—and he promptly delivered it to the camera crew, who had what they needed to flash on the screen for the evening news. That evening, the television station reported the story with shots of the outside of the company's facility and a graphic showing our written statement.

No confrontation. No hand over the camera lens. No "no comment."

This was an unusual circumstance, but the handling of the matter is a good encapsulation of the mechanism that needs to be put in place whenever a company or its legal communications team is thrust into a legal matter that is going to put it under the harsh glare of the media spotlight. I call this the "Control, Information Response" method, or CIR. It perfectly describes the method of handling such incidents—hopefully not, as in this case, when a camera crew is waiting by your side—but any time a legal matter requires immediate action in the court of public opinion.

THE CIR SYSTEM:
CONTROL, INFORMATION, RESPONSE

The essence of handling of communications in litigation is the CIR Approach: Control, Information, Response. We want *control* over the points of communication, we want better *information* than anyone else has, and we want to have a *response* mechanism in place—one that is tailored to the overall business goals of the client and the litigation goals put forth by the legal team.*

In the previous example, as soon as we received the phone call from the company official about the camera crew standing by his side, our first thought was to *control:* We needed to get a handle on a situation that had the potential to explode right before our eyes. Media is, of course, inherently uncontrollable, but I'm not talking about *absolute* control here—I'm talking about as much control as we can have in the situation—enough in this case to ensure the camera crew wasn't going to start the cameras rolling right in front of Mr. Agnello's face.

Whether on the plaintiff or defense side, a client or legal counsel—often working with internal and external public relations professionals—will want to put CIR into effect at the earliest possible moment. Usually, this means when the company has any inkling that a lawsuit is possible and that the suit has a likelihood of winding up in the public arena. For plaintiffs, it should occur when the business strategy dictates that the client should move forward with legal action (or threatened legal action); for the defendant, it should occur when there is a sense that this is where the other side is moving. (In practice, unfortunately, as we've seen in many cases, it usually occurs when the complaint is about to be filed or when the first camera crew has shown up at the company's door.)

Through the course of this book, we have examples from a variety of lawsuits describing when and how the CIR response was put into effect—and times when it wasn't—and the consequences. But

---

*As an aside, in developing the CIR approach, over the years I've tried to come up with a descriptive acronym for what we do, something that is memorable and describes perfectly the kind of approach we like to take when handling legal matters. Something like R.E.S.P.O.N.S.E. or C.O.N.T.R.O.L. In many cases, I have seen management and communications professionals use this approach successfully, but in this case I couldn't seem to do it—everything I spelled out was either a dirty word or the name of a member of 'N Sync. In the end, I dispensed with the cutesy acronyms and decided to use initials that describe *exactly* what we do: hence, CIR.

briefly, what follows is a description of each of these areas and the practical application to your case or controversy.

Part One: Control

A confession: My name is Jim and I am a control freak. Almost obsessively so, as anyone who has worked with me can tell you. I always want to have my finger on the pulse of what is happening at all times. Uncertainty—that feeling of not knowing what is happening at any given moment—is my greatest foe. That's part of the reason, I think, that I have chosen to work in such a small firm—in a two-minute lap around my office, I can get the lowdown on what's happening in any number of matters and client assignments we are handling at any given time.

This is similar, I suppose, to a litigator's desire to control the course and flow of litigation. Any good lawyer wants to make sure that he or she is handling a case in a manner that allows for continued exercise of ethical and professional responsibilities at every step of the process. In the heat of a difficult legal battle, there's no room for surprises.

From a communications standpoint, the first task when stepping into a high-profile legal dispute is to *secure the points of contact:* the places and people that the media and other audiences will go to for information about your case or legal dispute. Not in a nefarious way, mind you—we're not talking about hiding things or otherwise restricting access to important information about the case. Instead, we are talking about exerting some measure of control over who is saying what to whom and when.

Why, you may ask? Isn't this unfair? Shouldn't you let the information and sources flow freely, and the truth will come out—through the "so-called marketplace of ideas."

If you've read this far in the book, you know the answer to this question. Particularly in a lawsuit—where documents flow like water and the legal issues are often as deep as the ocean—a reporter or other interested party who is speaking to the wrong person isn't getting the full picture of the facts and legal issues in the case. Like Rashamon, everyone will be telling a different version of the story. This may be true even within your own legal team. They may have their own pet issues or concerns that they want to address, or they just may not be particularly good at telling the reporter what is really important about the case. As discussed in Chapter Seven, there is a single unified message you ideally want to convey about your case, and unless your side is exerting discipline in the telling, the message is going to meander—not usually into areas that are outright damaging to your side and the case, but rather just off-point. But this can be just as damaging to the "presentation" of your case to the public audience.

Now in a "physical crisis"—such as a construction accident, for instance—the first thing you want to do is secure the location of the incident to ensure that no one slips onto the site before you can correctly ascertain exactly what happened. Again, not for the purposes of hiding anything, but rather to make sure that your communication is conveying a complete picture of what has happened. So, too, in litigation, which is the ultimate "virtual" crisis—it exists solely in documents, in other evidence, and in the recollections of parties and others with knowledge of the facts of the case. The first step is to exercise control over the flow of information to ensure the right message is getting out.

In the example that opened this chapter, there were many ways we could have let control over the communications aspect of the situation get away from us. Suppose, for example, we had just thrown the camera crew off the property—a perfectly *legal* solution, by the way. Besides providing damaging video coverage of a physical ejection (again, just what the local news would want), the video crew could simply have waited outside the facility for employees to come out. They could have approached the employees as they left the facility at the end of the day and asked them: "Hey, do you know anything about the suicide?"

Instead, we were able to give the news crew what they needed to file the story, and—more importantly—we gave them the sense that we were cooperating with them to the extent we could. Thus, they saw no particular reason to pursue different avenues of coverage, to wait around until employees left the building. They got back to the studio and filed the story.

Will this work all the time? Of course, not, nothing ever does. Sometimes you'll try to control the situation and give the media what they need to do their job—and they'll go interview employees outside the plant anyway. But what you are trying to do in the

Control phase of the CIR process is enhance the *probability* that the message that gets out is your message.

Who or What Are the Points of Contact

Who or what are the various points of contact you are looking to control when communicating regarding litigation? The *what* is easy enough—files, documents, and other physical evidence need to be in a secure place, and odds are this is being done in anticipation of the litigation anyway. The *who* is the trickier part. It can include:

- Attorneys working on the case.
- Senior executives with knowledge of the facts of the case.
- Other employees, particularly in a workplace-related story (such as a discrimination claim, a labor union issue, or a corporate fraud issue).
- Internal and external public relations personnel who have their own reporter contacts.
- Shareholders and other investors.
- In certain cases, users of the Internet and other technologies (in chat rooms, on investor sites, etc.).
- Other "influentials"—which might include pundits, consultants, and others in a position to comment on your case.

Each of these groups may be called on by the media before or after they speak to you—and may even be called *instead* of you, and pressed for information on a background basis or off-the-record. Your ability to control each of these audiences will differ, and it's important to understand exactly how it will differ in order to push the right buttons and maximize your ability to control the communications in the case.

We have been discussing the difficulties attorneys face when handling the media throughout the course of this book, and sometimes the legal team can be the hardest to control—particularly in a big case with a large team of high-profile litigators. In Chapter Six, we discuss our core legal/communication team, which includes representatives from the legal and communications departments and, hopefully, resolves some of the issues involved with attorneys establishing independent lines of communication with the media and other audiences.

But to look more closely at control issues, let's again use the case of the foreign company that opened this chapter. The first thing we wanted to do was ensure that the executive confronting the news crew was not put in the awkward position of having to comment on the two major elements of the case—the suicide itself, or the discrimination lawsuit that preceded it. Among other things, given the recent tragic events, it probably wasn't the time to comment on anything *except* to offer sympathy and condolences. Clearly it was not Mr. Agnello's responsibility to accurately handle all of the many legal and factual elements of the case, and when employees are put before the media spotlight, sometimes it can cause difficulties from both a communications perspective *and* from the standpoint of overall employee morale. Thus, controlling employees' communication during this case was key.

Which brings us to an important point about controlling communications in a lawsuit: Most often, you can control the points of contact by providing information *yourself* to all of the parties mentioned earlier: shareholders, employees, partners. Obviously, the information will be different depending on the audiences—shareholders will want to know more about the effect of litigation on stock price, for example—but the key is to make that information available to each of the points of contact. The more they know about the situation and the legal issues involved, the less likely they will be to engage in speculation, rumor, and gossip.

In addition, if you provide a mechanism for referring a reporter or other outside audience, this opens up another avenue for a response that coordinates with your overall litigation strategy. That is to say, if an employee, for example, has the option to say to a reporter: "You know who you should call . . ." they are far less likely to feel compelled to start answering questions themselves. Again, not 100 percent, but at least it creates a situation where the ability to control the points of contact are enhanced.

In the case of employees, for example, it is standard that we advise clients to issue an internal memo to employees regarding the case, generally along the lines of the following:

> As you know, there's been a considerable tragedy involving one of ForCo's employees, Mr. Bartow. Our great sympathies go out to the Bartow family during their time of personal tragedy.

Given the nature of these events, there is a possibility that ForCo employees may be approached by representatives of the media and asked to discuss the incident and Mr. Bartow's employment at ForCo. If you are contacted by a representative of the media, please respond as follows:

- Very politely take the reporter's name, the media they are working for, their phone number, and ask if they are working under a deadline.
- Indicate that this information will be forwarded to ForCo's press representatives, Mr. Jim Haggerty and Ms. Liz Hall, who will get back to them promptly (contact information is below).

Again, it is very important that all personnel be polite and helpful, *without* answering any questions from the reporter.

If asked: "Can you just answer one question?" the response should be "I cannot answer any questions myself, but I will forward your request to our representatives who will be happy to assist you in any way they can."

As you can see, the memo describes the situation to the employees in as much detail as possible (given the legal confines), explains that they might be approached by reporters at some point, and gives clear instructions for referring the reporters to the designated place for response. The first element is critical: If you just say "You may get called by a reporter, please refer him to . . ." without some sort of explanation as to what is going on, you are likely to lose the trust of your employees—and then the rumors and conjecture begin. It's almost as if you are saying: "Don't ask us why, just do as you're told"—and there's no better way to get people to do just the opposite.

Attorneys, it should be noted, have traditionally been resistant to providing any sort of information like this when communicating with employees, as with the media. "Don't say anything," or "say as little as possible" is often the lawyer's credo. It is important to get past this—the client and their public relations representatives should walk the lawyers through this process carefully, to alleviate concerns that if you say anything, you are saying something that is confidential or may otherwise damage your case. Just the opposite is true: If you say too little, your employees will have no idea what is going on—and the Control function of the CIR process will be undermined. In many cases, the attorneys must be convinced of this fact, just as we did when creating the statement for the foreign company in the opening example to this chapter. Attorneys, their clients, and anyone else involved in the process should start by thinking "What *can* we say?" rather than "What *can't* we say?"

There may be concern that the media may actually come to your door instead of calling (again, as in the ForCo example). Remember that *ignorance* is the greatest enemy—if employees aren't aware what is happening and a camera is shoved in their faces, problems ensue. In this circumstance, it is important to have a procedure in place should the news crew show up in the reception lobby. We suggest a variation of the previous memo, along the lines of the following:

> If reporters or a video crew come to the ForCo facility, reception and security personnel should:
>
> - Bring the news crew to a private area of ForCo's offices—preferably a conference room just off the reception area.
> - Very politely inform the reporter that it is the policy of the company not to allow media to enter the premises without an appointment.
> - Offer to take the reporter's name, the media he is working for, his phone number, and if he is working under a deadline.
> - Indicate that this information will be forwarded to ForCo's press representatives, who will respond promptly and provide any information he needs.
>
> Security and reception personnel should answer no questions and, above all, remain as cordial and friendly as possible while politely referring the media to ForCo's press representatives. If the news crew refuses to leave, security should notify Mr. Agnello immediately.

An important element of the procedure is *bringing the news crew out of the "public" area of the office and into a conference room* or other private area—where they're more comfortable and you are more comfortable. The reason is twofold:

1. Leave a news crew in your reception area even for a few minutes and they'll begin to suspect they are getting the runaround.

2. You don't want your employees to stroll past the reception area and think: "What's that news crew doing in our reception area? Something bad must have happened!" Misunderstandings and ignorance by any of the points of contact are fertile ground for miscommunication.

Similar tactics can be used for any of the key audiences, but the idea behind these tactics is the same: You need to establish some measure of control over all of the various avenues of communications—and, to do that, you need to reach out to the points of contact, give them an idea of what's happening and what the procedure should be for responding to inquiries.

Part Two: Information

Given the complexity of legal issues, one of the first things I want when thrust into a litigation situation is information—information about the case, the facts and the law, the lawyers involved, the business issues that underlie the legal dimensions, and the particular reporters that are covering the case. *Information is the foundation of strategy*—whether you are planning strategy months before the first reporter calls, or while the news crew is waiting next to you or your client.

Even in the scenario that opened this chapter, you can see how my mind was on the *information* I would need to make the right choices in a very difficult situation. While I was on hold with Mr. Agnello, I was already online to see what I could find about the situation facing the company. In most cases, there's a little more time than this, and we're able to collect much more information about the dispute, including:

- All legal documents, briefs, memoranda, letters of opinion, and so on.

- A litigation timeline: what will be happening next, and when.
- Background information about the company and its history—including the company's treatment in the media (and the reporters who routinely cover the company).
- Information on the legal team, including internal and external lawyers and nonlawyer executives who will be involved in the case.
- Information on the other side—who they are and who their attorneys are.
- In the same vein, information about the other side's propensity to use the media to advance their side of the case—i.e., do they have a public relations firm and, if so, how skilled are they; do the lawyers have "media savvy," or are they otherwise skilled at using the media to advance their position?
- Information on the media that has covered the case thus far—as well as information on reporters who *should* be covering the case.
- Information about nonmedia audiences that need to be reached with our communications message (i.e., employees, shareholders).
- Information on other "influentials"—politicians, regulators, business leaders, thought leaders—anyone who may have an effect, negative and positive, on the conduct of the case.

These are just some of the areas that we cover depending on the situation and how much time we have to coordinate strategy. As you can see, it's pretty comprehensive, and many times we pull together far more information than is needed. But all of my clients—be they lawyers or the actual companies themselves—are advised to provide me too much information, rather than too little. I *never* want to be in a situation where I'm caught off guard—by not knowing the latest legal development, for example, or not knowing the other side has a skilled litigation publicist working on their behalf. I'd always rather be safe than sorry, and when handling the communications component of high-profile litigation, there's no substitute for information.

Part Three: Response

The third element of the CIR process is the response. Much of this book and the examples we use are about proper response to the communications challenges that occur during litigation. But I want to emphasize that, along with the exact content of the response, the intensity, and particular vehicle for the response is critical. Again, we're not talking knee-jerk press releases or a press conference for every significant (or insignificant) legal development. Instead, we're talking about a measured, controlled response to the situation at hand—a thinking-person's response, if you will—one that takes into account the overall legal and reputation goals that the client and their attorneys have outlined in developing the litigation strategy. In many ways, responding to the particular developments in a legal dispute requires an "artisan's touch":

- You need to know when to respond with guns a-blazin'—for example, with a press conference or a satellite media tour.

- You need to know when to respond selectively (i.e., with a short statement as in the example of the foreign company at the beginning of this chapter, a single interview with the appropriate media outlet, or simply a background call to the right reporter).

- You need to know when *not* to respond at all.

The last point may be the most nuanced of the three. As I've mentioned, my background is in government and politics, and the mindset is completely different from what you need when managing litigation. In politics, if they hit you, you hit them back. Hard. They schedule a press conference at noon, you schedule one at 1 P.M. to refute whatever was said. They do an op-ed piece in the *New York Times*, you do one in the *Washington Post*. And so on.

Not so in litigation. It is *not* a political campaign. The goal is not 50.1 percent of the electorate or enough votes to pass a piece of legislation. In many situations, you need to step back and consider what's important in terms of the underlying lawsuit and let that dictate the level and content of the response. There may be times when no response at all is the best move—you'll find any other action is just not conducive to the litigation as a whole. Remember, the overall goal is to use communications to manage the litigation itself and the reputational ramifications of that litigation. If you're just looking for press clippings—"media by the pound," good or bad—you're not thinking about overall litigation goals. You don't have to win *every* battle—and, in fact, sometimes it's ill-advised—not just from a public relations standpoint, but from a legal standpoint as well.

Consider the following example: We had a large industrial client who was engaged in continuing litigation with its main competitor. There were several suits, countersuits, third-party interventions—and all the other kinds of activity that surrounds a legal dispute of this kind. At one point, the parties settled a particular piece of litigation peripheral to the main case, but one that was somewhat embarrassing to my client. As part of the settlement, each side had a confidentiality agreement—neither party could talk about any aspect of the case or settlement, in the media or otherwise.

The following week, an article describing the settlement appeared in a small trade publication—obviously placed there by the other side. My client and their lawyers were livid. They wanted to go to court to enforce the gag order—then hold a press conference of their own to announce that the settlement was void.

After analyzing the situation, we recommended they do no such thing. Not even the court action. This was, after all, a lawsuit far removed from the major elements of concern to my client—and one that would continue to give them a black eye the longer it remained front and center in the media. A press conference—or even filing papers with the court alleging a breach of the settlement agreement—would bring the whole story to the front page of the major media, rather than the back pages of a minor trade publication. Although the law was in the client's favor—the breach would have been easy to prove—the damage to my client's reputation would have offset any value gained through aggressive enforcement of the settlement agreement.

Instead, we had the client draft a short letter to the other side's attorneys, stating that it had come to our attention that their client had breached the settlement agreement, and that if they did so again, we would consider the settlement agreement void, and would go to court to seek appropriate remedies. The other side never breached the settlement agreement again, and that was the end of it.

The lesson here is that the usual method of proceeding in legal disputes can sometimes backfire when your court case is the subject of media scrutiny. If you do things "the way we've always done it," with no thought to the broader ramifications of your actions, you'll likely get burned—and your legal cause is going to suffer.

For another example, let's take a look at a small part of another sensational New York case—the Lizzie Grubman affair, where the publicity princess backed her SUV into a crowd outside the Conscience Point Inn in the Hamptons.

The facts: Late on the night of July 7, 2001, Grubman—whose small entertainment-and-party public relations firm was so high-profile that she was featured on the cover of *New York* magazine—was parked in a no-parking zone outside the popular Long Island nightspot. A bouncer asked her to move her vehicle. Grubman allegedly cursed and disparaged the bouncer as "white trash," then (presumably accidentally) put her Mercedes SUV in reverse and backed into a crowd of club-goers and Conscience Point employees. Grubman then fled the scene, surrendering the next day to police. Criminal charges were filed (with Grubman eventually pleading guilty and serving time in Suffolk County jail), along with personal injury lawsuits against Grubman and her father (entertainment attorney Allen Grubman, the lessee of the SUV). Among the civil lawsuits was one for more than $30 million filed by the Conscience Point promoter, Adam Wacht, who was injured in the accident.

Now, in personal injury cases, a standard part of the defendant's answer is to plead what are called affirmative defenses—including contributory negligence (which asserts that the plaintiff was also at fault in causing his or her own injury) and assumption of risk (asserting that the plaintiff assumed the risk that an accident of this type would happen). Most attorneys will plead these defenses whether or not they have evidence at the time to support the claim. Why? Because if you don't plead these defenses at the outset, you have little, if any, chance to add them later. Attorneys who practice personal injury defense generally throw in all the affirmative defenses they can, then hope that through the process of discovery they find evidence to support their claims (if they don't, the defenses are removed later on in the court proceeding). Very standard stuff—so standard that most defense firms have prepro-grammed, "boilerplate" pleadings that allow them just to insert the names and facts of the case, and print out an entire answer brief—including all the affirmative defenses.

In the civil lawsuit against Grubman and her father by Wacht, this standard method of legal practice proved a huge embarrass-ment—and likely cost Lizzie Grubman, both in her civil and crim-inal actions. In response to the lawsuit, her father's attorneys filed answers alleging various affirmative defenses against Wacht—in-cluding that he had somehow contributed to the accident. Again, standard stuff in a personal injury lawsuit—but this was no ordi-nary lawsuit. To reporters who read the pleading, it appeared as if Ms. Grubman's father was blaming the victims—reinforcing the notion that Lizzie Grubman was nothing more than a spoiled Daddy's girl who blamed everyone but herself for her woes. The re-sulting coverage was brutal, as you can see from the following front-page story in the *New York Post,* under the headline "Lizzie's Dad's Defense: Victims Are to Blame":

> Lizzie Grubman's dad is using a "blame the victim" defense—saying one of the people run over by his daughter was responsi-ble for his own injuries.
>
> Allen Grubman—a lawyer and the leasee of the Mercedes SUV that the publicity princess backed into 16 people—charges in court papers that victim Adam Wacht's injuries "were caused in whole or in part by" Wacht's negligence or "culpable conduct."
>
> The papers also claim that by being at the Conscience Point Inn in Southampton on July 7, Wacht knowingly assumed the risk of being hurt. The papers do not spell out how Wacht, an enter-tainment promoter whose leg was shattered, was negligent or culpable.
>
> The papers were filed as a response to Wacht's $30 million civil suit against Lizzie and her dad—and were made public as a sixth victim filed suit in the case. Wacht's lawyers were furious about Allen Grubman's charge.
>
> "That's pouring salt on open wounds," fumed one, Howard Hershenhorn. "It's absolute nonsense. Any logical person knows that there was nothing any of these victims could have done to avoid this accident."

But Lizzie's criminal lawyer, Stephen Scaring, told the *Post,* "I think you're making more of it [her father's papers] than it deserves."

Scaring said the language blaming Wacht "is boilerplate and routinely inserted into answers" to lawsuits.

That "boilerplate" explanation didn't wash with another of Wacht's lawyers, Anthony Gair.

"Given the egregious nature of this accident, it's totally un-called for, because there's absolutely no basis of fact to assert that Wacht was to blame," he said. Lizzie, 30, claims the crash was an accident, but police who arrested her on felony assault charges said she intentionally ran down the victims and fled the crash scene.[1]

Now let's think about this for a moment. What are the chances that a defendant in a civil action is going to prevail in a lawsuit by asserting that the people she backed over in her SUV were negligent themselves? Or that promoter who accepts a job at a club is assuming the risk that he will, at some point, be run over? These are long-shot arguments, at best, especially when considering the potential publicity damage you are doing to the client and the case by asserting them. But again, the standard operating procedure in a personal injury case is to preserve these defenses by asserting them in your answer—then abandoning them, if you have to, later.

This is not necessarily bad lawyering, but it is the result of lawyers not adequately considering the effect of their legal actions in the wider public arena. It is also an example of Grubman's public relations advisors not being "tight" enough with the legal team to counsel them properly on the potential negative effects of asserting such defenses. Had they read the pleading beforehand, any PR pro worth his or her salt would have raised a red flag when they got to these affirmative defenses, particularly if they understood the legal realities—that is, how much of a long shot these defenses actually were in this case.

Did this really hurt Grubman's case all that much? Well, consider: Did the front-page story reinforcing Grubman's alleged disregard for the blue-collar denizens of the Hamptons raise the media hysteria to a whole new level? Absolutely. Did it embolden the plaintiff's lawyers—and the prosecutors in the criminal case, for that matter—ensuring that they would take a harder line when negotiating plea bargains or settlements? Likely. Did it encourage copycat civil suits and an array of other legal maneuverings. Probably.

So did it ultimately damage Grubman in both her criminal and civil proceedings? What do you think?

Now go back to the example that opened this chapter and consider the response we chose: a written statement. Why did we choose this? We could have called a press conference, allowed an interview with the CEO, or rushed an attorney to the scene to respond. But we knew:

- There wasn't enough time to prepare a spokesperson for response.
- At this point, the response would entail nothing of substance, only an offering of sympathy and condolences.
- We knew a written statement—which the TV crew could excerpt and put up on the screen on the evening news—would be sufficient from their standpoint.
- We knew "No comment" was out of the question.

In managing communications during litigation, there are few straightforward "write the press release, send the press release" situations—which is why so many companies and their attorneys have so much trouble. But no matter where you come into the litigation process—be it before the first paper is filed or after the first reporter is in your office—the level and appropriateness of the response component is going to be key to ensuring that the CIR system has the appropriate effect.

TAKING DECISIVE ACTION

Just so that you don't get the idea that I'm always a super-nice guy when handling the media—always accommodating, always looking to please the media and others who might show up for information—I thought I'd include an example of a case where decisive action prevented a story from becoming larger.

In late 2000 and early 2001, the Pacifica Radio Network (a left-wing network of radio stations founded shortly after World War II) was embroiled in a series of contentious, high-profile internal battles that featured everything from court action, to lockouts, to behind-the-scenes power plays, to outright intimidation and violence. On one side was the Pacifica Board and its management, which was looking for ways to "professionalize" the network and its mission; on the other, longtime listeners and some station personnel—including Amy Goodman, the popular host of the program *Democracy Now!*—who feared the corporatization of Pacifica, that the board had clandestine plans to turn the last voice of freedom and free speech into a corporate monolith like . . . gasp . . . NPR!

At the center of the dispute was a board member at Pacifica named John Murdock, a thoughtful, good-natured health care attorney and partner in the law firm Epstein Becker & Green. Epstein Becker & Green is one of the nation's leading law firms in several different practice areas—including health law and employment law—and Murdock thought board membership might be a nice way to give back to the community. But three different California court cases charged the board with all sorts of improper action, and John Murdock in particular became a focus of the board's opponents (part of the reason was that Murdock's firm had been hired to defend Pacifica in these cases). Racist caricatures, WANTED posters, and threatening voice and e-mail greeted Murdock at every turn. His firm was also threatened, and several of the Epstein Becker & Green's seminars were disrupted by angry protestors. In prior disputes, shots had actually been fired at a director's house by a protestor—so these were not matters to be taken lightly. We were called in by the law firm and Pacifica to assist in the crisis and communications elements of the dispute.

A week or so into our work, I was on the Staten Island Ferry traveling to my Manhattan office and received a call on my cell phone from a colleague: Epstein Becker & Green's offices in San Francisco was on the line; they had a problem that they needed our help with. I was patched through—and found out that Pacifica protesters had invaded the Epstein Becker offices and were staging a sit-in in their reception area.

"What should we do?" the office manager asked. Her voice was almost overwhelmed by background noise.

"I can barely hear you," I said.

"Oh yeah, the protesters are chanting something in the background. They're peaceful, but we need to know how to get them out of here."

I thought for a moment. Again, this was an unusual occurrence, to say the least—and remember, up until then I was floating peacefully across New York harbor on the Staten Island Ferry.

"Are any media there?" I asked.

"No."

"Photographers?"

"No."

"Okay. Call the police and have them arrested."

"What?"

"Have them arrested. They're trespassing in your offices and won't leave. But do it quickly before the media arrives."

Obviously, the final decision didn't rest with me, but that's exactly what the firm did—and, it should be noted, Epstein Becker & Green handled the incident in a highly respectful manner. The arrests were, as they say, orderly and without incident. Most importantly, from my standpoint, the office was cleared before the media arrived. No small accomplishment, because video and photographs of the arrests would certainly have made the news in San Francisco—and maybe elsewhere as well. But lacking compelling visuals to complete the story, there wasn't a single article in the media the next day about the sit-in and subsequent arrests. By taking decisive action (and legal action, by the way, since the protestors were trespassing on Epstein Becker & Green's property), we were able to shut down any possibility that the sit-in would evolve into a media circus—which was exactly what the protestors were looking for. Ideally, clients are never put in the position of making arrests, but in this instance, aggressive action put a stop to the kind of coverage the other side desperately wanted.

To be fair, Pacifica's management and board of directors seemed to be making public relations mistakes at every turn—doing everything in their power to give the perception that they were the very secretive, free-speech-stifling power grabbers that the opposition said they were. For example, we arranged for John Murdock to appear on Amy Goodman's *Democracy Now!* program to debate left-wing journalist Juan Gonzales, who writes for New York's *Daily News*. John Murdock himself, it should be noted, was the impetus behind holding this debate: His view was that to avoid the perception of secrecy, he'd speak to "anyone, anywhere" about the issues—so long as violence and intimidation were not part of the discussion. John went to the Pacifica station in Washington, DC, to appear on the program.

The debate went well and was quite lively, and—despite the fact that moderator Amy Goodman was herself an avowed critic of Pacifica's management and board—John Murdock more than held his own. But halfway through the program, we found out that the station manager in Washington, DC, had pulled the plug on his own board member's interview, deciding that it violated a board policy of not airing the station's "dirty laundry" on the air. This was the very station John Murdock was broadcasting from! Talk about censorship! Instead of the live program, they were airing a taped rerun of *Democracy Now!* Not a good move, and it was the one part of the debate that John Murdock didn't have a good answer for.

Lesson to be learned: Decisive, aggressive action is sometimes vitally important—so long as you don't hurt your "case" in the process. By having the protestors arrested at Epstein Becker's offices in San Francisco, we were ensuring the story of the "sit-in" wouldn't become a huge part of the debate; by pulling the plug on John Murdock's interview on *Democracy Now!*, Pacifica management was doing exactly the opposite—handing ammunition to the other side and offering evidence to support the premise that, even when a board member was involved, Pacifica management was "the man," a corporate monolith interested only in stifling free speech and progressive debate.

WADING IN TO THE PERELMAN/DUFF DIVORCE

Although it is always effective to begin coordinating the public relations aspects of litigation as early in the process as possible, the right techniques can have an effect no matter where you come in—or how battered your side has been in the media and before other public audiences up until that point. As we'll learn in Chapter Seven, once Microsoft started to take the perception aspects of their antitrust case with the U.S. government seriously, they were able to make great headway in turning around what had been an absolute mess from a public opinion standpoint. (As we'll see, perhaps the worst handling of litigation communications by a major corporation in history.) Another excellent example of how public perceptions can be changed is a case that we were involved in that lit up the pages of the New York tabloids in early 1999: the Ronald Perelman/Patricia Duff child custody battle.

The Perelman/Duff case, which dragged on for more than five years (longer than the marriage, actually), was an unusual case in many respects. First, the size: the case had the distinction of being the largest child custody and support proceeding in history, based on the net worth of the father. Second, although the official name of the case was *Anonymous v. Anonymous,* the case became public in December 1998 and was splashed across the pages of the tabloids for months, off and on, until its final resolution in October 2001. My firm for its part, represented Ms. Duff in the first half of 1999— not coincidentally, one of the few times during the long history of the case that Ms. Duff received any positive media coverage at all.

Finally, it was not the typical case for my company. Sensational, personality-driven public relations is not our usual forté. Over the years, we have worked on numerous cases that were unusual—even sensational—but generally our work has been in the area of run-of-the-mill corporate legal disputes. Celebrity-driven lawsuits are the exception, not the rule, in my practice.

Yet, despite all of these anomalies, when my firm* was brought into the case in January 1999, we immediately began to have a positive effect—within days, really—by using the same techniques that we use with our corporate work. And as we were dropped into the middle of the nastiest of media frenzies, we used the very same CIR techniques that we describe in this chapter (although we didn't have a name for it yet)—techniques that, I believe, are applicable to all manner of litigation and other legal disputes. Hence, the importance of looking at a case like Perelman/Duff, since—among other things—it destroys the "but my case is different" excuse that any of the readers of this book might have.

One other point, by the way: the Perelman/Duff case also highlights the hazards of losing control of the communications portion of your case: as discussed, in the three to four months or so that my firm worked with Ms. Duff, the case started turning her way. When we stopped—and her side stopped following many of the guidelines I describe in this book—Ms Duff wound up getting beaten again,

---

*Which was then a part of The Kamber Group, a large Washington, DC-based public relations firm.

ultimately losing custody of her daughter and, in the end, receiving less child support than she was receiving on a *temporary* basis.

Moreover, the sad fact is that, after we had become involved, Patricia Duff had a chance to win the case by settling with Perelman on highly favorable terms—keeping custody of her daughter in the bargain. This was when Perelman was at his weakest, at the end of January 1999, when we had him on the ropes after several weeks of drubbing in the press. In addition to custody, thanks to some skilled negotiating by Duff's attorney at the time, William Beslow, Duff would have received a monthly support payment that would have been among the largest in history, more than double what she eventually received. *

And let me make this clear at the outset: although she has been portrayed in media reports as some sort of gold-digging, socialite Mata Hari, I believe Ms. Duff is a good person and a good mother. Certainly, both mother and child deserved a better resolution than they got. I don't know Ronald Perelman and I can't definitively vouch for his qualifications as a father, but I can say that everything I saw of the celebrity corporate raider indicated that his daughter was no different to him than any other asset. He wanted control. He wanted to win. And he did.

Around him, Perelman had assembled a supporting cast that represented the cream of the legal community, as well as two of the best-known public relations pros in New York—Howard Rubenstein and the late John Scanlon (whom we discussed in greater detail in Chapter One). Perelman also had an array of bodyguards, investigators, security personnel, and assorted other hangers-on. He arrived in the courtroom like a visiting head of state. Quite a show, actually.

And quite a formidable adversary—it's not often that your client is worth upwards of $10 million but is still considered the underdog. But money was the least of Duff's problems. Ultimately, she could be her own worst enemy—and again, I believe she is an intelligent, thoughtful woman who, above all, seemed to love her daughter very much.

---

* We'll get into more detail about this aspect of the case in Chapter Nine, in our discussion of handling communications when your case finally reaches the courtroom.

This is not to say she wasn't being driven nuts by the time we got involved in her case—a time just after her "secret" psychological evaluation had been leaked to the *New York Post* and she had successfully sued to have *Anonymous v. Anonymous* opened to the public—thinking the fresh daylight of public scrutiny would tend to prevent the sort of favoritism that the justice system tends to afford billionaires—especially in the New York family court.

However, with Perelman's built-in public relations might, once the case was open to the public and the media, Patricia Duff began to receive a systematic shellacking that was painful to watch, as every aspect of her life became fodder for tabloid display. And her legal team, while excellent at what they were good at—divorce law—were helpless to defend her, and in fact were making matters worse.

All of this should sound very familiar, given what we've discussed throughout this book. Very often, the parties to a lawsuit believe that if they just shed public light on the case, the truth will prevail. It's a very Lockean ideal—that the "marketplace of ideas will rule"—but as we've seen, it doesn't always work that way. The best idea, left uncommunicated, withers on the vine. It is what happens in countless corporate lawsuits, and it was what was happening in the Perelman/Duff case when we were brought in, introduced by my friend and sometimes-colleague, attorney Howard Teich. Howard is a brilliant man and among the most well-connected people in New York, particularly in Democratic political circles. It was no coincidence he made the introduction to Duff, who at the time was one of the most prominent female Democratic fund-raisers in the country.

In our first conversation, Duff anxiously described the series of things that Perelman was allegedly doing to her, including how his court-approved security arrangements had put her under *de facto* house arrest (albeit in one of the best suites in the Waldorf Towers); how his side was in the midst of a smear campaign designed to ruin her; and how he had threatened on many occasions to "crush her" if she ever tried to fight back. Yet, no one in the media seemed to be listening to her side.

That morning, in fact, a devastating article had appeared in New York's *Daily News:*

PERELMAN BLASTS EX'S BID—
HER MONEY GRAB IN BITTER BREAKUP IS EXCESSIVE, HE SEZ

The ex-wife of billionaire Ronald Perelman is making "excessive" financial demands for child support after pocketing $30 million from their divorce deal, his lawyer charged yesterday.

Patricia Duff wants $7 million for a new home for her and the couple's 4-year-old daughter, Caleigh, and $68,000 a month in child support, according to Perelman's attorney, Adria Hillman.

"Given what she has already received and that she also receives $1.5 million a year in maintenance for herself, these requests are excessive," Hillman told a court referee yesterday. But lawyers for Duff, 44, called the Perelman camp's claims "false and distorted."

"Their numbers are a complete fiction," said Kenneth Warner, an attorney for Duff.

The high-stakes legal battle was back in Manhattan Supreme Court for a hearing to determine how much money the 55-year-old Revlon boss should pay to support his daughter.

The referee, Lori Sattler, granted Duff an adjournment while her lawyers ask a state appeals court to order the resumption of the couple's bitter custody trial over Caleigh.

Last month, just before Perelman's scheduled testimony, a judge abruptly halted the custody case and ordered the hearing on child support.

With an estimated net worth of $6 billion, Perelman runs a business empire that includes cosmetics giant Revlon, Sunbeam, and Golden State Bancorp.

Duff was a Democratic Party fundraiser when she wed the cosmetics king in 1994. The marriage lasted about 18 months.

Under the couple's prenuptial agreement, Duff received cash, real estate, and jewelry worth $30 million when the couple split in 1996. Among the real estate was a Southport, Connecticut, mansion worth $8 million.

As part of that deal, the makeup mogul pays Duff $1.5 million a year in alimony.

The prenup did not cover child support. Under a temporary court order, Perelman pays $12,000 a month in child support and picks up such additional costs as Caleigh's schooling, medical bills, and summer camp.

"The implication that she is sitting on $30 million is a deliberate misstatement of her financial position," said William Beslow, another member of Duff's legal team.

Beslow said Duff should not be expected to sell her property or her jewelry to support herself and her daughter.

He said Duff had asked Perelman to purchase a residence in Manhattan, which he would own, so that she and Caleigh can comply with the mogul's wish that they live primarily in the city.

Source: Salvatore Arena, *New York Daily News,* L.P., January 5, 1999, p. 3. Reprinted with permission.

Duff kept publicly emphasizing that she had received nowhere near $30 million in the divorce—that the settlement was "more like $10 million"—and she had already spent millions on divorce lawyers. I pointed out that to the average reader of the *Daily News,* it mattered little whether the number was $30 million or $10 million—millions are millions, especially if you ain't got 'em.

This was central, I think, to what her side was doing wrong— they were arguing for and against facts that were important to them, not important to the wider public audience. They were also letting the other side dictate the debate, spending their time quibbling over millions while any broader message went flat. Again, not unlike many of the my corporate clients. In a way, this was no different than two conglomerates battling it out.

Over the phone and in meetings later in the day, my advice to Ms. Duff was similar to what I'd given scored of clients involved in corporate lawsuits over the years—and the advice that is sprinkled throughout this book:

1. *You need to exercise control over the information getting out to reporters.* The media she was speaking to, who was speaking to whom, and the types of information that were being given to the media. Specifically, in this case, I guessed that no one was listening to the legal victories and arguments of Duff and her legal team because the lawyers were just sending the attorneys the legal briefs and decisions—hundreds of pages of documents for a reporter who needed to file 500 words

that morning. As we've seen, this is not putting the message into a package that can be used.

2. *You've got to start "framing" your message properly.* Change the story to one of Perelman attempting to circumvent some very real legal principles governing child support payments, and the like. Right now, what was happening is that the story was being written as framed by Perelman's side—that of a greedy wife trying to steal a hard-working billionaire's fortune. To the male reporters, some of whom had no doubt been through a divorce or two themselves, there was no way to win this argument. Ms. Duff needed to reframe the argument to highlight "her" story—that she was being victimized by a paranoid, controlling dictator of a corporate chieftain who was trying to destroy her.

3. *You've got to open other fronts in this battle.* Get Mr. Perelman backpedaling, responding to your advances on the media battlefield.

4. *Your audience is the other side as much as the public at large.* If you appear weak, you will embolden him; if you convince him you are strong and he is in for a fight, he'll start to think about exit strategies (as all corporate raiders do).

PUTTING THE CIR SYSTEM TO WORK

Immediately after being hired, we began to put the (as-of-yet un-named) Control, Information, Response (CIR) system into action. The first step to this effort was *control:* We needed to get a handle on the information that was being given to reporters—again, not in some vain attempt at spin, but to ensure Duff's story was not being bogged down by thick legalities and muddy, "he said-she said" disputes over the exact amounts that had been paid to either party.

Exerting control in a case like this is no easy task. In any important piece of litigation, there are going to be tremendous egos involved, and in this particular case, Duff was surrounded by lawyers and other advisors—most quite capable, but virtually all with a dilettante's grasp of handling media and reporters during high-profile litigation.

Again, since I'm both a lawyer and a public relations man, I can tell you one great difference between the two: Nonlawyers generally don't believe they can practice law, but every attorney in town who's been on CNN once or twice thinks they know how to handle media strategy (we discuss this more in Chapter Six). Of course, some attorneys and clients are skilled at handling media and do it quite well (hopefully, many more will be more skilled after they've read this book). But if a PR person is going to exert any control over the course of communications in a lawsuit, the first thing they have to do is convince the lawyers involved that *they* are the expert, not the lawyers. In high-profile litigation, this is sometimes easier said than done.

Now, I'm a realist. I knew there was only so much control we could have. Important people are still going to call reporters when they think they have the idea that's going to generate the positive coverage they need. We didn't expect, nor did we have, 100 percent control. But we understood the value of setting up controls over the information being given to reporters—and control over access to Ms. Duff herself.

My colleagues and I began working with the legal team to establish such control. At the time, Duff was being represented in the child custody proceedings by William Beslow, a tall, Yale and Columbia Law School-educated divorce attorney famous for his representation of Marla Maples and Judith Regan. Duff was also working with the husband-and-wife team of Ken and Rita Warner of the well-regarded firm Coblence & Warner. Ken is a skilled, seasoned corporate litigator perhaps best known for his successful representation of Joseph Jett, the trader who was accused by Kidder Peabody of stealing more than $100 million. His wife Rita is a divorce attorney drawn from central casting—with a rapid-fire New York accent and a persistence bordering on savant. Coblence & Warner primarily handled the appeals work, and they were having considerable success. But, little of that was being recognized—the media seemed more interested at this point in the gory details of the dollars: how many of them there really were, and how they were spent. We needed to move them ever so subtly toward the underlying legal issues and Perelman's egregious—sometimes borderline maniacal—behavior.

We started on the second leg of the CIR system—*information*. We immediately began gathering information on all aspects of this case, the parties involved and the reporters covering the case. We requested copies of all of the legal documents and picked through them carefully for the types of information that would not just be legally significant, but that would be "news."

Among these documents was an appellate brief about to be filed to contest the oppressive security restrictions that the trial court had placed on Patricia Duff and her daughter. It was Ken Warner's suggestion that there was a lot in there that could serve as fodder for news stories—if you could get the media interested, that is. But it was already into the afternoon, and we had just been hired. How could we find what was newsworthy in the information presented and communicate it effectively in time to make the morning papers?

We did it by going back to the original tool of media relations, one I've been bashing since the beginning of this book—the press release.

Okay, I know I'm going to seem fickle here, since I've downplayed the effectiveness of press releases as tools for communicating in litigation. The problem with press releases is primarily that clients and their lawyers tend to think they are the *only* tool for getting information out there—and, as we've seen, very often a far more effect presentation of your message can be made in a *Media Brief,* a written statement, or simply with a phone call to the right reporter with the right information. But press releases *are* effective for announcing *new* information—information like a legal victory or, as in this case, a substantial appeal.

I felt a press release was particularly appropriate in this circumstance for the following reasons:

- It was an excellent way to give the news a "time hook"—we were announcing that the appellate briefs had been filed—and there's no better way to do that than in a press release.

- Up until now, this was a case that had been communicated to the media through whispers, rumors, off-handed comments, and sensational press conferences—we felt a press release would have an "official" look, it would lend decorum that would shore up its legitimacy.

- It was a good way to say to the reporters involved—"hey, we're handling the media now, and it's going to be a little different from the circus of whispering and sleaze you've become used to."

So we worked to draft a quick press release announcing that Duff's lawyers had appealed the security decision, pulling from the appeal itself language that would really resonate with the newspapers we were aiming for—in this case, the *New York Post* and the *Daily News*. Getting the press release approved, however, was another matter.

This highlights another problem with press releases: The parties involved, particularly lawyers, will see the press release as an "official" document, similar to the legal documents they've been creating all along—in this case, similar to the appellate brief itself. Try getting that approved in an hour!

But persistence paid off. While working the phones with the attorneys—and Duff herself, of course—as they noodled endlessly with the fine print of some less-than-critical paragraph buried deep in the press release, I was in touch with the reporters at the same time, assuring them that indeed the press release was on its way and it would be worth the wait.

For my part, as with all press releases, I was interested only in the following:

- That the press release have a compelling headline and subhead.
- That the lead paragraph really catch the reporters' attention.
- That we unleash a real "corker" of a quote from one of the attorneys involved.

Here's what we produced:

ATTORNEYS FOR PATRICIA DUFF APPEAL ORDER ON SECURITY ARRANGEMENT

Appeal alleges that, in an unprecedented power move, Ronald Perelman has convinced the court to virtually imprison his daughter and her mother under 24-hour security watch.

NEW YORK, NY—Attorneys for Patricia Duff have filed an appeal of a court ruling in their child custody case that allows Ronald Perelman to virtually imprison his daughter and wife under 24-hour armed guard, supervised in part by his own private security force.

The appeal states that Mr. Perelman is using this tactic as part of a multifaceted attempt to "harass, monitor, invade, and ultimately, bend her to his will."

The appeal alleges that Perelman is using this oppressive and unprecedented tactic to intimidate his former wife, invade the privacy of both Ms. Duff and her daughter, and monitor her movements. The appeal points out that security experts agree that the risk to Ms. Duff's daughter is "low," and that there are far less invasive ways to protect the security of her child, including arrangements such as those the couple had prior to separation, which were far less onerous. Further, no divorce court in the United States has *ever* ordered any restriction of a parent's fundamental rights, in the absence of gross neglect, which has been shown not to be the case here.

"For a capitalist, Mr. Perelman appears to have learned a few things from the former Soviet Union," said Rita Warner of Coblence & Warner, attorney for Patricia Duff. "Ms. Duff and her daughter are actually living with an armed guard who follows them day and night everywhere they go. It is oppressive, unprecedented, and un-American."

The appeal to the First Department Appellate Division of the Supreme Court of the State of New York (a copy of which is available upon request), filed on Monday, January 4, 1999, reveals a series of mistakes made by the lower court in allowing these draconian security restrictions to go forward. As detailed in the appeal, the court required an armed guard be placed inside Ms. Duff's temporary living quarters in a spare room formerly reserved for the couple's nanny, with regular walk-throughs of the entire living quarters, thereby preventing any privacy or comfortable family environment for Caleigh. The court has also required that the outside security firm hired for this purpose monitor all Ms. Duff's visitors.

"We are asking the appeals court to remove these unprecedented and oppressive security measures," said Ms. Warner. "The lower court has violated the mother's right to autonomy and privacy—as well as the right to make decisions about the security and protection of her child—in a way that serves no useful purpose except to further Mr. Perelman's litigation agenda of harassment and intimidation against the mother and daughter alike."

Now in my view, press releases are the "sausage-making and not the sausage"—that is to say, we're not interested in what the press release says, but what the resulting news coverage reports—that, after all, is what your audience will read. But to see the ways in which you can break free of existing news coverage—open a "new front" using military terminology—it is important to look at this press release along with the articles that resulted, so you can get an idea *why* the three points I mentioned—the headline, lead paragraph, and quote—were so important. As you'll see, the lead paragraph of the press release framed the entire tenor of the media coverage of the appeal. Also, the resulting coverage vindicated many of the precepts set forth in Chapters Two and Three—by giving the reporters what they wanted, we were able to influence the coverage to a far greater degree than might normally be expected. Moreover, the resulting articles the next morning were a testament to the fact that the CIR approach could have an immediate effect, even in the most sensational of cases.

The following from the *New York Post*, was typical of the resulting news coverage:

PERELMAN'S EX CONTESTS "OPPRESSIVE" SECURITY

Ron Perelman has ex-wife Patricia Duff and daughter Caleigh living "in a jail . . . harassed and intimidated" by armed guards who watch their every move, court papers charge.

Duff's lawyers made the claims in a filing with the Appellate Division seeking to overturn Manhattan Supreme Court Justice Eileen Bransten's approval of the Revlon head's "Orwellian" security measures for his ex and their 4-year-old girl.

"For a capitalist, Mr. Perelman appears to have learned a few things from the former Soviet Union," said Duff's lawyer, Rita Warner. "Ms. Duff and her daughter are actually living with an armed guard who follows them day and night, everywhere they go. It is oppressive, unprecedented, and un-American."

The papers say Perelman, 55, "is using the trial court in a multi-faceted attack on the mother to harass, monitor, invade, and ultimately, bend her to his will."

The guards are posted—by court order—inside Duff's Connecticut home and two-bedroom Manhattan apartment whenever

Caleigh is there—security far tighter than what was in place while the couple was married, the filing claims.

"The practical effect of the order is that [Duff]'s life has been turned upside down. Every facet of her and her child's life is under a microscope with little or no freedom of movement," the papers say.

"A guard is posted within their home 24 hours a day, seven days a week . . . No classmate or other visitor can simply 'drop by' to see [them]" and "the mother is required to submit lists of visitors to the guard in advance."

The papers also argue that Perelman's main concern isn't Caleigh's welfare, but "to obtain a day-to-day inside view of everything [Duff] was doing, everywhere she was going and everyone she was seeing."

New York's richest man has also ignored a court order to pay for the security, the papers said.

Perelman's spokesman, Howard Rubenstein, said the cosmetics king refused to comment.

Source: Dareh Gregorian, *New York Post,* January 7, 1999, page 6.

One other key fact to note about the coverage of the security release: As we learned in Chapter Three, reporters are writers at heart—they love language and generally can't resist a good turn of a phrase that sums up the story in a compelling manner. Thus, we spent some time thinking about it and wrote the following for Duff attorney Rita Warner: "For a capitalist, Mr. Perelman appears to have learned a few things from the former Soviet Union . . ." We knew that finding a pithy way to compare Perelman's security regime to the former Soviet Union would catch the reporter's and editor's attention—and figure prominently in the resulting story.

Thus, two days into our work, Patricia Duff was already beginning to turn the tide. But things were about to get hotter. And further along in this book—in Chapter Nine, dealing handling the media when a case finally makes its way into the courtroom—we'll look at exactly how hot things can get for all of the parties involved, including the hardworking publicist the other side decides to make an example of in court.

ACTION POINTS

✔ Although planning for communications in litigation should occur well in advance, very often clients, their lawyers, and their communications professionals are thrust into the case after the first reporter has shown up at your door.

✔ Even in the most chaotic situations, "No comment" is never a good idea. There is always a way to make a comment to the media *without* divulging confidences or tipping your hand as to strategy. This gives the media what they need—and shows a willingness to cooperate that will help establish legitimacy and credibility with your audience.

✔ Key to developing communications strategy in litigation is the CIR process—Control, Information, and Response. No matter where in the litigation the communications strategy is begun, the CIR method will help lawyers, clients, and communicators in ensuring the *right* message gets to the *right* audience at the *right* time.

✔ When thrust into particularly chaotic high-profile cases—especially cases where your client is getting beaten—it's important to put the CIR process into place, then look for opportunities to "open a new front," thus reframing the story in the media's mind.

CHAPTER FIVE

The Litigation
Media Checklist

Is there a businessperson or lawyer out there who doesn't rely on systems and procedures to manage the day-to-day aspects of the work that they do? It's not just General Electric with its Six Sigma we're talking about. Common knowledge dictates that, regardless of the size of the organization, flying by the seat of your pants is a sure recipe for disaster. Yet, in handling the communications aspects of litigation, this is exactly what is often done. Most business executives and lawyers rely on gut instinct, intuition, and chance—hoping that someone, somewhere along the way, is going to notice the case before it explodes into a public relation's nightmare.

In this chapter, we look at a key tool for putting a system in place for analyzing your case for potential impact in the media and before other public audiences. And we learn about the surprising way unexpected cases can find their way into the court of public opinion.

In 1994, I was sitting with a prominent labor and employment lawyer in Washington, DC, discussing the various cases that he was currently involved with. This particular partner—easily among the top dozen or so in the country is his particular field—specialized in employment discrimination and sexual harassment cases, and his plate was, as usual, full of cases that could be considered "newsworthy." My job was to analyze the cases he was handling to see if there was anything particularly media sensitive—a standard practice in the work we do.

Over the course of a good 90 minutes of conversation, the lawyer discussed cases at various levels in the court process—this case is at the DC Circuit on Appeal (very interesting legal issues), that one was about to come to trial in New York (and may eventually make it to the Supreme Court on the question of which party has the burden of proof in certain actions), and so on. All pretty interesting stuff.

About 70 minutes or so into the conversation, he mentioned—almost as an aside—what he called a "little" case he had that I should be aware of.

"It's nothing too big," he said, "just a small case, it hasn't even been filed yet and there's nothing new legally, but it has some interesting facts. It deals with sexual harassment by e-mail." He then went on to another case that was before the Fourth Circuit in Virginia and may create some new law in the area of . . .

Wait—sexual harassment by e-mail?

This was 1994, remember—back then e-mail was just becoming common in corporate environments (if I recall correctly, my entire small company still had only one e-mail address at the time). The true implications of this new tool were just then beginning to come to light. No one had ever heard of using computers to sexually harass.

I stopped the lawyer's discussion of the Fourth Circuit case and went back to e-mail case.

"Tell me more . . ."

He proceeded to tell me how e-mail and voicemail technology that was becoming common in corporate offices was now actually making certain forms of harassment *easier*. In the old days, if you wanted to harass a coworker in an office, you would have to get up, walk to the coworker's desk, and make your move there. Or, at the very least, call the person on the phone—and risk a very painful rebuttal. But now, in the age of e-mail and voicemail, all you had to do was hit the "send" button on your computer (or in the case of voicemail, leave a message when you knew the coworker wasn't around).

"But it's the same old discrimination law," he said, "from a legal standpoint, there's nothing unusual at all about the claim."

In hindsight, you can see how he was correct as to the law, but dead wrong as to the wider public arena. In 1994, sexual harassment by e-mail may not have been new law, but it was *big news*. This, I warned him, was the case we needed to watch out for. Sure enough, it was, with stories appearing in *BusinessWeek*, the *Wall Street Journal*, and numerous other publications.

Lesson to be learned: What is *legally significant* is often quite different from what is *newsworthy*. As a result, cases that your legal team may not pay much attention to could be the cases that attract the most attention in the wider court of public opinion.

Hence the need to review all cases very carefully. As we'll see in this chapter, one of the tools that can be used to do this is the *Litigation Media Checklist*.

Let's go back to the sexual harassment case and discuss it a bit more. The lawyer I was meeting with had a very good sense as to the *legal* significance of the cases he was working on—"this is new law," "this case is at the DC Circuit," "this case could go to the Supreme Court," and so on. However, it was almost at the end of our conversation before it ever occurred to him to mention the harassment by e-mail case. Why? Because by his standard—that of the law—there was nothing new about it. It was simply a new application of old law—the fact that it occurred in an area (the Internet and technology) that was of growing interest to the media at the time was of no particular importance to him. It was a case with little legal significance, but one that was enormously important to a wider audience, with their sights on the broader business and public ramifications of the case.

In my experience, this is a problem lawyers often have when analyzing their cases for potential media effect—which is the first step toward being prepared when facing public relations issues in litigation. The reason is simple: Lawyers have been trained in law school to look at the *legal significance* of cases. They have worked for years—first under the direction of older lawyers, then as the lawyers directing the work themselves—again, looking at *legal significance*. Legal significance is the frame of reference through which they see all cases.

Thus, it can be highly difficult for attorneys to step back from the "trees of their own expertise" and see the forest—what will be of interest to the media and other stakeholders, including investors, politicians, regulators, and others. This is similar to the concept we discussed in Chapter Three in our *Rules of Media Procedure:* Since lawyers and the clients are often immersed in the complexities of what they do, they often need to sufficiently "decompress" to refocus on big-picture issues.

It's usually just as hard for clients to do this as it is for their attorneys. Very often they are buried hip-deep in the complexities of the lawsuit as well. Beyond the pending legal issue that has demanded their attention, business executives spend the rest of their day looking at business issues, usually with the same intensity as lawyers look at legal issues. Wrapped up in their own day-to-day concerns, CEOs, CFOs, and other top corporate executives may miss the significance of issues that will wind up on page one of their local newspaper if they're not careful. Such "blinders" are not limited to lawyers by any means.

Thus, the importance of stepping back and considering issues from a distance.

WHAT IS NEWS?

From the *New York Daily News,* July 16, 2002:

> A Long Island man gave a pit bull a taste of its own medicine when he bit the dog to save his own pooch's life.
>
> Dutch the pit bull was sporting teeth marks on his head yesterday courtesy of Richard Robbins, 44, of Melville, who locked jaws on the vicious animal to rescue Gina Marie, his Siberian Husky.
>
> "I had no choice," Robbins told the *Daily News* yesterday, "She [Gina Marie] is like my daughter."

From across the breakfast table, my wife looked up at me and said: "I guess it's true what they say . . . 'Man bites dog' is news!"

For those of you who don't know, "man bites dog" is one of the oldest and most venerated answers to the question "What makes news?" The answer is stated thus: "Dog bites man isn't news, but man bites dog—now that's news." In other words, the unique nature of the activity is what makes it news: Dogs bite men all the time; rare is the man that bites the dog back! It is more than just that the event doesn't happen very often—it's also the fact that the event seems to turn conventional wisdom on its head. It's the opposite of what you would usually expect to happen. That, too, is what makes "man bites dog" news.

In this example (which doesn't really have anything to do with litigation—except I'm sure a lawsuit or two will flow from it), the aphorism was literally true. Usually, of course, it is used in the figurative sense.

Moreover, as we've seen in previous chapters, this is only one of the factors that make an event a story. The underlying theme is important, however: Particularly with regard to litigation and other legal matters, it's rarely just "new law" that makes a case newsworthy. What made the O. J. Simpson case news, for example, is not that he allegedly murdered his wife—husbands murder wives all the time—but that he was a celebrity actor/sportscaster/corporate spokesman/Hall-of-Fame football player who murdered his wife. Hence, news.

Where do cases come from?

Depending on who you are, lawsuits and other forms of legal proceedings come to your attention in a variety of manners:

- If you are a lawyer at a law firm, cases come from your clients.
- If you are an in-house lawyer at a large corporation, there are a steady stream of legal matters crossing your desk from all of the different divisions of the company.
- As a CEO or CFO at a large corporation, cases usually come to your attention through your general counsel's office—who likely reports to you the state of legal affairs and any particular cases or matters that deserve the executive's special attention.
- If you're the owner of a small business, it's likely you or your top assistants are the first line of defense when a lawsuit comes in.
- If you are a high-profile individual, you or your personal attorney likely receive notice of a pending legal action.
- If you are in the public relations department of a corporation or if you are an outside public relations advisor for a corporation, organization, or high-profile individual, hopefully you learn about cases as early as possible—but usually, I'm

sure, you learn about the legal matter just before, or just after, the first reporter has called.

Why is this important? Because if you are going to set up a *system* for analyzing lawsuits for potential public impact, you need to first take a good look at how these cases are coming to your attention. Depending on who you are and where you fit into your organizational structure, how you find out about lawsuits can differ considerably:

1. It can happen when an external actor—such as the media, protestors, or regulators—lets *you* know that the case is of interest to them (sometimes quite noisily).
2. It can happen when someone in the legal department or your law firm—or the CEO or business owner if the organization is small—happens to notice that the case may have a wider impact.
3. It can happen in a systematic matter, as each case is run through a system for analyzing potential impact in the public arena.

Now which do you think is preferable for clients and their lawyers who really want to be prepared for handling the communications aspects of their legal disputes?

How do business executives and their legal counsel work together to identify those cases where the media might take an interest? How do we ensure that every case coming in is, at the very least, screened for public elements that may put you in the court of public opinion?

Some cases are easy—corporate fraud, SEC or Department of Justice investigations, a particularly salacious sexual harassment claim. But other cases are questionable—and, as noted earlier, at first glance some legal matters may seem to be less-than-noteworthy to the lawyers and business executives close to the situation. Then, when the media arrives at your door, all hell breaks loose.

The answer, again, is in systems. There needs to be a screening system in place so that each case is "filtered" through what I call the *Litigation Media Checklist*—to see if it may be susceptible to media coverage or other forms of public interest.

THE LITIGATION MEDIA CHECKLIST

This concept may not be entirely revolutionary to you. If you are very experienced at handling lawsuits—lawyer or not—you may already be informally running legal matters that come your way through such a screening process—and you think that this works just fine. Whether you are a CEO, CFO, top communications officer, or a corporate lawyer, you may do this intuitively as each matter comes to your attention. You feel you just *know* which cases are going to put you before a wider public audience—and these get special attention: perhaps referred to your top communications officer or tagged for special consideration by the chief litigator in the general counsel's office. Perhaps the managing partner or head litigation partner at the law firm puts in a call to the firm's outside public relations advisors to let them know that a case of particular note may be in the offing. Again, as media has become more interested in these sorts of legal matters, informal systems have sprung up, and some of those CEOs and lawyers with particular experience in the area have developed considerable expertise in spotting and tagging public opinion cases.

However, even if you are the most media-savvy attorney or client around you still need help, you still need to have a *standardized* way to filter your cases for potential media interest. You demand such systems in every other aspect of your business or legal practice—why should analyzing cases be so . . . intuitive?

Moreover, since we are all specialists these days, we are often inclined to look at legal issues from the wrong perspective: from a litigation management or regulatory compliance standpoint if you are a lawyer; from a contingent liability standpoint if you are a CFO. It takes a special skill to step back and look at a legal issue from a wider perspective: the vantage point of public opinion, where many of these cases will ultimately be won or lost. Thus, the importance of a system like a Litigation Media Checklist—which should be a standard component for analyzing legal cases as they come in.

A suggested Litigation Media Checklist follows. It is a very basic checklist, one that can be adapted depending on your own needs. As in all elements of litigation PR, flexibility is key. Depending on your particular industry or circumstance, your Litigation Media

Checklist might vary considerably. If you are in a highly regulated field like telecommunications or health care, for instance, you may want more questions on regulatory concerns. No matter. Our example gives a basic format that should guide clients and lawyers as they develop their own individual checklists, and other systems tailored to their own organization's needs.

LITIGATION MEDIA CHECKLIST

- Is the lawsuit unique, out-of-the-ordinary, or otherwise "man-bites-dog"?
- Does the case involve sensational facts?
- Does the case involve, or potentially involve, a large sum of money?
- Are the parties to the suit well known or otherwise high profile?
- Is it a case that will merit attention in the regional or trade media?
- Does the case make new law?
- Does the case involve a new application of old law?
- Is the area of the law considered "hot" by the media right now?
- Does the case have a compelling "human face"?
- Is the case indicative of a trend?
- Does the case have broader implications as a business story?
- Is there a political or regulatory aspect that will attract interest in the case?
- Does the opposing counsel have a history of publicizing his or her cases?

Let's look at each of these criteria in the checklist in a bit more detail. Although most seem straightforward at first glance, the nuances of each criteria warrant further consideration if clients and lawyers are going to properly use the Litigation Media Checklist to isolate those legal matters that may be of interest to a wider public audience.

Is the Lawsuit Unique, Out-of-the-Ordinary, or Otherwise "Man-Bites-Dog?"

Applying the maxim, "man bites dog" is likely the clearest criteria for determining whether a case will be of interest to the media or other public audiences. Is there something unique about the facts of your case that make it distinctive or unusual, against conventional wisdom or otherwise *contra* (as lawyers say) to all of the other cases that are out there? Is your case the opposite of what you might usually expect?

For example, several years ago we advised on a financial services case involving a man who worked at a bank and who had been sexually harassed by his superior. Okay, that's interesting enough—since men are far less likely to be harassed than women, but otherwise it was a typical example of *quid-pro-quo* harassment (in other words "You'll get ahead in this company if you . . ."). But here's the kicker: The harasser was also a man. Same-sex harassment is still relatively rare—and definitely "man bites dog." Hence, a natural for media coverage and other public interest.

Does the Case Involve Sensational Facts?

There are all sorts of sensational facts out there, but suffice it to say, if your case involves:

- Nazis or klansmen,
- Political figures,
- The Mob,
- Rich versus poor, or
- Sex.

You can expect a call from the media. And if you've got a case of a wealthy politician who is a former Nazi with connections to the Mob, who has fathered a child with his maid—well, call me. We need to talk.

Seriously, there are facts and then there are FACTS. The more sensational your facts, the more likely they are to catch the interest of the media. Never has this been more true than today—in the era of Reality TV, Howard Stern, Jerry Springer, and so on. This may sound like simplistic advice, but there are many times when sensational facts are dismissed by lawyers because the underlying elements of the particular lawsuit are the same.

For obvious reasons, sexual harassment cases in particular lend themselves to "sensational" facts. But in most cases, the law is the same throughout—this is where many lawyers, and many of their clients, get tripped up. Almost a decade ago, for example, we were involved in a case on behalf of a major insurance company—one of the most staid and conservative institutions in the country, in fact. They had been sued in what seemed to be another run-of-the-mill sexual harassment claim. The facts were as follows: A superior and one of his employees entered into a relationship that eventually went sour. Now the woman was threatening to sue, alleging that the man had blocked her advancement in the company as retribution.

If these were the only facts, there would not have been much to the case—although it still may have been noticed by the legal and regional media, as well as in publications catering to the insurance trades. But now . . . the rest of the story. It seems the relationship between the man and woman was, shall we say, unusual? There was a mask involved, along with third parties and at least one videotape (that the client knew of). And this, remember, at an old-fashioned, conservative institution that staked its reputation on its history and values.

Take those facts, mix 'em up—and you've got a real media circus on your hands, regardless of whether the case is, in all other respects, the same as any other.

Does the Case Involve, or Potentially Involve, a Large Sum of Money?

I have a brother who, unlike the plumber you met in Chapter Four, doesn't quite understand what I do. He thinks that because I'm in the public relations field, I'm in the business of promoting "the largest"—you know: the largest pizza, the largest line of tap dancers, the largest bagel ever slathered with cream cheese. All of the stuff that you see at the end of your local news—usually as the anchor chuckles and says: "And, finally tonight . . ."

Besides hoping that he reads this book (we are related after all), I bring this up because although it's definitely not the business I'm in, it's absolutely true that the "largest ever" makes news. To go a bit further, the larger the sum of money at stake, the more likely the media interest. In fact, "how much" is usually the first question out of any good reporter's mouth. Isn't capitalism great?

Thus, for example, we work with a very prominent patent attorney, who, in 1989, won the largest patent verdict in history. Big news? You bet. Less than a decade later, he was successful in *over-turning* the second-largest verdict ever. This, too, was of great interest to the media. Admittedly, there was also a little bit of "man-bites-dog" interest in that it was the same lawyer involved in both cases. It was the amount of money, however, that put both cases over the top as news stories.

Over the years, my firm has been involved in many of the largest cases of their kind in history—including what was at the time the largest employment discrimination class action in history (the Home Depot case of the mid-1990s), the largest child custody case in history (the Ronald Perelman/Patricia Duff divorce), and, currently, the largest, single-family Holocaust restitution claim in history (on behalf of the heirs of Berlin's famed Wertheim department store chain—a case we'll learn about further along in this chapter). In each of these cases, the stories themselves were interesting, but the explosive media interest was clearly stoked by the tremendous numbers involved.

When working with plaintiffs, therefore, one of the things we do—since the actual damages may not be apparent at the beginning of the case—is try to get the client and their lawyers to determine just how big the claim might potentially be. When you are a plaintiff, nothing works better than to say to the media: "This case has the potential to be the largest case of its kind in history." On the defense side, we want to know whether the other side is going to use that bullet to generate media interest—so we can more accurately gauge how to counteract it.

It's not always easy to get this information, particularly from the attorneys in the case, who do not want to over-promise the client on the plaintiff's side, or embolden the plaintiffs lawyers (and scare the hell out of the client) on the defense side. But such information can be critical for proper planning of media response.

I can remember one example in a patent case against some major players in the electronics field, dealing with a ubiquitous piece of computer equipment. The question arose as to the size of the case. Our questioning of the attorneys went something like this:

"So how big is this case?"

"It's impossible to tell at this point. We're very early on, so we'll really know better after discovery."

"Well, what are the potential damages here? Millions."

"Well, potentially, yes."

"Billions?"

"A billion anyway."

"Is it fair to say that this has the potential to be the largest patent lawsuit in history?"

"Well, if it went to trial, yes. But we don't think it will ever get that far. We think that at least some of the parties will settle . . ."

And so on. Whether or not it would actually ever make it to trial, it was perfectly accurate to say that this case had the potential to be the largest patent lawsuit in history, and it was important to make this part of our message. But it was difficult to squeeze that information from the attorneys involved, since they are always squeamish about attaching a "hard" number to a case, especially so early on. But, again, we knew that the first question out of any good reporter's mouth would be "What's the potential liability here?" The right answer to this question can make a routine case a "story." Whether you are plaintiff or defendant, you need to know the value of the case beforehand so that you can properly gauge the level of interest the media is going to show in the case.

Are the Parties to the Suit Well-Known or Otherwise High Profile?

This is perhaps the easiest question to answer. Shoplifting is shoplifting, but Winona Ryder is news. Celebrities immediately make a legal matter newsworthy—and although I have said "now more than ever" more times that I'm comfortable with in this book, let me say it again: now more than ever. We live in an age when Anna Nicole Smith is "must-see TV." If O. J. Simpson hadn't been O. J. Simpson, maybe you get five inches in the *Los Angeles Times*—depending on what kind of news day it is otherwise. Sad to say, but it was only the fact that he was O. J. Simpson that made the O. J. Simpson case the "trial of the century." The bloody glove, car chase, blood-soaked dog howling in the night: yes, they were sensational details, but they made the case only one in, say, a hundred murder cases that year with sensational details. He could have done it in the library with a candlestick—it wouldn't have mattered if it wasn't O. J. Simpson holding the candlestick. In our celebrity-obsessed culture, names make news.

But here's something to remember about this whole "celebrity issue." It's a relative term. Depending on where you are and the audience you reach, a party to a lawsuit can be a celebrity without even knowing it. If you're a prominent CEO or a leading lawyer in Kansas City, you're a celebrity in Kansas City as sure as Brad Pitt or Julia Roberts is nationally. This is true whether you're thinking about regional audiences such as the *Kansas City Star,* or trade audiences covering your field. If you're the founder of one of the nation's largest medical products manufacturers, expect a call from *Modern Healthcare.* There's a fairly good chance they are going to be interested in your case, no matter whether the story is newsworthy otherwise.

Is It a Case That Will Merit Attention in the Regional or Trade Media?

Building on that last point, there may be cases that don't necessarily involve a celebrity, but still will be of interest to the regional media in your hometown, or the trade media that covers your business or industry. Although *Larry King* may not be banging down your door, if you own a company in, say, Tampa, Florida, coverage from the *Tampa Tribune,* the *St. Petersburg Times,* or the *Tampa Bay Business Journal* may be just as important to you, your customers, and the overall health of your enterprise as anything that might appear nationally.

Similarly, a case that won't necessarily make *Newsweek* may be of interest to *Information Week*—if that's the trade publication covering your industry. The heat may not be as intense as that which accompanies a case of major national importance, but the effect of media coverage on the course of the litigation and the company's overall reputation can be just as devastating.

We worked on just such a case, for example, involving a defense contractor who had declared bankruptcy and laid off hundreds of workers without pay. A rotten move on many levels, and the resulting article covering the case was bad. But it was a local, regional newspaper covering the layoffs, and the company officials at first thought they could withstand a bit of negative coverage from a newspaper that no one at the company particularly respected anyway. Until the article found its way to the state's Attorney General, and pretty soon a full-fledged investigation was underway. Clearly, that regional coverage mattered a bit more than was originally believed.

Does the Case Make New Law?

I hesitate to include this item in our sample checklist, simply because it is usually the only criterion lawyers look at when considering the import of a particular case. But it is an element of media coverage, and it's important to take this into consideration when planning media strategy. Potential new law can raise media interest—particularly if it is combined with another criterion, such as a trend (see below), a celebrity litigant, or a large amount of money.

In the Home Depot employment discrimination case, we were called in to work with the company on an issue involving new law in the area of class actions, and many of the elements on our Litigation Media Checklist were present. First, there was the issue of the law—The Home Depot executives and lawyers were hoping the Supreme Court would take a look at loose rules for class action certification (the process by which individual litigants are grouped together as a class). In addition, this was a case that was potentially the largest employment law class action in history, and a case that featured a "celebrity" company and founders—The Home Depot was perhaps the greatest retailing success story of the late 1980s and early 1990s, and its founders, Bernie Marcus and Arthur Blank, were business celebrities of the highest order. The legal issue itself would likely have generated media interest in only the legal media—and perhaps trade media covering the home improvement industry. But combined with the other elements of the case, it was, quite naturally, front-page news.

Does the Case Involve a New Application of Old Law?

This is very different from the last criterion. In this category, the case takes established law and applies it to a new area. A perfect example is the case that opened this section—that of sexual harassment by e-mail and voicemail. Again, old law applied in a new area.

It is true that many cases that cross lawyers' desks involve slightly different applications of old law. No two fact patterns are the same. This is why we have lawyers, after all—or else we'd just have computers applying the law to the facts of each case and spitting out a verdict. Lawyers take fact patterns that differ slightly from the precedent-setting case in some key element and try to fit them into an established pattern of law. Then the other side differentiates, that is, explains why the precedent-setting case is different and does not apply here. Then, in the courtroom, a value judgment is made.

Similarly, the client and the legal and communications team need to look carefully at the case to determine if, indeed, the facts have enough "freshness" to them to warrant media coverage. Very often, the right facts—combined, perhaps, with some of the other criteria we've discussed, are enough to warrant media coverage in their own right.

The same-sex sexual harassment case is a perfect example of this. Only a single fact changed—the harasser and the subject of harassment were of the same sex. Change any of the other facts of the case—the type of company, where the harassment took place, the type of *quid-pro-quo* the party was looking for—none of this, in and of itself, would have made the case newsworthy. It was the "freshness" of the new fact that made all the difference. Old law applied in a new way.

Is the Area of the Law Considered "Hot" by the Media Right Now?

Sitting here in late-2002, I can barely even remember quite what "convergence" was, but in 1999 and 2000, it was hot. I do know it had something to do with combining television and the Internet, because the client we were working for had a joint venture agreement that prevented one of the world's biggest media moguls (a bona fide business "celebrity," by the way) from getting into Internet-related ventures without paying a hefty fee to our client. But the mogul had stopped all payments under the original joint venture agreement, so my client was going to court to enforce his rights. In 1999 and 2000, this generated instant media interest.

What's "hot" right now is one of the key variables that will influence whether a case receives media interest. Consider the flip-side of my convergence client: We are currently working with a shareholder fraud lawyer who is on CNN and CNBC twice a week regarding the cases he's involved with. In the late 1990s, we couldn't have booked him on public access cable. No one was doing corporate malfeasance or fraud stories then—now you can't get away from them. Conversely, nobody's doing convergence anymore, after the dot-com crash and the subsequent recession. These days, it's all corporate malfeasance all the time. White-collar perp walks are where it's at.

This is, at bottom, grossly unfair, isn't it? But right or wrong, it's the reality of news coverage, although the media, at times, is hard pressed to admit it. It reminds me of what someone once said about *New York Times* reporters: They act as if they go up to the roof of their building each night, and God delivers the news directly to them. Unfortunately, it's far more arbitrary than this, far more dependent on what the reporters are interested in, what they're hearing at the cocktail parties they go to, what they're reading in other media and seeing on the network news each night. News is far more dependent on "what's hot right now" than many in the media care to admit.

Does the Case Have a Compelling Human Face?

In the summer of 2000, Barbara Principe, a grandmother from southern New Jersey who fled Nazi Germany and grew up in poverty on a chicken farm, discovered she was heir to Berlin's famed Wertheim department store dynasty—one of the largest fortunes ever plundered by the Nazi regime. Moreover, the Wertheim's family's assets were stolen at the direction of Hitler himself—who took the land the family owned in downtown Berlin to build his Reich Chancellery, private living quarters, and infamous bunker complex. Mrs. Principe must battle the combined might of Germany's largest retailer and the German government itself to reclaim what was systematically taken from her family both during and after the war.

Heck of a story isn't it? It gets better (and we'll learn more about the Barbara Principe case, and the fascinating extra-judicial battle for the stolen Wertheim fortune, in Chapter Eight). But for now, just consider the amazing human face we've managed to put on the story. Here's a grandmother, living quietly in a one-story house not two miles from the small chicken farm where she grew up. Suddenly she's thrust into the middle of an international legal dispute that involves everyone from Gerhard Schroeder, to Condoleeza Rice, to the captains of German industry . . . to Hitler himself! All centered around a New York-based lawsuit over the alleged 1951 theft of the restitution right to shares in the Wertheim company, shares stolen from Barbara Principe's father. There is a tremendous human element to this case, but as I showed the complicated documents to reporters—complete with legal actions in both New York and Berlin and intense lobbying in Washington—more than one commented to me: "When it comes right down to it, this is just a fraud case, huh?" And it is.

But it's not the fraud that made the case newsworthy. It's the facts surrounding the fraud—and the incredible human story of a "regular" grandmother fighting to reclaim her past. You don't need to be an executive at the *Lifetime* cable network to see the human side of this fraud case.

But we could have missed it. Our story could have been presented as follows:

> In the wake of World War II, Gunther and Fritz Wertheim were fraudulently induced to give up their rights for restitution of their shares in the Wertheim Department Store company for an amount far less that the real value of the claim. Gunther Wertheim's daughter is now suing Germany's largest retailer, KarstadtQuelle, alleging that executives knew, or should have known, that the Wertheim brothers' shares were acquired through fraudulent means.

Not a bad story. But is it the story that opened this section? Absolutely not. It is the same case—but it's definitely not the same story. Not even close. It lacks the "human face" that made Barbara Principe's story so compelling—that of a plucky New Jersey grandmother taking on the world to reclaim her family's stolen legacy. Plaintiffs need to be constantly looking for ways to give their cases a "human face," while defendants need to be on-guard against those facts that lend themselves to such compelling narratives.

Is the Case Indicative of a Trend?

One case, you've got an anomaly, two cases, you've got yourself a trend. A bit simplistic, but it highlights a key point: If you can identify two or more cases that are similar, odds are the reporter's going to begin to see a trend—and trend reporting is one of the major types of news reporting out there.

I don't just mean trends in the legal sense. Lawyers use the term as in: The law is trending toward more protections in the workplace, or the Supreme Court has been trending away from its century-long erosion of states' rights. We're talking other types of trends as well—industry trends, factual trends, trends in the types of "human" stories reporters are seeing out there each day. Just look at some of the sample cases in this book, for instance. Could the cases be indicative of a trend toward:

- An increase of same-sex sexual harassment?
- A rise in the number of patent claims—or the size of the potential liability?
- Increasing discovery of fraud perpetrated against Holocaust survivors *after* World War II?

In any of these cases, the answer may well be "yes"—an indication that such trends will make the cases themselves far more attractive to reporters covering these stories. From a plaintiff's perspective, litigants and their lawyers want to undertake background research to see if there are other cases with similar fact patterns that reporters could use to indicate a trend. Defense needs to do the same to discover whether this is the type of story they need to guard against.

Does the Case Have Broader Implications as a Business Story?

The media love stories of lawsuits that somehow hold a deeper meaning in the business world. An example of this type of story is the media mogul case discussed earlier. In that case, a small integrated media company had a joint venture agreement with one of the true giants of the media world. Despite the age of convergence, this agreement prohibited our mogul from integrating television and the Internet—a move he desperately desired. The mogul had violated his agreement with my client, and my client had gone to court to enforce the mogul's prohibition from getting into interactive television. From the perspective of my client, it was a contract dispute over a joint venture agreement.

But from the mogul's perspective, it was far different. This was the core of his business model, and he was well aware that the service's closest competitor had already made moves that would bring it into the world of convergence. Moreover (as discussed above), this was a "hot" issue for the media at the moment, and the conventional thinking was that, as a business issue, the mogul had to be engaged in convergence to succeed. Without this underlying business issue, unrelated to the actual case itself, the story would not have garnered any interest in the media.

Is There a Political or Regulatory Aspect That Will Attract Interest in the Case?

There are various aspects of state and federal investigations and regulatory proceedings that bring special problems and issues when managing the communications aspects of the claims. There are also many cases that have significant public policy ramifications—and cases like these will also engender considerable public and media interest. Examples of these types of cases might include:

- A shareholder fraud action against one of the nation's largest investment banks.
- A medical malpractice lawsuit against an HMO over a decision to deny an "experimental" treatment.
- Tobacco and other product liability cases.
- Workplace-related cases, such as those involving sex, race, or religious discrimination or harassment.

Each of these types of cases could attract wider public interest—based not on the case itself, but on the wider public policy ramifications of the case. The SEC might become interested in a shareholder fraud case and launch an investigation of their own. The EEOC might see repeated claims of discrimination and decide to take a closer look at a particular company and its hiring and promotional practices. A politician might seize on a medical malpractice case to push for reform of HMOs and their treatment decisions. In each instance, the litigant is fighting two separate issues: the investigation or regulatory or political action on the one hand, and the increased media attention that such activity will bring to the original lawsuit on the other. In the glare of political or regulatory investigation, even the most run-of-the-mill business lawsuit can wind up as fodder for the nightly news.

Does the Opposing Counsel Have a History of Publicizing His or Her Cases?

When working for the defense in a case, one of the first things we check on is opposing counsel and their predisposition and willingness to use the media in the course of the lawsuit (this is the "information" part of the CIR process discussed in Chapter Four). Just as litigators want information on the general techniques the other side uses in court (and in the pretrial stage), so do we want information on opposing counsel's ability to use the media, and whether this is a weapon in this particular litigator's arsenal. In addition to all the factors cited earlier, this is a key factor in determining how much media interest will be generated by the lawsuit—or how little.

For example: We worked on a case with considerable innate media interest—a figure at the center of a major corporate fraud scandal at a large industrial corporation was now filing wrongful termination charges, claiming he was fired because he was a whistle-blower. We were called in to determine whether the corporate executive in question was going to take his case to the press—and coordinate the proper response should he do just that.

As part of our CIR response, we first briefed all senior executives on the need to *control* the lines of communication with the outside world—and most importantly, to bring to our attention any phone calls or other contact that might indicate that the other side had begun the media onslaught. All employees were instructed on the basic response mechanisms we discussed in Chapter Four. In the meantime, we began assembling *information* on the plaintiff, the facts of the case, the prior corporate fraud case that the plaintiff was at the center of—and, importantly, who the plaintiff had chosen to represent him.

Now some plaintiffs' attorneys are particularly skilled at using the media to their advantage. Some seem to have their media fingers constantly "a-twitching," ready to pull the trigger at the earliest sign of a newsworthy case. But on investigation, we found that this particular plaintiff's attorney was not one of this ilk. He was an older gentleman, and when reviewing the prior cases he had been involved in, we could find no prior evidence of situations where he had used public opinion to advance his client's interests. In 30 years, not one. For whatever reason, this was not this particular attorney's style (as you see through the course of this book, I feel that he was doing his clients a disservice in this regard). This clearly focused our response strategy. It became obvious to the legal and communications team that this lawyer was chosen by the plaintiff because he wasn't thinking of media coverage of the case. In fact, we surmised that the corporate fraud case the business executive had been through several years earlier had been quite painful and—whether or not it would have ultimately helped his case—the plaintiff did not want to rehash all of the old charges, no matter the payoff.

Thus, we advised the defendant corporation that it was unlikely that there would be any major media interest in the case—unless a reporter happened to stumble on it and connect the dots, independent of anything the plaintiff was doing.

This doesn't mean, by the way, that we did nothing. There still was a potential exposure, and we prepared the company by assembling a short statement denying the charges, and also set a system in place to monitor media interest in case a media outreach effort was launched by the other side. But because of our analysis, a base level of preparedness could be undertaken because it was unlikely that a full-fledged media campaign built around the case would ensue. A smaller fee for my firm, to be sure—but it supplied the legal team and the company itself with the right level of readiness without going overboard.

You've run the checklist—now what?

Ideally, this is how a company and its communications and legal teams should work with the Litigation Media checklist:

- First, filter each case through the checklist. For some—or even most—cases, this may take about 10 seconds, as in: "Routine auto accident case involving a company vehicle. No litigation media exposure." End of story. At other times, more thought and investigation may be given as to whether the case is the type that will generate public interest—and if so, how much.

- To those cases that merit media coverage, a commensurate response is prepared. As we've discussed in Chapter Four, this is where the CIR system comes into play, with determination of the exact nature and intensity of the response. As in the example cited earlier where we determined the plaintiff's lawyer was not the type to take steps to publicize a case, the exact response depends on just how much news a particular case will make. Take the auto accident example above and adjust the facts slightly:

  —Routine auto accident case involving a company vehicle that hit Jennifer Aniston on Hollywood Boulevard . . .

  —Routine auto accident case involving a company vehicle that hit Jennifer Aniston on Hollywood Boulevard while being driven by the company CEO . . .

  —Routine auto accident case involving a company vehicle that hit Jennifer Aniston on Hollywood Boulevard while being driven by the company CEO's mistress . . .

You get the point. To be effective, the response needs to be commensurate to the level of media interest you might expect, using the criteria outlined in our description of the Litigation

Media Checklist, and the elements of the CIR system outlined in Chapter Four.

The Baseline Response

Any case that lends itself to media interest, even at low levels, needs to have a baseline response—that is, a minimal level of preparedness to handle whatever public scrutiny may come your way (from a plaintiff's perspective, you may be looking to beef up the media interest—and in Chapter Eight, we'll look at ways to do that). This will vary depending on your circumstance, but in general, such a baseline media response usually consists of:

- A strategy memo outlining possible responses.
- Development of the "message"—a written statement or message points that allow your spokesperson to respond effectively.
- Media monitoring, so that you can immediately identify any increase in media interest in your story, and respond accordingly.

But this begs the question: Who handles this? The legal department? The communications department? Outside advisors? And how do we get them all working together?

In the next chapter, we'll look at how to put together teams of lawyers, business executives, and public relations professionals to look at these issues—and the peculiar cultural and philosophical differences that often cause difficulties in getting the members of these teams working together.

ACTION POINTS

✔ Immersed in the complexities of their legal issues, lawyers and business executives sometimes have a hard time seeing which cases will be of interest to a broader public audience.

✔ What is *legally significant* is not always what is *newsworthy*—therefore, when plotting communications strategy, lawyers and their clients need to consider not just the cases that have the most legal import, but those that have the most public import.

✔ *Systems* are key to managing the public relations aspects of legal matters—systems such as the Litigation Media Checklist, which offers a convenient, flexible framework for considering whether a case or legal matter will be of interest to a wider audience.

✔ All cases should be run through a system like the Litigation Media Checklist—and for any that have a public component, an appropriate level of response should be determined.

CHAPTER SIX

Lawyers, Clients, and Public Relations Professionals: How We Can Work Together

Generally speaking, the two people who are most unbelievable when put before the media are lawyers and public relations professionals. Unfortunately, this may be all they have in common.

Often it seems as if the legal and public relations professions are constantly at odds—but when handling the communications aspects of major litigation, it is critical that they work effectively together for the overall strategy to be a success. In this chapter, we learn about the peculiar mindsets of lawyers and public relations professionals and why, at times, they seem so divergent. We'll also look at the creation of the core legal communications team—a strategy for creating a team of lawyers and communications professionals charged with enacting the systems we have discussed throughout this book.

It is in everyone's interest (except, perhaps, the readers) to pretend that PR consultants are not involved in stories. It behooves the journalist, because it suggests that he has penetrated a rarified realm; it behooves the star, because he looks fearless and unattended by handlers; and it behooves the publicist, because it always behooves the publicist if the star is behooved.

—Tad Friend, "This Is Going to Be Big," *The New Yorker*, September 23, 2002

Journalist Tad Friend was writing about celebrity public relations, that strange world of press junkets, premieres, and publicists who can handpick the writer for the next cover story about their star. But even in the context of litigation and legal issues—about as far away from Hollywood public relations as you can get—I'd still say Mr. Friend is on to something. Except I'd add to the last sentence ". . . it behooves the lawyers, since they want the public to believe it was their legal skills, and not the publicity, that actually won the case."

Lawyers and public relations professionals can, at times, make for very strange bedfellows. In this chapter, we examine exactly why that is and what can be done about it. This is not, by any means, an academic exercise. It is critical that these two species of professionals work well together to ensure that the communications component of the litigation is handled effectively. It is in the best interest of the client and it is in the best interest of the case. If you really want to use public relations techniques to "win" your case, cooperation between your legal and communications advisors is essential—despite the often fractious relationship between the two disciplines.

COUNSELOR VERSUS COUNSELOR

Why can't lawyers and public relations people just get along?

Whenever I give speeches—to either legal groups or public relations groups—the first question I'm usually asked is: Can you teach us to work better together?

As someone who is both a lawyer and a public relations consultant, I have some insights in the mindset of both groups. I also feel that, given my professional credentials (and having worked for so many years alongside both lawyers and public relations people), I have the right to bash both groups of professionals unmercifully . . . in the interest of scholarship, of course.

THE GREAT DIVIDE

At one end of my midtown Manhattan office are my bar admission certificates—New York and Florida—with New York proudly declaring me "Attorney and Counselor At Law." At the other end, a certificate from the Public Relations Society of America Counselor's Academy, declaring me a Counselor in the practice of Public Relations.

This is, perhaps, symbolic of the deep divide between public relations practitioners and lawyers: Both see themselves as *counselors* in the highest definition of the word—yet each come from training, education, professional culture, and discipline that could not be more different.

It's a little like "Spy versus Spy" from *MAD* magazine—each side launching bombs at one another from behind the corners of buildings, never quite realizing just how closely they resemble each other.

Traditionally, the legal and public relations departments in corporations have wanted nothing to do with each other. The legal department (again, traditionally) sees a company's communications department—and the public relations people who populate it—as shallow wordsmiths, ex-reporters and wanna-be novelists or screenwriters who barely understand business and certainly don't understand legal issues and affairs. They're good for arranging parties, announcing new products, and maybe preparing the CEO for a speech or an appearance on the evening news. During a crisis or legal matter, they—at best—can run interference with the press until the "real" thinkers can decide what to do. But that's about it. Law is a substantive business, and most public relations people, lawyers feel, lack just that: substance.

To public relations professionals, on the other hand, the word *lawyer* could be synonymous with another word: *roadblock*. The legal department is seen as an impediment, something designed to get in the way of communication, not facilitate it. Lawyers, in the professional public relations person's view, exist mainly to screw things up—as in "legal will never let us do this," "legal will never let us say that," or "wait until legal gets hold of this . . . it will be unreadable!"

And unbusinesslike? In the mind of the public relations professional, the lawyer is the most unbusinesslike person in the organization—thinking not about the overall needs of the organization as a business, but rather of the strict legalities of the situation. Always thinking about liability, always thinking: "We can't do this?" rather than "How can we make this happen?" Lawyers would compromise business success in the name of legal rectitude every time. To the public relations professional, lawyers will stifle any business advantage that effective communication and properly executed public relations programs bring.

I have no doubt, by the way, some of the lawyer's attitudes toward public relations departments are gender-based. Not all . . . but certainly some. Law has been a profession dominated by men; public relations, by contrast, has traditionally been more open to women. Over the years, there's been a lot of the "this is too complicated for the public relations gal . . ." mentality among lawyers. If you need proof, look at the marketing and public relations departments that have developed at law firms and the respect they engender from their own partners and associates (although some, to be fair, are highly respected, both internally and externally). Public relations departments, like human resources departments, have long been places where women are over-represented—and both areas, not coincidentally, suffer from a certain amount of second-class citizenship in the corporate world. But the paradox of this is as follows: Given the increasing importance of human capital to business organizations *and* the enhanced importance of communications in the business environment, there are likely no more important departments in a company these days than human resources and public relations. Let's go even further: Organizations and business enterprises now succeed or fail based primarily on the strength of their human capital and their ability to communicate to their target audiences. Thus, the two departments most historically open to women have become among the most critical to the organization's mission. Can pay equity be next?

Back to our question: How do you get lawyers and public relations professionals working together—as more and more they will have to as legal issues and litigation increasingly become public relations concerns?

For years, I'm sure that question was never asked. There just never was much of an opportunity for a corporation's legal department and their public relations department to work together. But as media coverage of legal issues and lawsuits began to grow, these two groups were thrust together like never before. Like Felix Unger and Oscar Madison, the question of whether they can live together without driving each other crazy is still very much open. But the first step to cooperation is to understand—at some level, at least— how the other side thinks.

THE DIFFERENCE BETWEEN LAWYERS AND PUBLIC RELATIONS PROFESSIONALS

To start off, here's an interesting fact that highlights the difference between law firms and public relations firms: Lawyers at law firms, by and large, will always invite you to come in and meet at *their* offices. Public relations agency people will always suggest that they come to *your* offices.

What does this mean? Well, besides the fact that lawyers tend to have nicer offices than public relations people (and that public relations has always been more "service-oriented" than the legal profession), this fact is a little more telling than you would think. Despite lawyer jokes, a perceived erosion of professional standards and other recent changes to the legal profession, there is an aura of prestige surrounding the practice of law that influences the way lawyers think and act. Public relations, by contrast, arose much more recently, at the beginning of this century, as "press agentry"—first in the promotion of vaudeville acts and other forms of entertainment for the lower classes, and then in the counseling of corporations on their public conduct by people like Ivy Lee and Edward Bernays—themselves just one step up from the ranks of vaudeville press agents. Thus, you are summoned to an attorney's office, but you summon your public relations firm to you.

Think about this dichotomy and the way it affects the relationship between lawyers and public relations counselors. American lawyers have John Adams and Abraham Lincoln and Clarence Darrow and Thurgood Marshall to look up to (just to name a few).

Public Relations? It's pillars are—shall we say—slightly less stellar: Sydney Falco of *The Sweet Smell of Success,* Samantha Jones of HBO's *Sex and the City,* and Lizzie Grubman come to mind. This is not to say that esteemed counselors in the field of public relations don't exist—most, I'd wager, are every bit as professional as the most ethical lawyers practicing today. But there just isn't a level of reverence for the profession that you find in the practice of law. Put another way: It will be a long time before we hear a U.S. president say the following in his inaugural address: "As John Hill, the founder of Hill & Knowlton, so rightly put it . . ."

Now, let's look at it from the opposite perspective: Law is seen by some as a profession in decline. Whether this is actually true or not is open to question, but the perception is certainly there. There are lawyers on every street corner battling for business. Ethical and even criminal abuses abound. The profession is run by the billable hour. Stories of law firm billing abuses are rampant, like the partner who billed more than 24 hours in one day because he was on a plane that crossed several time zones. Many lawyers—even ones that came of age in the idealistic 1960s—now see the practice of law primarily as a way to make lots and lots of money. Bill, baby, bill.

Public relations, on the other hand, is on the way up, struggling out the primordial ooze to take its place among law, accounting, management consulting, and other so-called "legitimate" professions. Moreover, with the rise of media, public opinion, and technological access to information of all kinds, communications firms are no longer the houses of ill-repute, but temples of reputation—guardians of a corporation's most precious asset: its name and goodwill in the marketplace. Again, these differing mindsets work to inform the way the different professionals think, work, and interact. Whichever view of the various disciplines you subscribe to, you can see how divergent they are in history, culture, and outlook. There's no doubt about it: Law is from Mars, public relations from Venus.

Finally, another example of the difference between the two disciplines. My mother once asked me what I do for a living. I thought about it for a moment and told her: "I get people in the newspaper . . . and I keep people out of the newspaper." She looked at me like I was crazy.

So when people ask her what her eldest son does for a living, what does she say?

"Oh, he's a lawyer."

ALL ABOUT LAWYERS

Lawyers compete. Every engagement is an opportunity to seek advantage. A meeting with the partners at one of New York's major plaintiffs' law firms a few years back crystallized my view of the way lawyers think.

Granted, plaintiffs' lawyers are a theatrical breed to begin with, and maybe not typical of the type of litigator you encounter in a business setting. But on the other hand, litigators are litigators, and I found the exchange emblematic of how lawyers operate in most situations.

The law firm in this case was about to undertake a major class action against the airline industry on behalf of air travelers, and they were hoping for considerable publicity on the case. My colleague and I sat down for a meeting with three of the partners to discuss the ways our services might be of assistance.

The first partner in the firm greeted us warmly and led us back to his office, which was among the most well-appointed attorney's offices I had ever seen. This partner was a charming man and all was going well, until two other partners arrived. Neither shook our hands, and one of the partners carried a sheaf of documents and proceeded to read through them as we were talking, without ever looking us in the eye. Occasionally, he would look at a letter and chuckle, shake his head, and mumble to himself: "What is this . . . ?"

Partner #2, for his part, launched into a line of aggressive questioning: "So what do you think you can do for us that we can't do ourselves? We have somebody here who can write press releases, you know."

I explained that we weren't talking about writing press releases, but strategy for managing the media during the course of the litigation. He ignored me.

"What reporters do you know? Can you get this story on the front page of the *Times*?"

I explained that we know many, if not all, of the major legal re-porters in the country, but that didn't matter much—they still hang up on me if I don't have a story that's of interest to them. As to the front page of the *New York Times,* I said we'd need to know more about the case, but it certainly wasn't out of the question.

All the while, Partner #1 smiled amiably, while Partner #3 ig-nored us, rifling through his documents, signing letters, reviewing other correspondence, seemingly not paying attention at all.

"So what is it, exactly, that you do?" Partner #2 asked.

I explained that we work closely with lawyers in the case to plot communications strategy, including crafting the proper messages that are going to be of interest to the media and making sure that the messages are getting in front of the right audiences in the most effective manner possible—so that the public relations effort really helps in winning the case. "It's like any other area of litigation management," I said. "You've got to make sure it's handled prop-erly, or you run the risk of getting damaged in the media so badly that it will hurt the other portions of your case."

"I don't know," said Partner #2, "I just don't believe you can do anything to manage the media. We'll just send them the complaint. After they read it, they'll see how important this case is."

Suddenly, Partner #3 dropped his documents, slammed his open hand down on the conference table, and glowered at us.

"This is horseshit!" he screamed, "I don't think this stuff works at all, and I'll be damned if I'm going to sit here one second longer and listen to this crap!" With that, he picked up his assorted pa-pers, letters, and legal briefs and stormed out of the room.

Partner #1 looked back at us and smiled.

"Now let's talk about your hourly rates," he said.

Clearly, we had been set up. The litigators in question had care-fully choreographed the entire meeting to knock us down on fees. Needless to say, we didn't take the assignment.

Lawyers always seek the advantage. To a lawyer, each meeting is an adversarial encounter, and at times they will beat you up even when they agree with you. Understandably, this can be quite a turn-off, particularly if you don't know where it is coming from. But to lawyers, this is all part of negotiation, collaboration, and learning. Lawyers have been berated this way by other lawyers since as far back as law school (as you'll see in more detail next).

It is understanding the way lawyers think and act that allows public relations professionals (and the clients who have to deal with attorneys, for that matter) to work with the legal team more effectively. With that in mind, consider the following:

- *Lawyers like to argue—this is how they explore important issues and arrive at answers.* Lawyers learn by argument, by questioning—like Socrates on too much caffeine. I'm never comfortable when I go into a meeting with a lawyer if he or she just listens to our ideas and strategies, shakes our hands, and says "Okay, sounds good." Though this may be a verbal contract of some form, I know it will likely be broken before I even get back to my office. Why? Because I know the lawyer hasn't been listening.

The meetings that go much better are when the lawyer puts up a little bit of a fight—in fact, my firm has been very successful over the years in meetings where the first thing the legal team said was, "I don't believe this stuff works . . ." Then we go on to vigorously debate whether or not it does. This is the type of interaction with the legal team that leads me to believe they are interested. Like a justice in a Supreme Court oral argument, they are simply testing the parameters of my argument before proceeding. Which is good, because I know the argument is a winner.

Lawyers like to argue. It is the way they collect information. Thus, communications professionals, outside public relations firms, and business executives need to be able to put up with these arguments—and counter them—to make the case for the course of action that is being proposed. Otherwise, there is no "buy-in" from the legal team on the course of action to be taken. If there is no buy-in, communications strategy won't integrate properly with legal strategy, and in the end you will have just proven the lawyers' point: that this stuff really doesn't work.

- *Lawyers are taught to always have the answer.* Here's another telling sign about lawyers: Sometimes when I sit across from them at a table discussing communications issues, I get the distinct impression the lawyers I'm speaking to are thinking, "If I only had the time, I could do this—and I probably could do it better than you!" This is more than mere arrogance (or a reflection of the impression I give at meetings). It comes from lawyers' predisposition, drilled into them through law school and other forms of legal training, that the "form book" for handling every problem exists out there somewhere—and it's the lawyer's job to find it. Lawyers are taught to listen to a client's problem, then head to the law library and find an answer. This is particularly true in communications matters—since lawyers, by and large, perceive *communication* as something they do.

• *Lawyers thrive on precedent. Precedent* is a legal term for the cases that have gone before and set the legal rules we operate under. It is critically important to remember this because it is through the eyes of precedent that most lawyers see the world. You want new ideas, new ways of looking at old problems? Well, to be fair, some lawyers are very good at this, but I'd wager that this is *despite* their legal training, not *because* of it. Again, most lawyers are trained as follows: Hear the problem, then find the case law, statute, or legal form that gives the solution.

ARE LAWYERS SMART?

Many lawyers are creative thinkers, deep thinkers with considered, deeply held convictions on a variety of subjects. Some are even able to break out of the mindset I describe above. But are lawyers smart? Well, yes and no. There's certainly a presumption that they are. After all, law school is really hard, as is passing the bar. But in reality, I'd say that lawyers are just like everyone else in the business and professional world—some are smart, and some are not.

Moreover, even some of the most brilliant lawyers possess what I would consider a *compartmentalized knowledge.* A lawyer friend of mine who is the managing partner of a large law firm once told me that a good litigator is like a good auto mechanic: They have exactly the tools needed for the job, and they know how to use them. Just don't ask them how an internal combustion engine works.

I think this accurately characterizes a large percentage of litigators—they know what they know very well, and sometimes they don't know much else. That is key to understanding the lawyer's mindset and the way they act. Consider the old saying in legal circles:

- If the law is on your side, pound the law.
- If the facts are on your side, pound the facts.
- If neither is on your side, pound the table.

In interacting with lawyers, there's often a lot of table pounding going on. To work effectively with lawyers, you've got to understand this and know how to cut through it to reach the overall strategic business goals of the legal issue at hand.

LAW IS NOT AN INTELLECTUAL EXERCISE

In the end, legal training, for all its rigor, is not primarily an intellectual exercise. I can still remember my first day of law school (or night, actually, since I started at Fordham University Law School in New York in the evening program). I had no idea what to expect—growing up we had no lawyers in the family, nor any lawyer acquaintances. At this point, I hadn't even seen *The Paper Chase*. I expected law school to be an intellectual exercise the equal of anything I'd experienced as an undergraduate. Boy, was I wrong.

My first class was Torts. The professor at the front of the room was a scary man, vaguely reminiscent of Fred Flintstone in a really bad mood.

He entered the class on that first evening, and without saying a word, bellowed: "*Weaver v. Ward.*" The name of the case echoed through the room. The professor looked down at his attendance sheet and picked someone at random.

"Mr. Jones, have you read the case?"

A frightened student rustled in the back of the room. Meanwhile, I hadn't even bought the books yet.

"No I haven't," Mr. Jones replied. The professor scowled and looked back down at his attendance list.

"Ms. Adams?"

"Haven't read it."

The professor then went on to berate us for five minutes or so for not having read the case, until someone finally piped up and said that they had indeed done the assigned reading. In machine

gun fashion, the professor proceeded to grill her on the facts of the
case and the decision of the judges:

"Who were the parties?"

"What was the issue involved?"

"What was the holding?"

Each time, the student meekly answered the professor's questions. Then it was over and he went on to the next case.

"*Brown v. Kendall.* Mr. Smith?"

And that was it. No intellectual discussion of *why* the law was
like that, *should* it be different, or even what a tort was (and, honest-
to-God, at that point I still really didn't have a clue).

A few weeks into the class, my name came up. By this time I had
the book and had actually read the case in question on the subway
on the way up to the Lincoln Center Campus from my day job as a
low-level aide in the Koch administration.

"Mr. Haggerty: *Mohr v. Williams* . . ."

I dutifully struggled through my brief* of the case, responding
to the professor's questions with whatever I could recall from my
subway ride. At the end of the questioning, he glared at me for a
moment in silence, then said:

"Good enough for government work, Mr. Haggerty."

I was insulted, of course—not just for me, but on behalf of all
government workers. But this is what the study of law is like, to a
large extent, although maybe not as exaggerated as it was in this
professor's tort class. You learn what one case held about a particular issue of law, and then another one, and then another one after
that. Through this you wind up with two things:

1. You begin to discover the parameters of the particular area
   of the law you are studying.

2. You learn to "think like a lawyer."

Legal education indoctrinates law students into a manner of
thinking that remains with them throughout their professional careers. That's not always a bad thing: Law teaches a rigorous process

---

*You may recall from Chapter Two that a *case brief* is a short summary of the
major facts of the case, the law, and the holding—from which we derive our
own *Media Brief.*

of thinking and approaching problems that I find indispensable in many aspects of my business life. It is also true that legal education has loosened up a bit in the past decade, and in the later years of law school you engage in more practical courses (i.e., pretrial litigation, trial techniques) or theory-oriented classes (law and justice, perhaps). But, in the end, legal education is really not about thinking, it is about *learning*. This mindset permeates an attorney's thinking all throughout his or her years of practice.

PUBLIC RELATIONS PROFESSIONALS

On to the public relations profession and its many foibles. First, let's acknowledge the enormous number of highly skilled public relations practitioners out there, many of whom combine business expertise, creativity, and an appreciation of the nuances of the work in a manner that make them extraordinary counselors to their clients. But they are not without their own idiosyncrasies—some of which run directly counter to the nature of the lawyers they need to work with in a litigation situation. So here's the "down-and-dirty" about public relations and some of the professionals who inhabit the field:

• *Many public relations people never wanted to be in PR to begin with.* At the most elemental level, some don't like public relations and wish they were doing something else. They hate being called "the public relations guy (or gal)." They find calling a reporter and begging him or her to write a story to be demeaning. In fact, some say in conversation, with a measure of pride: "I haven't made a media call in years . . ." as if that somehow puts them above those public relations people who do speak with reporters on a regular basis. They append their firm names with euphemisms like "communications strategists," "reputation management consultants," and "public affairs specialists." Now granted, there's much that these firms do that goes well beyond the term *public relations*—including research, strategy, lobbying, government affairs matters, and so on. My firm does all that as well. But it's an undeniable fact that many public relations professionals started out wanting to do something else with their lives. Some wanted to be journalists, but found they just couldn't make a living that way. Others wanted to be politicians and change the world. Some wish they were management consultants, while others wish they had gone to law school. During the dot-com boom, many set up Web-based subsidiaries or were circulating business plans to get them out of the field of public relations entirely.

This is important for both clients and their lawyers to know. You need to make sure that the public relations professional you're working with doesn't have these insecurities. Make sure they like what they do, that they feel great pride in what they do, and they relish the opportunity to get the job done. In a conscious or unconscious way, an attitude of dislike for the profession will bleed through to all the work they are doing on behalf of your legal matter. Especially given the complexity and confidential nature of this work, a public relations consultant who is not fully committed to what he or she does is dangerous.

• *Some have doubts about the value of what they are doing.* I have a sneaking suspicion that, deep down, many public relations professionals don't feel that what they do is worth the money you're paying them. They have a hard time quantifying the results to clients, and there's no way to give the client any sort of guarantee as to what result they are going to get. It's not as if the public relations consultant can say: "I can get this on the front page of the *New York Times*/on *Nightline*/in *Time* magazine, by next Tuesday/next month/three days before the case goes to trial. There are no guarantees. The most a public relations consultant can do is assure the client of their best efforts to accomplish these tactical goals. Hence, at times, there can be a lingering sense that what public relations consultants do is . . . well, too speculative to be of any real value to the client. This is why they have such trouble with an attorney's argument-based way of working through the issues. In many cases, the public relations person doesn't quite believe the argument either.

This causes some unscrupulous operators to just give up trying, to take the client's retainer for as long as they'll pay it, pass the day-to-day contact on to as junior a person as possible, and then when no results come, say, "Gee, I guess it wasn't news." By then, they've moved on to the next client—thus reinforcing the notion to clients and themselves that this stuff just doesn't work.

I tend to tell clients: While we can't guarantee *exact* results, we can pretty much forecast the level of results you can *reasonably* expect. That is to say, if your story is interesting enough (and we do our job right), we certainly can't predict the *New York Times* for next Wednesday, but we can predict major media coverage *somewhere*—and again, in the work that we do, media coverage designed to advance our overall litigation goals. This requires a certain amount of confidence, but if you believe in the value of what you do and your ability to produce, that shouldn't be a problem. As Hall of Fame pitcher Dizzy Dean once said, "It ain't bragging if you've done it."

• *Some want to show process instead of results.* Meeting reports. Weekly reports. Monthly reports. Strategy memos. Maybe owing to the lack of perceived value in what they do and the uncertainty of the entire process, some public relations consultants are not in the business of getting results for the clients—they're in the business of telling their clients what they're doing. Early in my career, I worked at a public relations firm briefly (about two months) that did just this. They papered their clients to death with reports of their activities, but forgot all about the *results* their clients hired them to get. Another example of this papering includes reports and updates that say the following: "Dear Client: We sent out the press release regarding your story to the following publications:" They then list everything from *Accounting Today* to *Zoom!* magazine. The client is fooled into thinking, "Wow, that's great progress!" Progress, yes; but results?

• *Public relations consultants rue the lack of professional credentials.* Why do some public relations professionals feel so insecure about what they do? Well, consider this: To be a management consultant, you need an MBA. To be a doctor, an MD or PhD. To be a lawyer, a JD.

To be a public relations consultant? A computer, a telephone, and a fax machine.

This is a major problem that faces the public relations industry, and it creates at least three distinct problems:

1. Public relations people feel very insecure about their credentials, and this insecurity translates to how they approach their work.

2. People who have no business being in this field hang out a shingle and start "serving" clients.

3. Everyone who's ever watched television or read a newspaper thinks they can do public relations.

Good public relations counselors have the intestinal fortitude to dispense with these notions and to otherwise set up the relationship with attorneys and other members of the team on the proper level. Otherwise, the poor insecure public relations flack will be steamrolled by the argumentative, advantage-seeking litigator every time. Ultimately, it's the client's case that suffers.

THE POLITICAL ANIMAL

One last point on the field of public relations. Many practitioners start out in politics—in fact, many of the real stars of the public relations world—the grand "Spin Doctors" out there like Mike McCurry and Ed Rollins—come out of the political world (as I did, by the way, along with many of my partners and other colleagues). There's nothing wrong with a political background, but it does have its own particular mindset that sometimes can get in the way of working effectively with the communications issues a client might face during litigation.

In my early years, I worked as a low-level aide to Senator Daniel Patrick Moynihan of New York and New York City Mayors Edward I. Koch and David Dinkins, and certainly some of the aspects of a political campaign or a good public policy battle are present in litigation, but I find that the two areas of expertise diverge very quickly—and sometimes political-types are hard-pressed to recognize this.

This is a particular myopia of the denizens of politics and government that extends to many areas of their lives, by the way—they tend to think that the whole world operates like their little corner. I can't emphasize this enough: Working with communications and the media during litigation or other legal matters is not like a political campaign and shouldn't be treated as such.

Too often in my litigation consulting—particularly with powerful clients who have considerable political contacts—I would get input like this: "Well, I mentioned the case to James Carville, and he said I should . . ." or "I ran into Congressman John Smith at a fundraiser and he said . . ." Politicians and their spin-meisters may know more about polling, campaigns, and politics than I ever will, but God save me from their unsolicited advice during legal actions.

Why is communications in litigation so different from political campaigns? Consider the following:

- In most forms of litigation, you are not responding to an *electorate* in the same way you are in politics and government. Yes, you have *constituencies,* but these tend to be highly segmented and narrowly focused—thus, old political saws like "you must respond to every public attack," are just not true in the litigation context. If your target audience is not hearing it, you don't respond.

- Litigation can be dragged out over months and years, and public interest in the litigation tends to ebb and flow with the legal action itself. Political campaigns may start out slow, but they build momentum each day, every day, until election day. Thus, the "message of the day . . ." and similar techniques that just aren't relevant in the litigation context.

- In politics and government, the media come to you. This was one of the biggest changes from my days working in government—when reporters would call me—and my days working in the private sector—when I would have to call them. In most cases in the private sector or in a public relations firm, you go out and find the story, it doesn't find you.

Finally, politics differs from litigation—and from the rest of the "real" world, for that matter—in its glorification of the individual politician or government official. Whether senator, congressman, or local alderman, politics imbues the elected official with a certain sense of grandeur, of nobility—remember, most are not making much money at this, so the trappings of power become the coin of the realm. The political aides who scurry about feed this sense of privilege, this sense of entitlement, this cult of personality, and all of the "work" of the office—from political campaigns to legislative battles to administrative action—flows from the individualized perspective. That's not to say that the political power structure hasn't, over the years, produced some great leaders and great results. But it differs considerably from the world of legal issues and litigation, where it's not the parties but the *law* that is (generally speaking) elevated to this pedestal. This is not an insignificant difference, and having at various times trod the political path, I know it is a mindset that any litigant or attorney who is receiving advice from a congressional aide or political consultant should bear in mind.

Moreover, this cult of individual and personality exists as readily in the smallest of cities as it does on Capitol Hill—or for that matter the White House. When I started my career, I worked as a research associate (read "intern") for the Honorable Juanita M. Crabb, a very talented young mayor of the upstate city of Binghamton, New York. Binghamton was a small city, just over 50,000 in population at the time. Despite Binghamton's small size, power was power, and it was hoarded and wielded by the mayor and other machers in Binghamton just as surely as it is in the Chicago, New York, or any other big city. Thus, the various potentates would play power games with each other whenever they could. Every time Mayor Crabb would go to a meeting at the offices of the local assemblyman, for example, he would make her wait a good 10, 15 minutes before seeing her. When he would come to City Hall, she would reciprocate. I'd come to the office in the morning, and there he'd be—waiting impatiently in the reception area. This went on the entire time I worked there. It was nobody's fault. This is just how politics is.

Another example: As a low-level aide to Daniel Patrick Moynihan, I once spent an entire Saturday afternoon chasing the great man's sweater all across the Northeastern United States.

Let me explain. Moynihan had flown up from Washington, DC (from Dulles if I recall correctly), and had gone to his usual residence at the Carlyle Hotel on Manhattan's Upper East Side. This was during his re-election campaign, and each weekend one of his New York City-based political aides would staff his New York office in case he needed anything. So there I was, alone in his office on a

Saturday morning, when I received a frantic call from the senator's personal assistant in Washington. The senator had left his sweater on the airplane. Could I help track it down?

I called the airline public affairs office and they hurriedly hopped right on it. Green though I was, I can still remember being quite amused at the vigor with which the airline set about on the search for the senator's sweater.

About 20 minutes later, I received a call. The sweater was still on the plane, but the plane had flown to Cleveland.

Then, a short while later, another call: Before they could retrieve the sweater in Cleveland, the plane had taken off again for Baltimore. They were going to try and catch it there.

All the while, I was relaying my progress to the senator's personal assistant, who kept calling to ask: "Any word on the sweater? The senator was wondering."

The airline called again: As it turned out, the plane was now headed back to New York. The airline would retrieve the sweater at LaGuardia and have it messengered to my office.

Finally, quite late in the afternoon, the sweater arrived at Moynihan's office on Third Avenue in midtown Manhattan. I made arrangements to bring it to his room at the Carlyle.

When I knocked on the door, Moynihan himself answered, tieless and in shirtsleeves. He appeared to be in the middle of an early dinner with his wife.

Never much on formalities, Moynihan was nonetheless quite pleased we'd been able to find the sweater and greeted me rather warmly. I handed him the sweater. Since he barely knew who I was, I thought this might be an opportunity to make an impression.

"Here's your sweater, senator," I said, "and you'll be happy to know it now qualifies for frequent-flyer miles."

He stopped and stared at me blankly, obvious quite confused by my last statement. Moynihan, he of erudite, professorial demeanor and lofty, historical preoccupations, gave me a look as if I had just arrived from Mars—or better still, as if I had momentarily confused Disraeli and Gladstone. He was not a man for humor based on the then still-new frequent-flyer practices of the modern airline industry.

After a moment more of staring, he gave me a half-smile.

"Thank you," he sang out, then ushered me through the doorway.

An indignity, to be sure, but the following Monday I was lauded in the office for my good work in the hunt for the senator's sweater. And, thus, my career in politics was launched.

THE CORE LEGAL COMMUNICATIONS TEAM

So now I've pissed off virtually everyone I work with. But all of this is so that you can understand the incredible gulf between the lawyer's mentality and the public relations/public affairs practitioner's mentality. Now let's talk about bridging that gap.

Anyone confronting a particularly vexing legal issue that is going to impact both lawyers and communicators needs to put together a structure for melding the legal and communications functions of the organization. In other words, you need to create the core *Legal Communications Team* (LCT) that will facilitate cooperation between the two differing groups of professionals, both with their own distinctive way of analyzing issues and tactical approaches to problem solving. As you'll see, this team should be created regardless of the size of the organization or the particulars of the legal fight you find yourself in.

In smaller cases—where you have only one lawyer and one public relations professional involved, for example—it's easy: that's your team. In larger organizations, you need to identify an individual or individuals who are going to make up your core team, then bring them together with a mandate for coordinating the communications component of litigation strategy. Team members need to be dedicated to working across lines—both organizational lines and those of philosophy and culture—to ensure that both the legal components and the communications components are working in tandem.

Often in the heat of battle, this happens anyway. A core team—consisting, for example, of one of the outside lawyers, a member of the general counsel's office, and either internal or external public relations counsel—develops. They take it upon themselves to lead the litigation communications effort. This is fine, but as we discussed in the last chapter, proper *systems* are one of the most important factors in effectively managing the process. Moreover, several things can happen in these situations that hamper the effectiveness of the informal team, including:

1. The team is formed too late to have the desired effect.

2. Having never worked together before, the informal team immediately begins to butt heads—for all of the various reasons laid out earlier in this chapter.

3. The informal team doesn't have the blessing or authority of the decision makers handling the litigation, and therefore cannot have a real strategic impact on the course of the litigation. (They, in effect, nibble at the edges of properly managing the communication elements of the litigation.)

How can these problems be avoided? Primarily by creating an LCT that is:

- A permanent part of both legal and communications planning.

- Meets regularly to discuss legal issues facing the organization.

- Has the imprimatur of the top leadership of both the legal team and the organization as a whole.

The larger the company or organization, the more important this is. In smaller companies, these sorts of teams develop organically. In big corporations—where everything else is formalized—your LCT needs to be a formal part of the litigation management system as well, lest both the legal and communications members of the group become marginalized and therefore ineffective in managing the communications aspects of the litigation.

Assuming you are an average size corporation—that is, not a General Electric, but not a small mom-and-pop shop either—ideally, the members of your Legal Communications Team might include the following:

- The general counsel or the member of the corporation's legal department who is in charge of litigation.

- If it is a larger law department (and law departments at major corporations can run into the hundreds), a designated

litigation lawyer with a proclivity and sensitivity to communications issues.

- The leader of the outside law firm's litigation team.
- A senior internal or external communications professional
  with specialized skills in working with legal departments.

Let's take that last member first. Whether your public relations
representative is part of the company's internal marketing/public
relations/communications department or from an external public
relations firm that specializes in this sort of work, they need special
skills to deal effectively with various lawyers that make up the
LCT—and all of the other lawyers floating around the litigation as
well. This public relations person is a unique breed. It needs to be
someone who:

- If not a lawyer, at least understands the *process* of law—internal
  and external investigations, demand letters and notices of
  intent to sue, filings, motion practice, discovery, mediation
  and other alternative dispute resolution (ADR) methods . . .
  the list goes on and on. In other words, your public relations
  representative doesn't need to know the substance of the law—
  that is, the elements of *quid pro quo* sexual harassment, for example—but he or she does need to know the course the legal
  action is going to take in order to properly chart strategy.

- Your public relations representative also has to be someone
  who won't be intimidated by members of the legal team. This
  is not to say that public relations people are any more easily intimidated than anyone else—just that, given everything we've
  learned about lawyers and how they use argument to move
  their points forward, your public relations leader needs to be
  someone who isn't going to be backed down easily. This can't
  be emphasized enough: *Argument* is the way lawyers consider issues and reach conclusions. It's nothing personal, it doesn't
  mean they don't like you, it doesn't mean they're getting ready
  to rule against the course of action you're prescribing. To be
  an effective member of the LCT, the communications representative, whether internal or external, needs to realize this,
  lest his or her contributions be minimized.

- The public relations representative needs to be a *senior* member of the communications team. Again, this is true whether the public relations professional is part of the internal communications department or an outside firm. There may be a temptation to staff the LCT with a junior member of the public relations team—especially given the increasing number of lawyers now entering the public relations field. A senior public relations professional—in addition to being able to handle the first two criteria mentioned—will also need to have a breadth of business and strategic knowledge. Moreover, internal communications executives will have one eye toward the company's overall public relations and corporate communications strategy—a key element that should dictate the approach taken to a particular piece of litigation or other legal matter.

Each of these elements is critical for the public relations member (or members) of the team. What should the legal members look like? Well, ideally, they have the following background/credentials:

- First, like the public relations member, the legal component of the LCT ought to be senior members of the legal team handling the matter. By now, the reasons are becoming obvious—there needs to be a broad sense of the legal, public opinion and business issues involved, as well as senior-level buy-in of the strategies and work of the team.

- The legal members of the team should ideally have knowledge and background in media, public relations, or other aspects of public issues management. Sometimes this is hard to find, particularly since most lawyers went directly from undergraduate studies, to law school, to private practice, or to work in a corporate law department. But some level of skill/knowledge/interest in the world outside the law library is important to his or her understanding of the issues that the LCT will handle. In this context, even lawyers who have backgrounds in politics or government are preferable. In a situation where the lead lawyer, either in the corporation or in an outside law firm is not necessarily media-attuned, other members of the team need to make up the deficiency.

- Finally, the legal members of the LCT need to *believe* in the goal of properly managing the communications aspects of the case. I mean really *believe*. Some lawyers just don't (although I hope more do after reading this book). Others feel that it's "not their style" to attend to the public relations aspects of the case. A person like this on the LCT will sabotage the overall goals of the group. Remember, we're not talking about flashy promotional efforts here. In most circumstances, we are simply talking about properly framing public discussion of the issues, building relationships with outside audiences important to the legal action, and otherwise controlling all of those things that occur outside the courtroom during litigation. All of this should be acceptable to even the most conservative lawyer in the room—if he or she believes in the overall value of the effort.

If you are a smaller company with a "small" lawsuit (although few lawsuits are "small" to the parties in the middle of them), the decision as to who will be part of the LCT should be considered carefully. Many times, as the legal issues in the case multiply, so to do all the people working on your behalf. Before you know it, even companies or organizations of a relatively small size can find themselves working with handfuls of lawyers and public relations specialists—along, perhaps, with other consultants, experts, and internal and external executives who are a "part" of the legal action (in the broadest sense of the term). These other actors can include:

- Investor relations specialists who need to attend to the shareholder issues that are part of the lawsuits.
- Government relations specialists, since many lawsuits today have at least some level of governmental or political impact.
- CFOs, human resource people, and other internal financial and operational personnel, whose expertise and activity may be at the core of the legal issues involved.
- External consultants, experts, researchers, investigators, and other personnel who lend their particular expertise to the case.

I'm sure there are many others as well. But here's an important point: Although all of these groups should have *input* into the process of creating communications strategy for the lawsuit, they *should not* be part of the LCT. As your case grows, there is a propensity to create an unwieldy committee, with participants whose interest in the lawsuit may be quite parochial and whose endless debate over the various tactical moves that the LCT might undertake will all but ensure the management of the communications elements is hit-and-miss at best, and a downright disaster at worst.

I think it was Harry S. Truman who once said: "You want to make sure nothing ever gets done on an issue? Appoint a committee."

Is your outside public relations firm committed?

One final point regarding the makeup of the LCT. It is critically important that your outside public relations team be committed to this type of work. That seems elementary, but given the economic structure of many public relations firms—especially larger firms—this may not always be the case. Why? Because—as opposed to the many other types of public relations—it's just too hard to make money at this type of work.

Now don't misunderstand me—my hourly rates are as high as anyone's and I'm actually doing well, all things considered. But then again, I'm a specialist at this type of work—I could no sooner take on a large consumer products public relations account than I could argue a case before the Supreme Court. But many public relations firms face the following dilemma: They can take your litigation—an assignment that requires senior-level attention, which will ebb and flow over the course of weeks and months and years (thus being impossible to predict vis-à-vis cash flow), and could end via settlement or plea bargain at any moment—*or* they can take that new product launch that will be predictable and involve a large number of junior level staff (thus, enormous billing leverage), freeing up the more senior-level public relations executives to pitch other large consumer products accounts. Which would you choose?

Over the years, I've had many public relations executives tell me that they don't even like to work with law firms and legal issues for just that reason. "There's no way to make money at it" they tell me. And not just large public relations firms. The smaller public relations firms that are looking to be bigger will staff their matters in the same way the large firms do. Among other things, it makes it easier to sell your firm if the owner's senior-level expertise is not needed on every assignment. Again, as a public relations entrepreneur, it's certainly okay to one day have the goal of selling—so long as it doesn't get in the way of doing the job and doing it well.

This is a bit of an oversimplication, but the point is a good one: Your outside public relations firm has to be absolutely committed to this type of work for the relationship to be effective. That means they need to staff the work properly, with people who understand what they're doing and how the complex legal and factual issues relate to the whole. There are many good, quality public relations firms—of all sizes, by the way, despite my own personal bias toward smaller firms—that understand this perfectly and are committed to the process of getting the job done right. This is the type of firm you need to find.

The "big" case

Employment class actions. The Firestone/Bridgestone case. The Enron and Worldcom shareholder lawsuits. The Enron and Kmart bankruptcies. Tobacco and asbestos cases. All of these are examples of "big cases"—large, sometimes multidistrict lawsuits involving myriad plaintiffs and defendants and a litany of legal and procedural issues that can vastly alter the course and outcome of the case, and the company's ultimate standing in the court of public opinion. These cases can drag on for years, with numerous side actions, intervening parties, cross-pleading and amici briefs from nonparties of interest—including everyone from local environmental groups to the U.S. government. These cases create their own set of problems in terms of effectively managing communications across all the disparate elements of the case—and needless to say, are exactly the types of cases where the LCT needs to rise to the occasion.

But how do major lawsuits differ from smaller suits? How are they the same? Here are some basic rules:

- Although your litigation may involve numerous communications teams in various locations, it is imperative to ensure central coordination and control of both message and strategy throughout the course of the case.

- There is a greater tendency in these situations to look at the use of public relations teams as merely "litigation support"— that is, the "bodies" you throw at the communications portion of the case, rather than viewing communications as a central strategic element of the litigation. In fact, I would generally avoid public relations firms that call what they do "litigation support" for just that reason.

- Although at any given time there may be hundreds of "audiences of interest" to the dispute, there are only a handful of "influentials," including media, analysts, government and political leaders, and others who will drive the debate.

- The Internet and other technological resources become even more critical for both communication with other members of the communications team and communication to your ultimate audiences.

Considering all of this, one fact is clear: an effective Legal Communications Team and disciplined use of the CIR method discussed in Chapter Four—Control, Information, Response—becomes even more critical in the so-called "big lawsuit," given the elemental unwieldiness of the case and its various elements and parties.

WHEN TO FORM THE LEGAL COMMUNICATIONS TEAM

When do you bring your core legal communications team together? Ideally, as early as possible. Moreover, for large corporations, this core team bridging the gap between the organization's communications function and its legal function ought to be free-standing and permanent, since there is often a steady stream of legal issues with public components flowing through the corporation. This core team can meet on a regular basis to review the legal issues before the organization, those that may be coming on the horizon, and the immediate needs in litigation and other adjudicatory proceedings that are pending. (This is where the CIR discipline becomes so important.) Continual contact and interface on all of the many issues facing the organization is key.

For smaller organizations—those that aren't facing these types of issues on a continuing basis—initial preparation for a LCT should begin as far before the legal storm as possible. Ideally, even in mid-sized to small companies, the core legal communications team is assembled—and meets at least on an intermittent basis—independent of any specific legal threat. This way, the LCT is trained and ready to go into action whenever legal issues of public concern appear on the horizon (as they no doubt will in the operation of most organizations).

Look at it this way: You don't want to start digging the storm cellar after the twister starts ripping through the cornfield!

ACTION POINTS

✔ Lawyers and public relations executives are like oil and water—but for your litigation program to succeed, you need to make sure they mix.

✔ The key to the lawyer's mindset is "argument"—an aggressive attack on a program or idea isn't necessarily indicative of whether the lawyer is for or against you: it's the way legal minds sort through issues.

✔ Lawyers rely on precedent—what has gone before. They also are trained to believe that they can solve any problem—if they can only find the right "form book."

✔ Public relations executives can be insecure and doubt the value of what they do. It is critically important to work with an outside public relations firm that is confident and committed to the practice area of litigation public relations—which can be less lucrative than other areas of the profession.

✔ Political operatives often become stars in the public relations field—but the idea that communications in litigation is somehow like a political campaign is misguided and can do damage to your case.

✔ Key to getting lawyers and public relations people working together is the development of the core Legal Communications Team (LCT), made up of senior legal and communications "players" involved in the case.

◆

CHAPTER SEVEN

Building Your Message and the Credibility of Your Case

Preparing your message and conveying it effectively to the media and other audiences is the threshold challenge of effective public relations in litigation and other legal disputes. Yet it's the last thing lawyers and their clients often think of when attempting to communicate a message about their lawsuit or other legal matter.

"Just get us in front of the New York Times," they say, "we'll know what to say when we get there."

In this chapter, we take a look at why this is such a bad idea. We'll show how a litigant's ability to win his case in the court of public opinion flows directly from his ability to create a message that is compelling, straightforward, and—above all—succinct. Failure to work "from the message out" will hurt not just the message itself, but the organization's balance in what I like to call the Credibility Bank. To illustrate this point, we'll take a look at a company that failed to give its message and its credibility proper consideration: Microsoft, in its infamous antitrust lawsuit with the U.S. Department of Justice.

The media training, for a litigator at a major law firm, was going according to plan. The lawyer, based in Los Angeles, had just lost a case at the trial level, and was now filing an appeal. The case involved a Los Angeles industrial agency that had decided to expand their facilities without doing the required environmental impact research to determine if the local community would be hurt. These types of reviews are standard practice, so it was a surprising loss.

On my way into the room with the attorney, I asked him what had happened.

"The judge got it wrong," he said. "He said the defendant could build first and ask questions later. But that's not what the law says, and we're going to prove that on appeal."

For those of you who have never been media trained, the process works like this: Before the glare of the lights of a full television-style video camera, we lead the subject through a series of mock interviews, to sharpen skills and ensure that the message is getting across. We watch the resulting interview tapes and critique the subject's performance. I generally take the role of reporter and grill the subject far harder than most news reporters ever would. Be prepared, I like to say.

Sometimes (as in this case) we focus on a specific issue that is expected to come up in the coming weeks. Other times, the training is more generalized.

In the Los Angeles case, I sat the attorney down and began to play reporter.

"So tell me," I asked, "what is this appeal all about?"

"Well," the attorney started, "in its ruling, the court allowed the agency to go forward with an enormous expansion of the existing facilities, without the requisite environmental impact statements or any consideration as to the risks posed to the public, in terms of both additional acreage the facility will use and the additional diesel exhaust that will result . . ."

I interrupted and stopped the tape.

"Wait a minute," I said. "What happened to that simple explanation you gave me in the hallway?"

"Well," he said, "I felt I needed to explain it to the reporter in all of the particulars so that they would understand . . ."

I cut him off again.

"But you're not explaining anything to the reporter," I said, "you're trying to get your message across to the audience—just like you did for me in the hallway."

Welcome to the number one problem in communicating a legal message to a lay audience: the inability to say it succinctly, concisely, and in a manner that conveys the "big picture" to your target audience. And to do it in the four or five seconds you have on television, or the sentence or two you have in the print media. Or in the 10 or 15 seconds you have before you lose an influential party's interest. Or before initial opinions are formed by stock analysts, regulators, congressional investigators, or your employees and customers.

In 15 years of working with law firms, corporations, nonprofits, and governments, I am constantly amazed at the inability of otherwise intelligent people to communicate effectively with outside audiences. In a way that doesn't obfuscate or confuse. *Complexify* is the term I use. It's like they're all too smart—too smart to speak clearly. It reminds me of what the great college basketball coach and announcer Al McGuire once said: "I'd rather have a C student on the foul line than an A student." His point was clear: An A student thinks too much about the task at hand, and thereby messes it up. Words to live by.

Almost every lawyer I've worked with has this same problem. "My area," they say, "is far too complex to be summed up succinctly. There's just too much nuance . . . there's no way I can sum it up accurately and be true to the spirit of my work."

And it's not just a problem I've encountered in dealings with lawyers and legal issues. Lack of clarity when communicating complex ideas seems to be a problem throughout the business world.

But especially in the legal context, *we must build our communications program from the message out.* Too often lawyers and their clients leave the message until last (if they think about message at all). They do things backwards—that is, they begin with the tools and the staffing and the other logistical elements of the communications program. Only then do they think about the actual message they're trying to convey.

I think part of the reason is that, generally, clients and their lawyers and other advisors just don't understand the importance of the message to the communications effort. Deep down, perhaps, they know that the message is the hard part—media lists, logistics of events, staffing, these are comparably easy. The difficulty lies in figuring out what you are going to say to your target audience(s) to advance your overall litigation goals.

When I give presentations to corporations and organizations on the importance of effective communications, I start with a simple, but controversial message: The message is no longer the "icing on the cake," it *is* the cake.

Yet, when going into major litigation, I'll meet with lawyers and their clients and they'll inevitably want to talk about tactics rather than message, as in:

- "We need a press conference arranged."
- "What reporters do you know on the energy beat?"
- "Can we get Senator Clinton involved?"
- "How can we get an editorial in the *Times*?"

I usually ask, "Well what are you going to say to these people when you get there?"

"Don't worry . . . we know what to say."

If I press further, the client or lawyer will usually launch into a rambling, 10-minute diatribe about the case—one that even I find difficult to follow (and remember, they're paying me to follow it!). I think to myself, "How are we ever going to succinctly explain this to the media? I can't even understand it!"

WE ARE ALL EXPERTS

If communicating the message is so important, why are we all so bad at it? Part of the problem is that we're *all experts* these days—and not just the lawyers who argue the case or otherwise take the lead in a legal matter. CEOs, CFOs, division heads, line managers—they're all experts in the substance of what they do, no matter what product or service they're selling. Moreover, as we've learned in prior chapters, we're all immersed hip-deep in the intricacies of our specialty— whatever it is—day-in, day-out. We eat, drink, and breathe the stuff. As a result—and again, this is a common theme throughout the book—we're far too *close* to what we do to easily pull back and see the big picture, never mind communicate it effectively. Because of our closeness, there's no way to sum up the *essence* of what we do. Given the opportunity, we'll always go in depth, always give more detail—and our ability to actually *communicate* invariably suffers as a result.

Consider this example: When I train clients on message, the first thing I do is ask them, "What are the three most important points about your lawsuit (or service, or issue, or expertise) that you want to get across to your audience?" I write them down. Then I ask a series of questions—designed to knock the subject off message. Inevitably, I succeed—even though we just went over the message minutes before! They wander, they meander, they explore tangents and peripheries heretofore untouched. Of the three points we initially discussed, I'd say on average:

- Small-business entrepreneurs and marketing professionals remember between one and two of their points.
- Big company CEOs remember about one.
- Lawyers, academics, scientists, and others: Close to zero!

And this is not 10 minutes after going over the three message points with the trainee! Why does this happen? Because they're all too close to what they do to "stick to the message." They can't step back and sum it up for their audience. They can't resist "complexifying." They can't see the forest for the trees.

Again, this is symptomatic of a condition that seems to affect everyone, regardless of industry or professional training. We're far too close to the information to be able to sum it up, to get down to the key message we want to get across.

I see hope, however. Take the same group of lawyers, clients, or other experts, give them three message points on a case or legal issue they know little or nothing about. Tell them that no matter what they do, the answer to each question must come from one of the three message points.

How do they do? You guessed it: Invariably, they answer the questions better with less information than they do with more! In almost every case, with a little additional training I could put the person on *Nightline* and not break a sweat.

Here's why I suspect they do so well: They can no longer retreat into the safety of the details and complexities of their own expertise—in a lawyer's case, the legalities of the case at hand. They are no longer at the in-depth level that they deal with on a daily basis. They stick to the message because they *have to*. They have nowhere else to go.

The conundrum? When attempting to communicate the details of a particular piece of litigation, the ability to break through the clutter of conflicting communications and give the true story on your case is almost entirely dependent on the strength of your message. It's like AM radio. Through all the competing stations, static, and interference, the radio station with the strongest signal gets through.

I often ask clients and their lawyers when preparing the communications aspect of a legal matter: How strong is your signal? It can make the difference between success and failure in communicating the key messages at the heart of your case.

DEVELOPING THE MESSAGE

About a year ago, we worked with a client in the financial services sector who arranged loans to help individuals pay their high-interest debts. They had been sued by a government consumer agency over the wording of their contracts. The allegation was that a clause in the contract describing the loan process was written in such legalese as to be indecipherable to the general public. A major business publication reported on the case but, unfortunately, got many of the facts wrong. The client's lawyer decided to write a letter to the editor.

Here's the funny part: The letter complaining about the characterization of the contract as "indecipherable" was, itself, indecipherable! I read it three times and didn't have an idea what he was talking about. And I'm a lawyer!

This is the essence of the problem—much of the time, lawyers and their clients may have no idea what they're doing, to the extent that they can become confusing even in a case that involves whether they've been confusing!

To combat this, we have several techniques:

- We provide exercises that allow the client, their lawyers, and other members of the legal communications team to step back, isolate, and remove all of the language that obscures meaning and hinders the communication of what's important.
- We practice, practice, practice—through intensive media and message training, so that clients and their lawyers don't fall back on bad habits and, in the process, fail to communicate effectively.

WHAT IS THIS CASE REALLY ABOUT?

Isolating what cases are *really* about is what we've been doing throughout this book. With our CIR process, our Litigation Media Checklist, and with each of our case examples, you have seen the legal and communications team struggle with this key question. When you ask "What is this case about?" in the context of communications in litigation, you are really asking: "Why would anyone be interested in this case or our side of the story?" That is the core question that will help you determine what your message or messages should be.

When looking at a particular piece of litigation, step back and ask yourself the following questions:

- What's really at stake here?
- What's the underlying trend that the media or other audiences are interested in?
- What's the "human face" of this story?
- Who is this case hurting?
- Who is it helping?
- Is there an injustice here?
- What will the other side be saying about the case?
- What are the ramifications for the *next* case that comes down the pike?

Many of these factors are similar to the factors we outlined in the Litigation Media Checklist in Chapter Five. When looking to develop the right message for your case or other legal matter, it's important to run your case through a series of questions like these to find the answer to the penultimate question in all litigation communications: What is this case all about?

PARING THE MESSAGE FOR THE PROPER AUDIENCE

In the mid-1990s, I worked on occasion with a great public relations man named John Softness, whose Softness Group was one of the largest independent public relations firms in New York for a while. John is a great guy with an incredible ability to cut through much of the clutter and get to the real heart of every communication issue put before him. On one assignment, I drafted a letter to a reporter at *Fortune* and showed it to John for comment. He reviewed it quickly, then handed it back to me and said (in his own unmistakable style): "That looks great. Now just take out half the words!"

I often think of this when developing messages for the media and other audiences, and have incorporated the idea into the work I do teaching lawyers and corporate legal departments how to draft a message that will communicate, not obscure; clarify, not "complexify."

Here's the exercise:

- Run your case or legal matter through a series of questions like those listed earlier (you can also look through the Litigation Media Checklist for other questions you might ask).
- Come up with one to three message points that you think appropriately convey "what this case is all about."
- Write each of these message points down—then count the words.
- Whatever the final word count, divide it in half and make *that* the limit for the number of words you can use to get the message across.

So in other words, if you come up with a message point that's 20 words in length, figure out how to say it in 10. Yes, 10. No cheating now . . . it's no fair loading up your original message with extraneous language you can then trim off. The point is this: Whatever you thought the proper number of words was to accurately convey your message, I'll bet you can do it in half. Or come close anyway.

Let's take a message from earlier in the book and see how we do. From our description of the Wertheim Department Store case in Chapter Five of this book:

> In the summer of 2000, Barbara Principe, a grandmother from southern New Jersey who had fled Nazi Germany and grew up in poverty on a chicken farm discovered she was heir to Berlin's famed Wertheim Department Store dynasty—perhaps the largest fortune ever plundered by the Nazi regime.

That's a whopping 48 words! So let's cut it down to 24:

> New Jersey grandmother Barbara Principe discovered last year that she was heir to what is likely the largest fortune ever plundered by the Nazis.

Twenty-four words, exactly. And it was tough. First I got it down to 40, then to 27, and finally to 24. But does the message lose something? Perhaps, I'll admit, it loses a shade of drama, the "backstory" of poverty and so on. But it more than makes up for it in *brevity*—which is what you need when communicating legal messages to the media and other nonlegal audiences.

Remember, this is just an exercise. Perhaps at 30 words my Wertheim message would be perfect. But I can't underscore enough the importance of this exercise, because it forces you to think about how much you can say in the fewest words possible. Which means you are going to get creative about it, you are going to focus—and ultimately you are going to create a message that's better tailored for the media and other audiences you are trying to reach.

MEDIA AND MESSAGE TRAINING

Now let's make sure the message "sticks" in the heat of the most aggressive interview. How do we do that? We undertake rigorous training in remembering our message and delivering it flawlessly.

Two attorneys come to me to discuss an interview they are about to give on a high-profile case. The first says, "Look, I've done this before. I was on CNBC just last week. I talk to reporters all the time. This'll be easy. . . ." The second says, "I'm not very good at this. I don't like the process. I need to be prepared."

Who'll do the better job?

Inevitably, I put my money on the second attorney. Why? Simple: Those who take the process seriously succeed. Those who think it's easy tend to fail.

It is axiomatic that when dealing with the public relations aspects of major litigation—and more specifically in interviews and other dealings with reporters—preparation is key. It is true in all public relations, but especially in legal matters, which tend to be both contentious *and* complex. Yet, it is always shocking to me to see how little attorneys and their clients do before meeting the press about a case. Again, these are the same attorneys who lock themselves away in their office (or if the case is in another town, in a hotel room) for hours and days before a deposition and trial. They'll even prepare assiduously for analyst meetings, congressional testimony, shareholder meetings, and other forms of non-courtroom communications. Yet, for an interview, they simply pick up the phone or show up at the studio. Or hand it off to the client's regular public relations team, who are more experienced at promotions, events, and all the other components of "regular" public relations. Components that have little to do with communications in the litigation context.

I cannot put it more plainly than this: Preparation for media outreach is *essential.* It is as important as preparing for hearings, depositions, settlement negotiations, or the trial itself.

Further, we always recommend message and media training on the litigation before meeting the media for the first time. The extent of this training depends on exactly the situation—how much time you have before the news breaks, how hard it is to get the parties together before a case is filed, but the overall premise remains the same—whatever pre-interview training you can do before sitting down in front of a reporter, or a camera (or many reporters and many cameras), do it. You'll be happy you did.

Unfortunately, attorneys and their clients seem reluctant to heed this advice, and I suspect the reason for this is because the whole process, well . . . the whole process just seems so damn easy. Just say what's on your mind, what you believe, and you'll do fine.

Yes, but . . .

Besides, you reason, your side is *right*. And that's what's important, isn't it? Your side is going to prevail in this piece of litigation, and anyone who listens to you during an interview will hear that.

If they just listen to exactly what you're saying. If they just ask the right questions. If . . . if . . . if . . .

Again, I emphasize that if an attorney were to take that sort of approach with any other aspect of the case, he or she would probably be disbarred. But for some reason, in delivering your message, it's acceptable. I think this is because there's a perception that this stuff is easy.

Those who do it well feed that perception. Everyone knows a person who interviews perfectly on television. You know, the type of person who seems poised and natural in every situation, who always seems to have the right way of answering questions—perfect, pithy responses that get to the core of the issues involved. They seem born to do this.

That person is a natural, right?

Wrong.

Odds are that person has spent a fair amount of time preparing for the interview and is well-versed by the time they sit down before the camera.

You don't believe that those who come off as natural are well-rehearsed? Consider the example of Winston Churchill, perhaps the finest orator of the last century. Surely, there was no one more natural than he? Yes, but . . .

A remarkable fact about Churchill was this: Although he often seemed extemporaneous and unrehearsed, that façade was the product of extensive preparation. "In Parliament," Churchill biographer William Manchester wrote, "his wit will flash and sting, but members who know him are aware that he has honed these barbs in advance, and only visitors in the Stranger's Gallery are under the impression that his great perorations are extemporaneous."[1] On average, for a 40-minute Parliamentary speech, Churchill spent six to eight hours in preparation.

But there's more. Churchill was so interested in giving the impression of spontaneity that he prepared exhaustively for it. During a speech to Parliament, he would hold in his hand not notes, but the entire text of what he was going to say—including, incredibly, stage direction ("pause; grope for word" or "stammer; correct self").[2] This, by the way, is not a technique I would recommend for everyone, but the point is clear: The "naturals" among us have usually worked damn hard to get that way.

In virtually *every* case, that "natural" you're watching in the news interview or reading about in the business pages worked and worked, and it's paid off. Anyone who says otherwise, I'd posit, is either (a) lying, or (b) doing it so unconsciously as to be unaware. In other words, they're not naturals because they were born with it—they're naturals because they intuitively knew how hard they would have to work to make it look "easy."

That's why the interview subjects who scare me are the ones who come into my office and say, "Oh, this interview will be easy. I've been interviewed before . . ."

Those who do well usually come in and say: "Look, I'm worried about this interview. I find the process awkward and difficult, and I need to be prepared."

Attorneys and clients who take the process seriously do well.

Yes, but . . . they make it look so easy!

And Willie Mays made the outfield look easy.

The power of muscle memory

The harder I work, the luckier I get.
　　　　　　　—Yogi Berra

More baseball analogies. I'm a big New York Mets fan, but that doesn't stop me from quoting from everyone's favorite baseball philosopher, Yogi Berra. When dealing with the media, particularly during an important court case, his statement makes an enormous amount of sense. So much sense that I routinely compare training for media appearances to hitting a baseball. You spend enough time in the batting cage, seeing pitch after pitch after pitch . . . eventually you develop the *muscle memory* that allows you to hit a baseball coming at you at 90 miles an hour. And a curve, for that matter.

And the Mike Piazzas and Barry Bonds of the world—you can be sure that they've spent an enormous amount of time in the batting cage, honing their skills, sharpening their "eye," before ever stepping up to the plate.

Or—for those of you who aren't baseball fans—think of typing, or playing the piano. Practice enough, and eventually it becomes almost subconscious—so ingrained in the memory and the muscles that it is replicated without thinking.

This *media muscle memory* is essential for interviews about your legal matter. If you have done it enough—if you have practiced and prepared enough—you will be so accomplished that your ability to get your message across during an interview will appear seamless—perfectly natural, like you haven't practiced at all. And this has an enormous effect on the credibility of your message—and its ultimate resonance, with the media and beyond.

THE CREDIBILITY BANK

Ultimately, it's all about credibility—your credibility with the media will influence what is written about you and your side's argument, and will have an enormous affect on the way your case is reported, from prefiling to post-appeal.

Look at it this way—every litigant begins a lawsuit or other legal matter with a set balance in what I call the *Credibility Bank*. As you'll see, everyone's balance is different, but we all start out with something. With each interaction with a reporter, you make a deposit or a withdrawal. As your credibility increases—if you're constantly making deposits—so too does your ability to frame a story properly, to get your side heard, and to have an effect on the way your case is viewed by the public-at-large, the judge and jury, and even the other side. But too many withdrawals and eventually your account has a negative balance in the Credibility Bank. You're overdrawn. What's the practical effect? The next set of documents you send over to the reporter—or the next explanation you give on some point of law or fact—will bounce higher than a rubber check on April Fool's day.

So what is your opening balance in the Credibility Bank? Why does it differ from company to company? There are an enormous number of factors that can affect your opening balance—how you are initially perceived by the media (and other public audiences) at the onset of your litigation, including:

- *Prelitigation reputation.* Almost every reporter will do an on-line database search of stories in other media over the past few years to see what else your company has been up to. Suppose, therefore, you've been sued for racial discrimination in New York. "We're innocent," you protest. The reporter does a Nexis search, and it turns out you've been sued under similar circumstances in the past three years in Chicago and Miami. Your balance in the Credibility Bank is going to be near-zero.

- *Prestige.* It's unfair, but your company's existing *prestige* will also determine how it's perceived, initially, in terms of credibility. Most of the inhabitants of elite media outlets are Ivy-League or near-Ivy-League educated white people, from families of similar distinction—the elites of the world. It's an unfortunate fact that the more you are perceived as an "elite," the more you're likely to be believed—again, at least initially. So . . . are you "blue chip," or strictly "blue-light-special"? Harvard-educated, or community college? Do you vacation in the Hamptons, or at the Hampton Inn? This is grossly unfair, but it is the reality—and, at least at the outset of your case, it will affect the way you're perceived by the media.

- *Your lawyer.* The lawyer or law firm you choose will affect the initial perception of your case. If Floyd Abrams is your lawyer in your First Amendment case, or David Boies in your antitrust matter, rightly or wrongly, the initial impression is going to be: "Wow, there must be something to this." Many times, in fact, I've made that exact argument to reporters: "Look, Mr. Lincoln wouldn't be involved in this case if he didn't feel it was a winner." In most cases this is unfair, but it is the reality of the way your opening balance is determined in the Credibility Bank.

- *Personal relationships.* How well you know members of the media will have an effect on how your case is initially perceived—but, in all honesty, far less of an effect than you might expect. I often tell clients that I have a lot of friends in the media, and that they all hang up on me if I don't have a story to tell. Media connections mean nothing if you don't have a concise, compelling message that is of interest to both the reporter *and* his or her audience. Moreover, relying simply on connections can sometimes be counterproductive. I can't tell you how many times I've had a client or attorney say something like this to me: "I know a reporter at Associated Press (or wherever); let's give the story to him . . ." Then you find out it's the restaurant critic. Or the movie reviewer. I'd rather find the *exact* reporter for my story and reach out to her—whether we know her beforehand or not.

- *The case itself.* How sleazy does your case seem? How against the current (and ever-changing) mores of so-called political correctness is the issue? What's the current "flavor-of-the-week" in public opinion (and, thus, media coverage) in terms of what's in and what's out, who the good guys are and who the bad guys are? All of this is going to affect how your case is perceived, and therefore the credibility of your arguments and statements in regard to that case. As mentioned in Chapter Five, during the stock market run-up of the go-go 1990s, good luck in getting any reporter to believe a shareholder fraud case. By contrast, in early 2000, good luck in convincing those same reporters that every CEO hasn't been cooking the books. Defendant in a sexual harassment matter? Uphill climb. Does it involve "sleazy" details—swapping, videotape, call girls on the corporate credit card account, that sort of thing? Even worse. Defending an anti-abortion protestor or an anarchist? Good luck to you.

The good news is: This opening balance is not permanent. The bad news is: This opening balance is not permanent! Everything you do during the course of the legal matter, every public action, every contact with a reporter, is an opportunity to either add or subtract from your balance in the Credibility Bank. Over the past several years, we've seen company after company destroy itself during litigation by ignoring its public reputation, or being dismissive of the process as a whole. How well you monitor your balance in the Credibility Bank—and make the right moves to add to it—can mean the difference between the success or failure of your public message, and ultimately, your case as a whole.

SHATTERING WINDOWS

You wonder, as you watch this appalling performance, what in the world did Gates think he was accomplishing by taking this tack? Did he think he was winning the battle of wits? Did he believe his absurdist responses would aid his cause?

—Joe Nocera of *Fortune,* covering Bill Gates' deposition in the Microsoft antitrust trial, December 21, 1998

Which brings us to the best example in the past several years of a company squandering its credibility and otherwise making a fool of itself by delivering the wrong message in the wrong place at the wrong time: Microsoft, in its long-running antitrust battle with the U.S. government.

Reams have been written about the case, from all different angles—including a fair amount about the public perception aspects of the case. Still, the Microsoft case is a good example to look at for a number of reasons. First, it was certainly the most high-profile corporate litigation to come down the pike in years—the O. J. Simpson trial of the business world.

But beyond this, the Microsoft case is the perfect example of a corporation that "got religion" in terms of taking message seriously and working *with* media and other audiences to deliver that message. And there is ample evidence that Microsoft's revised approach in delivering its message effectively benefited the company enormously.

In the beginning, Microsoft was petulant, dismissive, ham-fisted . . . all of the things that we warn about throughout this book. This attitude was crystalized in the public consciousness thanks to Microsoft CEO Bill Gates' ill-advised, ill-tempered deposition, which was presented to the court in November 1998—and which is what Joe Nocera of *Fortune* is referring to in the quote that opens this section. This is where Gates bobbed and weaved around government litigator David Boies' questions for more than 20 hours—claiming ignorance of such elementary terms as "competition" and "market share" and even the word "concerned."

But soon after Judge Jackson's decision to split the company in two (a decision that was overturned by the Court of Appeals), Microsoft's approach to public relations and public opinion changed.

As we'll see, that "tin ear" seemed to soften considerably, and by the middle of 2001, a kinder, gentler Microsoft was turning the tide in the public relations battle—culminating with Gates' testimony in spring 2002, where he was helpful, deferential, and at times even downright charming.

What is all the more amazing about Microsoft's missteps is the fact that it was not as if the company was a stranger to public relations before the antitrust trial. In fact, the Microsoft public relations machine was considered one of the best in the business—remember the launch of Windows 95, replete with worldwide celebrations, the Rolling Stones, and Jay Leno as Master of Ceremonies at Microsoft headquarters in Redmond, Washington? In this way, too, Microsoft is a perfect example of one of the underlying themes of this book— that public relations in legal disputes is different than almost any other form of communication. Microsoft had proven through the years that they knew a thing or two about public relations—they just didn't know how to apply it in the litigation context. And that's where the trouble began.

At the start of the most recent antitrust case, it is not an exaggeration to say that Microsoft still believed it was above the concerns of "mere mortals." They were smarter than everyone else, Microsoft seemed to insist, and it was clear that Gates and Ballmer hated the fact that anyone—especially the U.S. government—would have any sort of influence over the conduct of their case. "We don't care what Janet Reno thinks," is a quote famously attributed to Steve Ballmer, now Microsoft's CEO.

At trial, Microsoft's dismissive attitude toward wider public opinion became even more prominent, primarily through the viewing of portions of Gates' deposition, which Department of Justice attorney David Boies shrewdly began each day with, knowing full well that not only Judge Jackson, but the whole world, was watching.

Gates' performance in his deposition was nothing short of stunning, dissembling brought to the nth degree, such as in this exchange over the meaning of the word "concerned":

Q: What non-Microsoft browsers were you concerned about in January of 1996?

A: I don't know what you mean "concerned."

Q: What is it about the word "concerned" that you don't understand?

A: I'm not sure what you mean by it.

Q: Is the term "concerned" a term you're familiar with in the English language?

A: Yes.[3]

Microsoft's lead trial attorney, John Warden, complained mightily to Judge Jackson about Boies' use of the deposition tape to start each court proceeding. According to *Fortune*, Warden charged that the government employed this tactic solely for the purpose of creating news stories. And news stories it created: in many ways, Microsoft still has not recovered from the effects of the trial on the company's overall reputation and corporate character.

And it was not just Gates' deposition testimony that was having a damaging effect on public perception of the case. For most of the trial, no matter how bad the day's testimony against Microsoft, a spokesperson would appear to discuss how it had been a "great day" for the company. It was pure Kabuki theater, as transparent as Saran Wrap—in essence, anything and everything that could be done to deplete Microsoft's balance in the Credibility Bank.

Joe Nocera of *Fortune* called Microsoft's version of events: "a reality where nasty e-mails don't mean what they seem to mean, where witnesses have dark and untrustworthy motives, where a company with a 90 percent share of the desktop operating market is not really a monopoly . . ."

After weeks of such self-inflicted damage, Microsoft belatedly wised up to the fact that what they were doing was not working, and Microsoft public relations chief Mark Murray decided that they would meet with reporters individually rather than participate in large press conferences. As Nocera noted in *Fortune*, "the company appears to have realized that its daily courthouse statements—in which it often seemed to be saying that black was white and night was day—came across as shrill and not believable."

But Microsoft won in the end, didn't it? The case is over, Bill Gates is still the richest man in the world, and in the midst of an unprecedented technology bust, Microsoft announced in the summer of 2002 that it was hiring. It's quite logical to surmise that in its protracted, half-decade antitrust battle, the beast from Redmond had the last laugh. So why does it matter whether they initially handled themselves poorly in the public arena?

Here's why: When considering the implications of the Microsoft antitrust battle, think about the cost of the litigation: seven years, untold millions spent by the company on lawyers, witnesses, and trial preparedness. Not to mention the time and brainpower of some of the top Microsoft executives, including Bill Gates and Steve Ballmer (remember Abraham Lincoln's statement from the Preface that opened this book). It was noted in the *Wall Street Journal,* for example, that "the stress of the trial . . . took a visible toll on Mr. Gates in the late 1990s. He was distracted in meetings, irritable with employees, and not fully focused on overall business strategy."[4] Ultimately, the *Journal* reported, it was the antitrust case that led Gates to hand over the day-to-day running of the company to Ballmer.

So consider how much richer, how much more dominant, Microsoft might have been if it hadn't been embroiled in the trial of the decade and so severely damaged its reputation? But for the nearly decade-long antitrust case, I might be reaching into my Microsoft refrigerator for my next can of soda, or maybe driving my Microsoft car to the supermarket when I run out. The opportunity costs of Microsoft's disdainful approach to the communications aspects of its legal travails have been severe.

Moreover, it is very clear that part of the reason the company has been able to get back on track was its turnaround in the court of public opinion—and that was no accident. Consider the growth of Microsoft's public relations apparatus, particularly in Washington, DC, where the antitrust battle was held. At the start of its momentous fight with the Justice Department, Microsoft had *no* representation in Washington. Zero. This for a company that controlled the market for computer software that served as *the* platform for much of United States' vaunted "information economy." For a company the size of Microsoft, this was unprecedented.

Even during much of the original trial, Microsoft maintained just a single representative in Washington—and not quite in Washington at that. No, this representative was located not with the Armani suits and tasseled loafers of K Street, but in a suburban strip mall in Northern Virginia.

After the Judge Jackson verdict? In the wake of the verdict, Microsoft muscled up. In short order, they had a large staff in Washington—downtown Washington, with everyone else—and had hired some of the best-connected lobbyists in town, including Haley Barbour, Tom Downey, and Ralph Reed. They hired major polling organizations and public relations firms to assist them with their credibility-building effort. Among the tactics undertaken were assistance with the creation of op-ed pieces by supporters of Microsoft, considerable relationship-building with reporters covering the Microsoft beat, and the financing of groups that could further the Microsoft agenda—groups with names like Citizens Against Government Waste, the Technology Access Action Coalition, and Americans for Technology Leadership. In the wake of the original verdict, Microsoft even created a television advertisement featuring Bill Gates and Steve Ballmer explaining themselves and the fact that they still felt the importance of their cause.

Thus, when the Microsoft chairman took the stand again, in April 2002, it was a very different Bill Gates the public was seeing. He was controlled, polite, and more mature, according to the *Washington Post*. The *New York Times,* for its part, noted that:

> Mr. Gates' performance was a stark contrast to the combative evasive persona Gates projected during a videotaped deposition played for Judge Thomas Penfield Jackson of the Federal District Court during the liability phase of the trial . . . Gates was quick to answer questions and strove to appear helpful, frequently responding "yes sir" to questions from . . . a lawyer who conducted the deposition.[5]

Clearly, Microsoft learned its lesson, and learned it well. But along the way, it took a public relations spanking the likes of which we've rarely seen. The company realized that to win their case in the courts, they first needed to get control of a public opinion crisis spinning out of control.

In the end, it appears the most significant result of the Microsoft case may have been the effect on Microsoft's—and Bill Gates'—overall reputation.

Indeed, the Microsoft antitrust trial will likely go down in history as the textbook example of the perils of ignoring public perception in major litigation, and how, with the proper changes to the communications program during litigation and other legal disputes, even a company on the ropes can turn things around. Even a battleship like Microsoft—not usually able to maneuver so adroitly. In its wake, it is likely that no major case will be handled this way again.

ACTION POINTS

✔ The ability to effectively create a message that the media and your other target audiences will understand is the number one roadblock to effective communications during litigation or other legal disputes.

✔ It is a great paradox that, in the information economy in which we live: It is getting harder and harder to convey messages in a manner that is simple, straightforward, and to the point.

✔ Developing effective messages regarding your case, and communicating those messages in a way that advances the goals of your litigation, requires thought, training, and hard work.

✔ Every litigant begins his case with a balance in the Credibility Bank, and with each contact with the media and other audiences, he either makes a deposit or a withdrawal.

✔ Companies that ignore their message and their dwindling balance in the Credibility Bank will pay the price—a lesson Microsoft learned after doing significant damage to the company and its reputation.

CHAPTER EIGHT

The Plaintiff's Perspective: Ensuring Your Case Has "Staying Power"

Much of this book has been focused on litigation communication's equivalent of not getting caught with your pants down—a condition primarily (although not exclusively) faced by defendants who find their legal matter under the glare of the public spotlight. But what about plaintiffs? How do they get their story out? How can they ensure that their communication strategy is designed not just to make a single day's news, but to affect the course of the entire litigation.

In this chapter, we look at the particular problems facing plaintiffs as they prepare their case for presentation in the court of public opinion. We do so by looking at litigation my company is currently involved with that's particularly high profile: the Wertheim Department Store case, where a feisty grandmother from New Jersey is fighting to reclaim one of the largest fortunes ever looted by the Nazis. Then we look at plaintiffs who have nothing but resources on their side: government officials. To illustrate the enormous power of the government as plaintiff, we look at one of the hot-button cases of 2002: New York State Attorney General Eliot Spitzer's investigation of financial services giant Merrill Lynch.

Most of the principles I've detailed in this book can be used by *all* parties in legal disputes, regardless of the type of case, the particular circumstances of the parties, or the level of damages (or criminal penalty) at stake. Techniques such as the Control, Information, Response (CIR) System, Litigation Media Checklist, Messaging exercises, and Media Briefs are specifically designed to be:

- As applicable to the large-scale lawsuit as they are to the smaller case;
- Useful whether the litigant is a corporation, a nonprofit enterprise, or a high-profile individual that finds him- or herself in the media spotlight;
- As vital in a lawsuit between two private parties as in cases involving government investigations and regulatory action; and
- As important for the plaintiff's side to remember and adhere to as the defendant.

There's no denying, however, that for much of this book, I have focused on *response*—how to react and control the message when your case "breaks" in the media. This chapter focuses on the particular issues plaintiffs face when promoting their case, and how to make sure the case gets the best media coverage possible.

IN THE PLAINTIFFS' CORNER

Here's the number one problem that plaintiffs face when trying to use public relations to advance their interests in a lawsuit: After one day of news coverage, the case "goes away." The defendants breathe a huge sigh of relief and go back to business-as-usual, safe in the knowledge that the bad news is behind them—that they have the resources to outlast the plaintiffs, or at the very least, weaken the plaintiffs to the point where a settlement can be had on highly favorable terms.

In many ways, plaintiffs, their lawyers, and their public relations advisors play into this trap by launching their lawsuit with huge fanfare—perhaps even with a big press conference on the courthouse steps—then letting the pressure die down over subsequent weeks and months. There's a notion that, if you make a big splash with the announcement of your case, it is going to have the greatest impact on the resolution. Nothing could be further from the truth.

This is true in cases of all kinds, from the run-of-the-mill to the most sensational. As an example, let's take a closer look at what is likely the most sensational case I've ever worked on—the Wertheim Department Store case we introduced in Chapter Four. The Wertheim case boasts a cast of characters that includes everyone from Hermann Goring and Adolf Hitler, to Gerhard Schroeder and Condoleeza Rice. But even with a case that has a fact pattern reminiscent of a Ludlum thriller, we had to be very careful not to make the media coverage of the case a one-day story—one that would have little, if any, impact on the ultimate course of the litigation.

THE BATTLE FOR HITLER'S BUNKER

As we've learned, at the center of the action in the Wertheim case is a New York lawsuit involving a New Jersey grandmother who fled Germany with her family before the outbreak of World War II and grew up in poverty on a chicken farm, waking up one morning to find out she was heir to one of the largest fortunes ever plundered by the Nazis. The Wertheim Department Store empire was once the pride of Berlin, and included land that was taken by the Nazis at Hitler's direction to build, among other things, the Reich Chancellery and Hitler's bunker complex. One of the Nazis who orchestrated the "Aryanization" of the company remained in power as head of the company after World War II, then allegedly stole the remaining interest in the company from the New Jersey woman's father—three months after secretly selling the company to the department store's biggest competitor.

Again, this sounds like a wartime thriller, but it is not. *Martin Wortham and Barbara Principe v. KarstadtQuelle*, et al. is now at the center of "what may be the largest single-family Holocaust-related suit ever," according to the *New York Times*. It is a case like no other and, although still pending as I write this, it is an excellent example of the perils and opportunities that all plaintiffs face when promoting their case in the court of public opinion.

An Extraordinary Case . . . with Everyday Lessons

What can the Wertheim case teach us about the media aspects of court cases? After all, it's not often a litigant will be thrust into so sensational a case. Surely we could just sit back and let the news stories roll in until the defendant crumbled, right?

Absolutely not.

In fact, the sensational nature of the story could have worked against us—we could have been lazy and just thrown the information out there to see who responded. Stories would have certainly resulted, but would we have advanced the overall litigation strategy of the case? Probably not. In fact, as you'll see, if the media coverage of the Wertheim case got some key details wrong, it could have actually hurt us—convincing the U.S. government that the case should be dismissed as one arising from Nazi-era behavior covered by the 1998 Slave Labor Agreements between Germany and the United States.

So, yes, the Wertheim case is indeed sensational, perhaps the most unusual set of facts in any case we've worked on. But like all the cases described in this book, if you break down the Wertheim case into its component parts, you realize that there are lessons for every plaintiff—particularly those plaintiffs facing a David versus Goliath-style match-up (as most plaintiffs are), where the other side has a level of resources that ensure it is going to be an unfair fight—unless the plaintiff can plead his or her case to a wider audience.

Here are some of the main lessons to be learned from this case:

- *Keep up the pressure.* It's a recurring theme throughout this book. In most cases, the plaintiffs will hold a press conference to announce the filing of a lawsuit; they'll get a day or so of news coverage—then never be heard from again. The way to keep defendants off-balance—and ensure that your case is taken seriously—is to keep the pressure on the defendant with a series of stories that reinforce the perception that the damage this case is causing is *not* going away.

- *Fight for your story.* In the course of working on the Wertheim case, we discovered an interesting fact—Nazis are still big news. Almost 60 years after the war, you'll find at least a Nazi story a day in the major media. In fact, in the month we filed our case, May 2001, a Lexis-Nexis search indicated that more than 100 stories were written on one Nazi lawsuit or another—this in a single month, more than half a century after the end of World War II. We estimated at one point in the case that about a lawsuit a week is filed in the United States over one aspect or another of the Nazi era. The key issue, therefore, is this: With all the Nazi stories out there, how do you convince the media and other audiences that your Nazi story is one that merits attention?

  In a more general sense, this is exactly the type of issue all plaintiffs face when bringing the case "public"—you've got to differentiate your case from all of the other legal activity on any given day, to rise above the static in a way that advances your coverage of the case.

- *A big case is fought in various venues—but the message must be consistent.* In the Wertheim case, we had separate legal actions in New York and Berlin, with intense lobbying by the German government and the possibility of administrative intervention by the U.S. Department of Justice. We were fighting on several fronts in various locations all at once, against a defendant with unlimited resources. Moreover, despite the compelling story line, the complexities and factual issues of the Wertheim case made our heads spin. Forming a consistent message in these circumstances was a difficult assignment—but it had to be done, over and over, in different forums and before vastly different audiences.

PUTTING YOURSELF IN THE OTHER SIDE'S SHOES

Over the years, we have done work for both plaintiff and defendants, and this gives us keen insight into the way each side thinks. Anticipating the other side's reaction to your next move is a key component in putting a strategy together and keeping that strategy in place throughout the litigation. As you'll see later in this chapter, this was a critical element of the recent lawsuit by New York State Attorney General Eliot Spitzer against financial giant Merrill Lynch over their analysts' conflicts of interest. The fact that Merrill Lynch was not thinking about the other side's reaction to their public moves actually may have forced Spitzer's hand. This is why you can't *just* be looking for the biggest public "bang" when you look to get your story out there. To effectively lay out strategy for your litigation, you have to be constantly thinking:

- How will the other side react to the step I've just taken?
- What will their next move be?
- How can my actions blunt, or even dictate, their next move?
- Will a "soft" touch lend to the desired result, where a more aggressive approach might backfire?

Given all of these issues to consider, you can see why I firmly believe the "Have a lawsuit? Hold a press conference!" approach usually doesn't work.

Why this tendency to hold press conferences at all? Well, for starters, it just feels good. A room full of people. A row of cameras. All of the major players given a chance to speak. It makes it feel like a big story to you, regardless of the tenor of the resulting coverage and the "legs" the story has a month, two months, or six months down the road. Particularly for those of us in the public relations profession, this is a tempting tactic. It shows results. We can say "See, Mr. (or Ms.) client . . . I've given you results. Look at this room. It's filled!"

That's exactly the problem, because more often than not the client believes it. When people ask how the press conference went, the response usually is "The room was filled!" Never mind the fact that the story only received:

- A short AP piece that wasn't picked up anywhere,
- Five seconds on CNN in the news roundup, or
- A squib in the "Digest" section of the *New York Times*.

A week or so later, when the coverage has all but dried up, the client sits back and thinks: Okay, I had a great deal of fun and felt important, but what did it do, really, to advance the goals of the litigation?

By contrast, a slow, steady approach—reaching out for feature stories in two or three key media outlets that are really going to make a difference—well, that's a much harder task, isn't it? But if the goal is to *really influence* the course of the litigation—and, in the plaintiff's case, to make the defendant feel that the case is for real, that it's not going away, and that the pressure is, indeed, building— the hard work of placing *exactly* the stories you want, *exactly* where you need them . . . this is where the rubber hits the road.

It's a little like playing chess. You've got to be thinking two, three, four moves down the board at all times, anticipating what the other side is going to do, then finding ways to counteract. Too many plaintiffs in lawsuits send their Queen after the defendant's King on the first move. It may work, but more likely it's just going to make it more of a spectacle—and a match you lose in the end.

WHAT DEFENDANTS ARE THINKING

When you are the plaintiff in litigation, you are looking at affecting the way the other side is thinking about the litigation, how hard it will be to fight, and what it will mean to the defendant's long-term reputation to have the lawsuit continue. Because coming into a lawsuit, here is what most defendants are thinking:

- This lawsuit is without merit (every defendant, it seems, thinks this—at least initially).
- Greedy plaintiffs' lawyers! They're looking for an easy target. I'll be damned if I'm going to pay for that lawyer's new boat!
- We're a large national (or multinational) corporation. They're no match for us. Our lawyers are universally recognized as the best in the country. The plaintiffs and their lawyers can never keep stride with us once we begin to throw the resources of our vast legal team at the case. They'll make a mistake.
- We had one day of bad press. It's over now, the stories have been written, and there's nothing else the plaintiffs can do

to us. We'll repair the corporate reputation: sponsor a golf tournament or an inner city jobs program. We have a huge public relations staff—they'll get us past this.

- If we can just keep this litigation going for two years—five years, eight years, a decade—we'll wear the plaintiffs down. They'll eventually go away—or at least they'll settle for far less than they would today.

If the defendant in your lawsuit is thinking this, you are likely in for trouble—no matter how good you think your opening day press conference was. Contrast this now with what *you* want the plaintiffs to be thinking:

- Hmm . . . there may be something to this lawsuit. All of the major media are talking about how important it is. We'd better check into it.
- I hate plaintiffs' lawyers, but in this case, the plaintiffs may actually have a case—and they may have us on the spot.
- Despite our resources, this may be a case that is difficult to win. Even if we do win, the long-term damage to our reputation may be too much to bear.
- Another call from the *Wall Street Journal?* Wow, this case is not going away!
- I don't think we can take two years of this. This is hurting our reputation and distracting us from our core mission. We've got to do what we can to end this, for the future of the company.

You can see the difference—and, as we've said throughout this book, you can see how this has nothing to do with influencing the judge and jury in a case (although it certainly doesn't hurt to have your judge thinking "The *New York Times* says this case has merit . . ."). Corporate defendants are always thinking about how hard it is to fight a lawsuit. Whether to settle is usually a cost-benefit analysis. They are weighing the cost of continuing against the long-term effects on corporate reputation, stock price, employee morale, and the financial and emotional resources that are being used in continuing the fight. If they feel it's worth it, they'll continue—and they'll fight like mad. If they feel it's not worth it, they settle. It's that simple. What you are attempting to do as a plaintiff is to get the defendants to start thinking along the lines of what I've described. That's how you bring a defendant to the settlement table with instructions to get this case out of the way!

THE BATTLE FOR HITLER'S BUNKER

Back to the Wertheim case. All of this strategy went into our thinking about how to move forward on the communications aspects of the case—and what results we could reasonably expect.

Other considerations included the following:

- *The international aspects.* The defendant, KarstadtQuelle A.G., is one of the largest retailers in Germany but has no base of operations in the United States. A front-page story in the *New York Post* would be nice, but it was not going to help our cause—the defendant would never see it, nor would any of the defendant's customers or any other interested party overseas.

- *The complexity.* What I'm calling the Wertheim case is actually two actions: one in New York and one in Berlin related to the Wertheim properties that were taken by the Nazis. Moreover, even the history of the Belin properties was convoluted. While most of the land in downtown Berlin wound up in East Germany when the Berlin Wall sliced through the Wertheim land, an error in mapping left one parcel on the West side of the Berlin Wall. This property reverted to the West German government in 1991—and was promptly ceded to the defendant in the New York lawsuit, KarstadtQuelle. KarstadtQuelle sold the land shortly thereafter for more than $150 million.

This gives you just a sampling of the complexity of the issues involved, and our challenge in attempting to convey all this information to the media and other audiences in a manner that would positively affect our case. No easy undertaking, even when Adolf Hitler himself is one of the supporting players.

- *The sensitivities.* As mentioned, a key fact is that the New York lawsuit involves a fraud that occurred in 1951 in New York. If this fact was missed, or obscured, in the coverage of the case, the resulting articles could make it seem as if the case involved conduct that occurred during the Nazi era. This would clearly place the case under the auspices of the 1998 Holocaust Slave Labor settlements, which were designed to assure "lasting peace" by allowing for the dismissal of all claims "arising from" the Nazi era. A mistake such as this could be deadly. We had to be very careful to ensure that our coverage clearly identified the case as one involving a 1951 fraud, not a Nazi-era "Aryanization" of Jewish property.

Given all the factors that stood in the way of this story, how could our strategy ensure that the case would get the attention it deserved?

We outlined the following strategy:

- First, we needed to initially target *only* media that would do justice to the complexities of the case—this meant longer form print media that could go into some depth on the various issues involved in the case (but remember that the best journalists out there will only have, say, 2,000 words in which to tell the story).

- We also needed to target media that would hit the German corporate defendant where they lived. Therefore, we decided to begin in Europe—initially Germany, France, and the United Kingdom—then use the imprimatur of those articles to begin seeking coverage here in the United States—again, in the types of U.S. media that would affect government decision makers and the corporate defendant back home in Berlin.

- We needed to rise above the din of competing Nazi cases in the United States—again, this required high-level media outreach that would result in articles that would have the legitimacy and creditability needed to let everyone know that this case was for real.

As you might have already guessed, we didn't hold a press conference on the courthouse steps to announce the filing of the New York lawsuit. We didn't even issue a press release. Instead, working with my assistant, Carol McKoy and Senior Account Executive Liz

Hall, we created considerable background materials on the case for reporters' use, including:

- Background press releases, designed to tell the Wertheim saga in "feature story" style.
- A timeline—key to reinforcing the fact that the New York suit involved a 1951 fraud that took place in New York.
- A fact sheet and Media Brief, for at-a-glance details that reporters could use when reporting on the case.
- Maps, charts, photographs, and other visual materials that would put the story in context and add the critical "human face" to the story.

Armed with these materials, we selected each media outlet and reporter carefully—then worked, sometimes for months at a time, starting a process of building momentum in the coverage of the case.

We began in Europe (working with an affiliated firm), arranging coverage in the *Times* of London, *Der Speigel*, Agencie Presse France, and other major European media outlets. We then moved stateside, culminating in a coveted front-page story in the *Wall Street Journal* and—within several weeks—major articles in the *New York Times*, the *Los Angeles Times*, and the *Washington Post*. All were major stories on the case and the issues involved with enough in-depth coverage to ensure not only that the communications outreach would have a major impact on the course of the litigation, but also that the resulting articles would do no harm to our side's position.

Typical of the coverage was an article that appeared in the *New York Times* in July 2002—more than a year after the case had originally been filed:

A Jewish Family's Stolen Legacy; Heirs Seek Restitution for Retail Empire Lost to Nazis

Barbara Principe remembers little of her early childhood in Nazi Germany.

After her parents fled with her in 1939, traveling through Britain and Cuba to a chicken farm in South Jersey, they spoke only fleetingly of her Jewish family's old life in an opulent home outside Berlin.

It was not until two years ago, at the age of 67, that she discovered that her family once controlled a profitable department-store empire in the heart of Berlin.

She also discovered that the Nazis had forced the family to give up everything they owned. Now Mrs. Principe and her nephew are suing the current German owners of the property for unspecified compensation and damages in Federal District Court in Manhattan, in what may be the largest single-family Holocaust-related suit ever. It is a legal battle over parcels of land in Berlin that are now worth hundreds of millions of dollars.

Lawyers for the main defendant, KarstadtQuelle AG, Germany's largest retailer, say the suit should be dismissed because of prior Holocaust-related settlements. The United States State Department is deciding whether to ask the court to dismiss the suit on that basis, and is expected to issue a statement in the next few weeks.

Mrs. Principe's father, Gunther Wertheim, who was struggling to make a new life in 1951, came to Manhattan to sign away all his rights to restitution for the property he had lost.

He did so after he and his brother Fritz began the process to seek restitution in 1950, a lawyer for Mrs. Principe said. A lawyer and former advisor to the Wertheim family, Arthur Lindgens, traveled to New York from Germany and paid Gunther and Fritz Wertheim $9,200 each for the rights to their shares, insisting that the Wertheim department stores were ruined and the company's properties in East Berlin had been seized by Communist authorities. Mr. Lindgens's estate is also being sued by Mrs. Principe and her nephew; the lawyer for the estate would not comment.

Using those shares, Mr. Lindgens, who was chairman of the company, and other German owners of Wertheim then quickly merged it with its main competitor, Hertie, another Jewish retailer that had also been taken over under the Nazis. KarstadtQuelle bought the merged companies in 1994. The company says it had $15 billion in sales in 2001.

The 1951 deal came to light just two years ago because of the dogged sleuthing of Mrs. Principe's lawyers and a German graduate student at the Free University in Berlin who chose the Wertheim family as her Ph.D. subject. It formed the basis of the lawsuit, first filed in March 2001.

Mrs. Principe, who lives in Newfield, NJ, a few miles from the farm where her parents settled half a century ago, stands to win hundreds of millions of dollars if her case succeeds. Her lawyers would retain one-third, but receive nothing if she loses.

Lawyers for KarstadtQuelle filed a motion to dismiss the suit in early May. They contend that it is preempted by an agreement reached two years ago by the German government and major German companies to settle earlier suits brought by victims of Nazi slave labor.

That agreement obligated the United States government to request the dismissal of future suits against German companies "arising from the National Socialist era and World War II." Although the agreement included a fund to compensate some Nazi victims and their heirs, Mrs. Principe's lawyers say she would not be eligible under the law.

But in a letter to American officials, the Jewish Claims Conference, which helped negotiate the slave-labor settlement, has said it does not apply to the Wertheim suit. "This is not a claim arising from World War II, because the fraud alleged took place in 1951 and afterward," said Gideon Taylor, the executive vice president of the Conference.

Several legal scholars familiar with recent Holocaust claims say they agree.

"Given the facts of the case, the family should have their day in court," said Ruti Teitel, a professor at New York Law School who has written on international restitution law.

Whatever the outcome, it is clear that the Wertheims, like so many European Jews, were cheated of their legacy. They founded the Wertheim corporation in 1875, which expanded until the 1930s.

After taking power in 1933, the Nazis passed laws making it difficult, and eventually impossible, for Jews to own or operate businesses. The Wertheim empire, with eight large stores in Berlin, was a special target. The family was forced to give up its shares in the company to businessmen deemed Aryan.

Several Wertheim family members died in concentration camps. Gunther Wertheim and his family survived, but he was in poor health and virtually penniless when they arrived in New Jersey in the early 1940s. He died in 1954.

His brother Fritz, a death camp survivor, found a job as a cook in a mental institution.

The loss of the stores might easily have been forgotten. Although Mrs. Principe's mother successfully sought restitution for the family's house outside Berlin, she did not tell her daughter the full story of the company. Her father was too bitter over his losses to say much about them, Mrs. Principe said.

But in the early 1990s, Simone Ladwig-Winters, a graduate student at the Free University, discovered documents in an archive in Potsdam that showed how the Wertheim company's original Jewish owners were forced to give up their shares. In 1998, the Berlin Restitution Authority, which had issued compensation rulings on many East German properties stolen in the Nazi era, made her research part of its archive.

In early 2000, one of Mrs. Principe's lawyers, Gary M. Osen, stumbled onto Ms. Ladwig-Winters's findings. The idea for the lawsuit was born when he found what he considers the most damning evidence: an agreement written by hand in New York City on August 12, 1951, describing the anticipated merging of the Wertheim company and its major competitor, Hertie. That was several days before Mr. Lindgens, the former family advisor, persuaded Gunther and Fritz Wertheim to give up their shares.

Mr. Osen said the company's new owners had kept that and other documents from seeing light because they prove that Gunther and Fritz Wertheim were cheated. It is true that no one knew how profitable the company would become in later decades. But even in 1951 dollars, the shares were worth far more than the brothers were paid, Mr. Osen said.

It is far from clear that Mr. Osen will prevail. But Mrs. Principe and her nephew, Martin G. Wortham, say the battle will be half won if the suit is allowed to proceed in an American court so that the full truth of their family's betrayal can emerge. (The family changed the spelling of its name to Wortham after coming to the United States.)

"These people are still making money off our family's name, and my father was told there was nothing left," said Mrs. Principe, who has 7 children and 16 grandchildren. She returned to Berlin last year and was astounded to find a vast department store with her parents' last name on it. "It leaves you feeling not only flabbergasted but really angry."

Source: Robert Worth, "A Jewish Family's Stolen Legacy: Heirs Seek Restitution for Retail Empire Lost to Nazis," *New York Times,* May 24, 2002, p. B1.

As of this writing, no one knows how the Wertheim Department Store case will turn out. But what is clear is that by applying the same strategic techniques we've highlighted throughout this book, we've been able to keep the case in the media spotlight for well over a year. I think it's fair to say that the Wertheim heirs' battle is now the most famous single-family Holocaust claim in history, and certainly the largest. The corporate defendant—who otherwise might have holed up in its corporate offices in Germany forever—now realizes it will be fighting this case in the court of public opinion as well as the court of law. And the German and U.S. governments now take the case seriously as well, realizing the authority granted to them under the 1998 Slave Labor Agreements cannot be used as a "safe harbor" to disrupt all manner of fraud claims against German industry—even those that occurred well after the war, here in the United States.

WHEN THE GOVERNMENT IS THE PLAINTIFF

There is one situation where the plaintiffs have a decided advantage, in terms of both making news and keeping a story going throughout the course of the legal proceeding: when the government is the plaintiff—as in criminal and civil investigations, regulatory cases, and administrative proceedings. No case better illustrates the inherent advantage political officials and government agencies have over the media and other audiences in litigation than the recent battle pitting New York State Attorney General Eliot Spitzer against financial services giant Merrill Lynch. The Spitzer case highlights the difficulties in going head-to-head with a government official in a litigation matter—even if your advocate in the public arena is, arguably, the most popular man in America.

SPITZER VERSUS MERRILL LYNCH

At a hastily arranged press conference on April 8, 2002, Eliot Spitzer launched an attack on Wall Street giant Merrill Lynch that was unprecedented, both in the history of Wall Street and the New York State Attorney General's office. It would take less than two months for Spitzer to wrest a settlement of more than $100 million from Merrill—amazingly, without arresting anyone or bringing a single indictment against the company. Spitzer's aggressive actions and the resulting settlement sent shockwaves down Wall Street and established Spitzer as the most feared prosecutor of financial impropriety since U.S. Attorney Rudolph Giuliani brought down the junk bond kings of the late 1980s.

Which is interesting, because—although no one seemed to notice it at the time—there's ample evidence to indicate that it was Giuliani's ill-timed intervention on Merrill Lynch's behalf that forced Spitzer's hand. In other words, it may have been the sheriff of 1980's Wall Street that forced the new sheriff to take up his badge. This makes the Merrill Lynch investigation a fascinating case for us to examine—as an example of the inherent power government officials have to use public opinion in litigation, and the difficulties even the most sophisticated defendants can face when they try to fight fire with fire.

First, the obvious: Spitzer's use of the bully pulpit not only forced a quick settlement with Merrill Lynch, it also appears to be bringing real change to the practices of Wall Street firms in general. After settling with Merrill, Spitzer turned his attention to Citigroup's Salomon Smith Barney, Credit Suisse First Boston (CSFB), and other major financial firms, forcing settlements with these firms in late 2002 that totaled more than $1.4 billion.

Spitzer's success is also particularly interesting because he was such an unlikely person to be waging such a war. The New York State Attorney General is primarily a pursuer of consumer fraud, not the typical "hard-nosed prosecutor" of lore, and before the April press conference on the Merrill case, he had been considered, at most, a gadfly circling around the edges of the growing investigations of financial misdeeds that had sprung up in the wake of the dot-com crash and other economic disasters. Moreover, historically, the New York State Attorney General has steered well clear of legal battles with Wall Street, one of the state's largest employers—and one of its biggest campaign contributors. So not much thought was given to Spitzer's ongoing investigation in the weeks before his press conference—in fact, up until April 2002, no one seemed interested at all. Spitzer revealed Merrill was the target of an investigation almost a year earlier—but except for a few articles that appeared in December 2001, precious little had been written about the case, and Spitzer's efforts to play sheriff in the canyons of capitalism had been greeted with, mostly, a yawn.

Contrast that with Spitzer's reputation *after* the Merrill settlement. As *Fortune* magazine put it in its September 16, 2002, cover story: "On Wall Street right now, there may be no person as feared as the Attorney General of New York State."[1]

"The report," the *Los Angeles Times* reported, "has made Spitzer an instant hero to many investors (and their attorneys), and an instant nemesis to Wall Street."[2]

And if the office of New York state attorney general was an unlikely platform from which to launch an attack on the practices of the financial world, Spitzer didn't exactly fit the profile of the classic prosecutor either. A product of a rich real estate family and Princeton and Harvard Law School, Spitzer is as much a part of the New York establishment as the investment bankers that now cower before him. He lives in a Fifth Avenue apartment with a view of Central Park and used his father's money to gain the New York State Attorney General's office in 1998, after losing—and losing big—in the Democratic primary for the seat in 1994 (Spitzer finished last in a four-way primary). He won the election by the smallest of margins in 1998, primarily due to alleged improprieties and other missteps by the Republican incumbent at the time, Dennis Vacco. Moreover, Spitzer didn't come up through the regular New York political ranks, and many regulars in New York Democratic circles resented him for it. It is, therefore, not an exaggeration to say that before his unprecedented assault on Wall Street, Spitzer was still recovering from the perception that he was a bit of a lightweight, a man who bought himself a statewide seat with Daddy's money.

He's not perceived that way anymore. The *Fortune* article went on to say: "he has persevered in his mission of shaming and compelling the investment banks and their executives—right up to Sandy Weill, the head of conglomerate Citigroup—to end the despicable practice of giving their clients investment advice so dishonest and fraught with conflicts of interest that it has become worthless."[3]

Egregious E-mails Come to Light

Spitzer's investigation of Merrill Lynch centered on Henry Blodgett, the Merrill analyst who allegedly touted stocks he didn't believe in to enhance the company's chances of getting investment banking business. Merrill Lynch's behavior was representative of the kind of conflicts of interest common among investment banks in the height of the dot-com era. But it was the content of several e-mails Spitzer's team came across in its investigation that made the case a story—and ultimately led to the settlement.

It is telling that much of the media coverage of Spitzer's press conference described how taken aback Merrill Lynch and other observers were that Spitzer had decided to go public with the many damning e-mails that convinced a judge to issue a court order forcing Merrill to disclose whether the stocks they were recommending were from companies that were clients of the firm.

"The brokerage industry was stunned," the Los Angeles Times reported the following week, "because it had been expecting, or at least hoping, that regulators' investigations of analysts' potential conflicts of interest in their stock touting could be settled without the release of inflammatory internal communications and documents."[4]

To say that Spitzer dropped a bomb on that day in April is an understatement. His 37-page report was filled with e-mails between Merrill analysts—especially Mr. Blodgett and those who worked with him—detailing how the stocks they were touting were really "dogs," a "powder keg," a "piece of junk," or otherwise had a "bad smell" about them. Other detailed misgivings on the part of the some of the Merrill analysts: "We are losing people's money, and I don't like it," and "the whole idea that we are independent from banking is a big lie." Some of the companies touted by Blodgett and company were among the biggest blow-ups of the dot-com era: GoTo.com, InfoSpace, Pets.com, and eToys.*

In the media frenzy over the content of the e-mails themselves, the underlying court order was forgotten—as was Spitzer's comment that the court order was "a small first step" in the investigation.

Merrill's response was initially a vigorous defense. They argued in statements that the e-mails were taken out of context, that they were only part of larger dialogue that the firm's analysts were having over the companies and their worth—the equivalent to spoken conversations. Merrill's statement also said the company was incensed at the very public way Spitzer aired the e-mails, and the fact that he had not given them a chance to make the case in court.

But all of this—the unlikely prosecutor, the hastily organized press conference that caught everyone by surprise, the unprecedented media explosion that accompanied the announcement and eventually brought Merrill to its knees—all raise the same question: Why had Spitzer come forward so aggressively at that particular time to announce what even he conceded was a small step in the investigation?

In the week leading up to the press conference, for example, there wasn't even an inkling that Spitzer would go public on the matter. It's not as if Spitzer wasn't in the news—he was just in the news for all of the types of cases that the attorney general's office had been traditionally known for. Typical of these stories was the following report on nursing home abuse:

> Attorney General Eliot Spitzer announced on March 15 that Rene Mitchell, a certified nurse's aide formerly employed at the Victoria Home, was found guilty of physically abusing an 85-year-old female patient on New Year's Day 2000 by hitting and grabbing the victim on her neck and chest.

---

* Blodget's conflict-of-interest was no secret—it was chronicled, for example, in Howard Kurtz' excellent 1999 book on financial media, *The Fortune Tellers*: "Blodget found himself spending more time on the road, pitching companies for their investment banking business. Merrill Lynch had clearly bought itelf a ticket to the Net sweepstakes and that ticket was Henry Blodget" (Howard Kurtz, *The Fortune Tellers*, Touchstone Paperback edition, 2000, p. 155).

According to Deputy Attorney General Jose Maldonado, director of the Medicaid Fraud Control Unit, after deliberating for less than an hour on Tuesday, the jury convicted Mitchell of the crime of Willful Violation of Health Laws.[5]

There were also stories about Spitzer's involvement in long-distance telephone scams and the regulation of Christian pregnancy centers that discouraged abortions, parking meter scams, Indian Reservation cigarette taxes, and landlord-tenant issues. There was even an indication that Spitzer might be enlisted into the battle between Cablevision and the New York Yankees over a blackout of some Yankees games to New York cable subscribers. But certainly nothing on the scale of the bombshell the attorney general was about to drop.

So why? Well, part of the answer may have been revealed in the *Wall Street Journal* about two weeks later, where Charles Gasparino reported:

> With scrutiny on its stock research intensifying, Merrill Lynch & Co. is pulling out the heavy hitters in an effort to blunt attacks of New York Attorney General Eliot Spitzer, who has threatened the firm with civil and possible criminal action over alleged conflicts in its research.
> The biggest name on the list: Rudy Giuliani.[6]

That was not the most interesting—and revealing—piece of information in the article. It turned out Merrill Lynch hadn't just hired Giuliani the day before. Further down in the article, the *Journal* reported, almost as an aside:

> Mr. Giuliani, in an interview, confirms that he called Mr. Spitzer two weeks ago, just hours before the attorney general announced the results of his investigation into Merrill, including the release of e-mails—some of them derogatory in nature—showing that Merrill analysts often harbored doubts about stocks that received high public ratings from the firm.[7]

And toward the end of the article:

> Mr. Giuliani concedes that in his conversation with Mr. Spitzer, both men spoke about "the merits" of Mr. Spitzer's case against

the firm, but he wouldn't elaborate. "There were points I made that he agreed with, but we did get into the merits, and he did not agree with that."

But the main part of his pitch to Mr. Spitzer was that Merrill is a good firm and a good corporate citizen, which, unlike other firms, returned to its headquarters at the World Financial Center in lower Manhattan after the September 11 terrorist attacks, just yards from ground zero. "I told him this is a more complex problem, and the way it's being addressed, it needs more time and reflection," Mr. Giuliani said. "It should also be part of a larger response by the SEC and regulatory agencies."

Mr. Spitzer's response, according to Mr. Giuliani: "I'll consider it." A few hours later Mr. Spitzer blasted Merrill with the findings of his inquiry.[8]

Clearly, there was a good reason why no one saw the Spitzer announcement coming: because the final decision to make the announcement wasn't made until *after* the Spitzer camp realized that Giuliani had joined the fray. Discussions with those close to the situation confirm Spitzer's extraordinary foresight in seeing that, in the wake of Giuliani's involvement, unless he told the "public" the story of his investigation of Merrill Lynch, Giuliani would. And while he might have eventually gone public with the damaging e-mails anyway, Giuliani's intervention was the reason he did it so quickly and so forcefully on that April morning.

At the time, remember, Giuliani was still the most revered man in America, the hero of 9/11, *Time* magazine's "Man of the Year." Spitzer rightly realized that if Giuliani, on Merrill Lynch's behalf, was able to strike first and thereby frame the debate, all of his efforts over the past year might have been lost. Instead, Spitzer seized the high ground with his hurried press conference on April 8, 2002, and the Merrill Lynch forces never recovered.

Would this have happened if Giuliani hadn't signed on, if he had not made that fateful phone call that forced Spitzer's hand? Hard to say for sure, but clearly nothing in Mr. Spitzer's history, or the media coverage in advance of the April 8 press conference, indicated that Spitzer was about to turn on Wall Street. At the very least, it was far more likely that he would have looked for compromise with Merrill Lynch, compromise that advanced his policy goals while still keeping the peace in an important sector of the New York economy.

Moreover, as we've learned throughout the course of this book, sometimes handling the public aspects of litigation requires a "hammer," and sometimes it requires a feather-light touch. Anybody who knows Mr. Giuliani knows he is the 10-point ballpeen of diplomacy. At some level, Merrill Lynch may have thought that what they needed was not strategy, but instead just to retain Mr. Giuliani, wind him up, and point him in the direction of Mr. Spitzer. But when dealing with government officials—the ultimate plaintiffs in the court of public opinion—you must remember that you are dealing with an adversary that has enormous built-in weapons that even the most powerful defendants do not have. Even if you're Merrill Lynch, and even if you have Mr. Giuliani, armed and ready, at your side.

ACTION POINTS

✔ The needs of plaintiffs in enhancing media and other public interest in a lawsuit can differ significantly from the needs of the defense—although the same general systems described in this book can be used to further the communications components of all types of cases.

✔ "Job One" for the plaintiff is letting the defendant know that the case will involve *not* just one day of bad news, but a continuing ratcheting up of the pressure in the public arena.

✔ The particulars of the case will dictate strategy for plaintiffs in communicating the story of their case—as in the incredibly complex, historically significant Wertheim Department Store case.

✔ Government officials are the ultimate plaintiffs, with a host of tools at their disposal and an inherent advantage in attracting media and other public interest to their case.

CHAPTER NINE

When Your Case Comes to Trial: Managing the Media Frenzy at the Courthouse

As we've learned, less than 10 percent of cases filed in the United States ever make it to trial—and that's not counting the huge number of cases that are settled in the prelitigation phase. But eventually, you may wind up in the courthouse, pleading your case before judge and/or jury as well as before public audiences—and you'll need special skill to deal with all the various communications elements of the case as it enters its trial phase.

In this chapter, we look at some of those skills—and also look at the ways the lessons we've learned throughout this book apply when a case moves into the courtroom for trial. Along the way, we examine one of the more sensational courtroom cases of the past several years—the vicious child custody and support case waged between Ronald O. Perelman and Patricia Duff. We consider how the techniques that were used effectively in this case can be used in all legal matters that eventually wind their way through the litigation system to the courtroom.

"Ron Perelman lives like the Sultan of Brunei and he has the nerve to quibble over how much he should support his child," a member of Duff's legal team charged.

—Dan Raviv, *Comic Wars*, 2001

That's me doing the charging, quoted in a passage from Dan Raviv's 2001 bestseller on the battle for Marvel Comics between Ronald Perelman and fellow 1980s-style corporate raider Carl Icahn. I wasn't involved in that battle, but as we've seen from Chapter Four, my company was deeply involved in a case that was just as contentious: the infamous Perelman/Duff divorce and child custody case.* Although I've reminded readers throughout this book that far less than 10 percent of court cases filed ever make it trial, Perelman/Duff case was one that did. It is a case that will serve well as the framework for a discussion of what to do if your case actually does finds its way to the courtroom.

I'm not surprised, by the way, that I'm not specifically identified in the Dan Raviv quote—in my business, you get used to being in the background (most times, it's preferable). Moreover, I'm flattered to be described as a member of "Duff's legal team." If nothing else, that goes to prove the premise of this book—that in high-profile litigation, the public relations function and the legal function are, at times, indistinguishable.

When we were brought on by Democratic fundraiser/socialite Patricia Duff to assist her in the communications aspect of the child custody case, the case was about to go to trial on the issue of support—that is, how much New York City's richest man would be paying Ms. Duff each month for the care of their young daughter. In Chapter Four, we described how we entered the case, put our as-of-yet unnamed CIR process—Control, Information, Response—into place, and almost immediately began to see results in terms of the tone of the coverage of the case and the way our side's message was getting through. As the support trial began before no-nonsense Manhattan Supreme Court Justice Franklin Weissberg, our efforts were about to pay off on an even greater scale.

---

*In an interesting coincidence, although I was not involved in the Marvel bankruptcy, a current member of my firm was. At about the same time I was representing Ronald Perelman's ex-wife in his child custody proceedings, my colleague Bruce Berman—whose Brody Berman Associates is now part of The PR Consulting Group—was representing Perelman foe Carl Icahn and the Marvel Trustee in the public relations elements of the Marvel bankruptcy proceedings. We now work together on many legal and litigation issues.

Let me reemphasize one point before we begin: Although this case was among the most sensational you'll ever encounter, it is highly relevant to any client whose case winds up in the courtroom—regardless of how large the numbers or how high-profile the parties to the litigation are. As we've learned throughout this book, even the most sensational cases offer keen insight for anyone whose legal action is subject to broader public scrutiny. By applying the techniques outlined in this book—including our CIR system, message development guidelines, Media Briefs, and Litigation Media Checklist—clients and their attorneys can have considerable impact on all manner of litigation.

Make no mistake about it, by the way: the Perelman/Duff child custody and support case was, in some ways, a *business case*—with the millions of dollars at stake and the parties to the dispute capitalized far better than most companies. High-profile clients are often corporations unto themselves, and the similarities between corporate lawsuits and lawsuits involving so-called celebrities are considerable.

I have not lost sight, however, of the fact that there was a child involved in this case. You can make your own judgments as to the morality of the parties and issues involved—I did, and felt comfortable with the fact that Ms. Duff was fighting for her daughter, not in spite of her daughter. In the end she lost, and as I've mentioned in Chapter Four, in my opinion this was both unfair and contrary to the prevailing trend in child custody law. The saddest part of this result was, as you'll see, Ms. Duff had a chance to settle her case on the *right* terms when Ronald Perelman was at his lowest, reviled in the media as "New York's cheapest billionaire." But she didn't.

To back up my claim as to what was deserved in terms of child support in the Duff case, consider the following, from an article in the *Wall Street Journal* on child support in high-net-worth divorce proceedings—an article written more than two years before the Perelman/Duff case was finally decided:

Rich kids from broken homes are getting richer.

Throughout the country, support awards for the children of a rich parent have soared in recent years, as courts have begun redistributing wealth in the name of children's rights. While divorced or separated parents in all economic groups are paying more in child support, the very rich are shelling out as much as 20 times what they were a decade ago. Albuquerque, NM, lawyer Sandra Little, for instance, says she has several clients paying or receiving $20,000 to $30,000 a month in child support.

In Haverford, PA, Michael Karp, who earns more than $5 million a year from real estate and telecommunications investments, is paying $23,266 a month in child support to his estranged wife, Amy, for their four children. Mrs. Karp, who has custody slightly more than half the time, contends she needs that much so the children, who range from 9 to 13 years old, won't feel "second-class" when they are with her.[1]

The article went on to state that ". . . [t]he idea behind the ballooning awards is to prevent children from favoring the wealthier parent—typically the father—or losing social and financial advantages they would have had if their parents had stayed together."[2]

This, I would argue, is an entirely reasonable proposition—and remember that Ronald Perelman was a billionaire several times over, as opposed to Mr. Karp, who brought in a measly $5 million per year. So if Mr. Karp of Haverford, Pennsylvania, was paying $23,000-plus per month, what did the daughter of Ronald O. Perelman deserve? $50,000? More? This was at the crux of the Perelman/Duff case. It was not what Patricia Duff did or did not have, or did or did not get from Mr. Perelman in the divorce settlement. It was about what her daughter *deserved*—in order to live in the lifestyle she was entitled to, the equivalent of Perelman's other children. A lifestyle that was her legacy as the offspring of New York's richest man.

We'll come back to the Perelman/Duff clash in a moment, but first let's take a more general look at some rules to follow when a case moves from the litigation room to the courtroom.

STICK WITH THE PLAN

The main point about handling the communications aspects of litigation when the case eventually makes it to trial is this: *Don't throw away the strategy you've honed over the past weeks and months (and in many cases, years) under the misguided notion that when a case comes to trial "things are different."* Yes, things will change once the trial begins—there'll be a different feel, a new flavor to the proceedings, a rush of immediacy, a vast change in style and speed. You'll need to respond in some manner to all of the myriad maneuverings that will occur in the courtroom each day. As you'll see throughout this chapter, it will at times require quick thinking and decisive action. Moreover, except for certain private areas of the courtroom, such as those reserved for attorney-client conferences, all the courthouse is your stage. The media will be watching the lawyers, the clients, and everyone else associated with the case at every moment: in the hallways, in the stairwells, in the restrooms and on the way into and out of the courtroom.

But these differences are cosmetic at best. The best advice I can give clients and lawyers when operating in the courthouse is to stick to the fundamentals. Many litigants, lawyers, and public relations professionals dispense with all of the crucial elements we've discussed throughout this book and instead concentrate on the immediacy of the proceedings, the trappings of the courtroom, and the rush of the press corps bearing down after a long session before judge and jury.

PRESS CONFERENCE FEVER

Just one example of the way the change of venue can make a client or his or her lawyer feel they need to change strategy: Once your case gets to the courthouse, you're going to have an incredible urge to do what I've urged *against* since the beginning of this book: hold a press conference on the courthouse steps. We've all seen *Law and Order*—that's the way the game's played, right? A phalanx of microphones, cameras, the mini-tape recorders, the lawyer making a strong statement in defense of the client's position. This is the essence of litigation public relations, isn't it? If you don't hold a press conference, won't it seem like you are hiding something—from the very media you're trying to influence?

If you're worried about your credibility with the media, I can see you've been reading this book carefully. But if you think that courthouse press conferences are the essence of litigation public relations, then you haven't been reading this book at all. Courthouse press conferences, I believe, are a relic of television-courtroom dramas, which over the years have influenced lawyers and their public relations representatives more than most would care to admit.

So I'll say it again: In most cases, *resist* the press conference urge. It will be hard—the media may actually *prefer* to get their information that way—but, again, resist the temptation. As we discussed in Chapter Seven, even in the Microsoft antitrust trial—one of the most covered trials of the past decade—Microsoft abandoned its daily press conference schedule once they realized what a negative effect it was having on the company's credibility and their ability to get their message out. It was a mistake to treat a trial like a political campaign, and it was a mistake to think a press conference was the best way to get information to the media. Toward the end of the trial, they abandoned the practice altogether.

Why do I dislike press conferences? They can't hurt, can they? Well, yes, they can. Primarily because there is an *uncontrollability* to the press conference format that can often lead client and attorney down a path to disaster. Not only are dozens of reporters firing questions at you, they're feeding off one another as well. Following up on another reporter's questions, latching on to a point picked up in the last question asked. Moreover, many times I've seen mainstream reporters influenced by the questioning of the so-called "fringe" media present at a press conference—with the views of the alternative press subtly working their way into the mainstream coverage. The more frenzied the trial, the harder it is to keep control.

But how do you make sure it doesn't look like you're hiding something? If you handle the media properly, you'll do fine. Remember, we're not talking about restricting reporters access to information—but why do you have to hold a press conference to give the media information? In most cases, I prefer one-on-one contact with key reporters covering the case. It gets the information to the reporters in a far more personal and far more controllable manner.

Moreover, in most courtroom situations, it's not that hard to do. At the end of a heated day in the courtroom, each media outlet is going to need, at most, five to ten minutes of your time. Television "stand-ups" (where you stand in front of a building and take questions from a reporter), require even less. This can be easily arranged in a courthouse conference room, outside the courthouse, or in an office nearby (many attorney's offices are within walking distance of the courthouse). Depending on the events of the day, it might take an hour, tops, to reach all the media you need to speak to in order to get your end-of-day message out. One-on-one sessions are far more personal and controllable that the circus they call a press conference.

One last point about press conferences and the silly notions we sometimes have about the "right" way to do things. Several years ago I attended a press conference—predictably, on the courthouse steps—at 1 P.M. Why is the time so important? Well, it was the middle of summer and it was hot—almost 100 degrees. The courthouse steps faced the sun. Next to the courthouse was a small park, with trees and ample shade. I mentioned to the public relations person handling the case, "Why not move the press conference to the shade of the trees, where everybody would be cooler?"

"Well, we've already put the podium on the steps, and besides, that's the way it's always done, isn't it?" was the answer I got.

Let me tell you: "The way it's always done" made for a lot of sweaty, grumpy reporters that day. And their questioning showed it. So much for value of press conferences on the courthouse steps.

But I Have No Choice . . .

Suppose you have no choice other than to hold a press conference. Suppose:

- There is information you need to get to *all* the media *immediately*—an hour from now won't do. (This can happen particularly in the case of publicly traded companies, where reporters and analysts are sometimes putting their analysis of the day's activities "on the wire" almost instantaneously.)
- It's a "trial of the century" and there are, quite literally, hundreds of reporters bearing down on you.

If you must hold a press conference, it is vitally important to lay some tight ground rules to avoid the carnival atmosphere that can develop. The litigant's lawyer or press spokesperson should ideally get up before any one speaks and give reporters the ground rules for the press conference. These can be things like:

- The attorney for ABC Corporation will read a prepared statement from the company's chairman, but will take *no questions.*
- Mr. Smith will read a prepared statement and then his lawyer will take five minutes of questions, but no more.
- The defendant will read a short statement regarding his contract dispute, and then answer five minutes of questions regarding the case. We will answer *no* questions regarding the defendant's involvement in money laundering through Leichtenstein or the Wen Ho Lee matter (this is in case the "alternative" press is hatching conspiracy theories— and don't laugh . . . I've been asked both questions in the recent past).

If you are forced to hold a press conference, you can lay ground rules that establish the format and the types of questions that the plaintiff or defendant will and will not answer. But you've got to be tough in sticking to those ground rules: if you say five minutes of questions, it's five minutes and off. If you answer one question regarding Wen Ho Lee, expect more.

LOGISTICS

At various points in this book, I have not-so-subtly bashed politics as a training ground for litigation public relations, but here's one area where political-types excel—in the logistics of your trial site.

What do I mean by logistics? Consider the following:

- How will you or your client get in and out of the courthouse? Will a herd of media crowd all entrances and threaten to crush the litigant? In a criminal case, is there a "perp-walk"? What are the logistics of that process and where will the media set up?
- Who will lead the client in—or, if you are a client, will you have an escort? Microphones in the face can stop a party short, and that spells trouble. Since I'm not exactly small—

and I take the New York City subway each day—I can usually push through a crowd as if I'm getting off the #4 train at rush hour. Do you have someone who can serve that function? Or will private security be needed?

- What kind of message are you sending through your dress, your manner, and the way you enter the courtroom? Are you wearing dark sunglasses that make you look guilty? Are you chatting on a cell phone as you enter the courthouse like a dismissive corporate yuppie?

- Once inside, where exactly is the courtroom? In larger courthouses, some courtrooms can be difficult to find. Whether you are the actual party or a lawyer, you don't want to be wandering the hallways like Spinal Tap in Cleveland. This, most definitely, will send the wrong signal to the media and to your ultimate audience.

- What's your exit strategy? How will you leave the building? Through a garage? Across the street to a parking lot? Is there a car waiting for you outside the courthouse? Where will the media be? Will there be a "crush" of reporters crowding in on you? How can you make your exit as quietly as possible?

In many cases, these issues won't be concerns—but you need to know the logistics to avoid sending the wrong message. Political pros are skilled at this: Their advance teams have been paving the way for politicians forever. Like a good politician, in preparing for the trial phase of the litigation communications management, you should leave nothing to chance. Thus, the importance of reviewing these physical details which have, up to now, been nonexistent in the communications component of your case.

THE TABLOID STORY OF THE YEAR

Control is the key here: To the extent possible, you've got to control all aspects of the message that is getting to the media, usually in a situation where time is not on your side, events and information are coming at you in rapid-fire fashion, and the pressure to give the media what they want has been ratcheted up a hundredfold.

The Perelman/Duff proceedings were a perfect example of this. On the first day of testimony, Mr. Perelman was scheduled to take the stand. So many things were happening at once that there was a possibility he might not testify at all. The morning began with a hearing on a motion to have Ms. Duff's lead litigators, the very talented husband-and-wife team of Rita and Ken Warner, disqualified for a conflict of interest. The motion was filed by Mr. Perelman's ex-wife, New York gossip queen Claudia Cohen. It seems the Warner's firm, Coblence & Warner, had represented Ms. Cohen years earlier in her divorce from Mr. Perelman. Speculation abounded that the motion was filed at the urging of Ms. Cohen's ex-husband, who still had many ways to make her life miserable. Judge Weissberg granted the motion—and suddenly Ms. Duff was down to one attorney, sole practitioner William Beslow.*

Among other things, by the way, this removed my chief spokesperson from the proceedings, as Rita Warner (whom you met in Chapter Four when she suggested that Mr. Perelman had learned some of his security techniques from the former Soviet Union) was no longer representing Ms. Duff, and in fact had been thrown out of the courtroom after passing notes to co-counsel Bill Beslow after being disqualified. Thus, as they say in football, I had to "call an audible," deciding from the back row of the courtroom that I would be the chief spokesperson for Ms. Duff when the media frenzy began after the case went into recess. Again, in the heat of the courtroom battle, snap decisions like this may be required at any time.

After considerable confusion, Ronald Perelman finally took the stand. He was expertly questioned by Bill Beslow over his lavish lifestyle: more than $60 million in real estate holdings, private jets, yachts . . . the works. Then the conversation moved on to questions of how much it cost when his daughter stayed with him.

"When Caleigh eats with me, she eats about $3 worth of food a day," said Perelman. "She eats chicken fingers, hot dogs, cereal for breakfast, hamburgers, and some pasta."[3]

In the back row of the courtroom, I was sitting next to *Wall Street Journal* reporter Margaret Jacobs. I scribbled a note on my legal pad: "$3 a day?"

---

*I believe Ms. Duff had been through some 16 attorneys at this point, so she was not only down to a single lawyer, she was running out of options.

She looked at me in disbelief. I knew exactly what the story would be in the next morning's newspapers.

Since I was now the chief spokesperson on the case, I realized I had better come up with a message. I quickly scribbled two or three message points on my legal pad and—as we describe in Chapter Seven—memorized them before Perelman's testimony ended and the case recessed for the day.

My goal: to make Perelman's $3-a-day comment as big a story as possible for the next day's newspapers.

To say the resulting news coverage—complete with my memorized commentary—was *big* is an understatement: It was quoted hundreds of times around the world and no more eminent a source than the *New Yorker* cited the story as the tabloid news story of the year for 1999. Put bluntly, all hell broke loose. Media coverage was similar to that in the *New York Post* story that follows—the cover story of that day's edition, under the banner headline "New York's Cheapest Billionaire":

PERELMAN: IT WON'T TAKE A LOT OF BREAD TO FEED MY KID

High-living billionaire Ron Perelman says he can feed his 4-year-old daughter on just $3 a day.

Perelman offered that figure yesterday after describing his lavish lifestyle from the witness stand in his bitter custody battle with ex-wife Patricia Duff.

New York's richest man offered his two cents' worth on the subject when Duff lawyer William Beslow asked him to estimate an "appropriate" cost for feeding his daughter Caleigh, who's at the center of the acrimonious dispute.

"When Caleigh eats with me, she eats $3 worth of food a day," Perelman said. "She eats chicken fingers, hot dogs, cereal for breakfast, hamburgers, and some pasta." "Three dollars? So about a $1,000 a year would be appropriate?" Beslow asked.

"Yes," Perelman replied.

Duff's spokesman, Jim Haggerty, said outside of court that the comment shows "What's really going on. He believes his daughter needs $3 a day, and that's what he's willing to give."

U.S. Department of Agriculture figures show $3.07 a day was the national average last year for a "low-cost" home-cooked food plan for a 4-year-old.

Perelman has a full-time chef on his staff.

Perelman was the first witness to be called in the child-support phase of the custody battle.

Duff is seeking more than $50,000 a month in child support, including $40,000 to rent an apartment in Manhattan, a second car, $60,000 a year for a full-time nanny, additional household help, and cash for trips and vacations.

She also wants him to continue paying for Caleigh's school, camp, and medical insurance.

Perelman currently pays $12,000 a month in child support, as well as $1.5 million a year in maintenance to Duff.

"We're in uncharted waters here," Manhattan Supreme Court Justice Franklin Weissberg told the Revlon chairman and his beauful socialite ex-wife. "There aren't too many cases where a billionaire and a multimillionaire slug it out."

Beslow opened his case by grilling Perelman about his finances in an attempt to show what kind of lifestyle Caleigh is used to.

Perelman said his net worth is "approximately $6 billion," and that he made over $100 million over the past two years.

He described his five-story East Side townhouse, his 60-acre East Hampton estate, his oceanfront mansion in Palm Beach, Fla., and $5 million corporate estate in Los Angeles.

He said Caleigh would often go with him to his various homes, traveling sometimes by helicopter to East Hampton or in Perelman's private jet to Florida.

"Ron Perelman lives like the Sultan of Brunei and he has the nerve to quibble about how much he should support his child," Duff spokesman Haggerty fumed afterward.

The testimony got off to a cantankerous start, with Beslow asking Perelman be declared a hostile witness and accusing him of "fraud and perjury."

Beslow was set to argue Perelman lied when he claimed in his divorce papers that he and Duff didn't have marital relations between September 1995 and September 1996, but the judge said he's "not interested in theatrics or cheap shots."

Earlier, Weissberg granted a motion filed by another Perelman ex, Claudia Cohen, to disqualify two of Duff's lawyers, Ken and Rita Warner, from the case.

The Warners had represented Cohen for a time during her split from the makeup magnate, and her lawyer, Karen Seymour, said they were privy to "sensitive and confidential information" which they were trying to use on Duff's behalf.

Asked if he thought Cohen's move showed the "Live with Regis and Kathie Lee" gossip reporter was in the powder-puff poobah's pocket, Haggerty said, "That motion should be dusted for fingerprints."

Weissberg later barred Rita Warner from the courtroom for arguing with him after she was disqualified.

Source: Dareh Gregorian, "Perelman: It Won't Take a Lotta Bread to Feed My Kid," *New York Post,* January 21, 1999, p. 7.

The next day, the story was all over the news, as far away as Australia. Radio disk jockeys ran food collection drives outside Perelman's East 62nd Street townhouse and Perelman even became a bit player in a daily comic strip originating out of Washington, DC. Ronald O. Perelman quickly became known as "Three-Dollar-A-Day Ron." And he was not happy about it.

One element of Perelman's response was to come into court the next day and set the record straight, proclaiming that he really spent more than $1,000 each day on his daughter when she was with him. The second part of Perelman's strategy? To try to rattle the public relations guy who made a fool of him the day before.

Before Perelman even returned to the stand, his lawyer, Adrian Hillman, addressed the judge. She stood up and forcefully objected that "someone named Jim Haggerty" was issuing press releases and making other public statements about the case. She was quite animated, and the court grew silent.

She then dramatically turned and pointed at me, sitting in the back row. "And your honor," Hillman announced, "Mr. Haggerty is here in the courtroom today!"

Now maybe I've seen too many courtroom dramas over the years myself, but from my perch at the rear of the room I could've sworn the entire crowd whirled around with a "gasp" and stared directly at me. It was a moment of pure theater, like something out of Perry Mason.

Judge Weissberg, to his credit, saw the theatrics for what they were. He took a deep breath. "We all know a Mr. Haggerty has been issuing press statements," he started, and then went on to remind the parties that although there was nothing he could do about it, he was sure each side would conduct itself with the appropriate "decorum" outside the courtroom. According to the *New York Post,* Weissberg warned both sides "not to try the case in the press," because "I don't think the publicity is helpful to the child."[4]

It wasn't doing much for my digestive system either. I'm used to staying in the background, remember. Perelman's attorneys knew there was nothing they could do about my public statements—they were just trying to shake me up, make me the issue, maybe even scare me a little. As the press surrounded me at the rear of the courtroom, I put on my best game face. It's a good thing I didn't try to drink a glass of water—I'd have been like Tom Cruise after he questioned Jack Nicholson in *A Few Good Men.*

But it wasn't me who was really rattled. I found out later that I was the subject of considerable discussion in the judge's chambers as well. Apparently, I'd struck a bit of a cord with the Perelman forces, and they were determined to do what they could to get me off the case. They knew I was an attorney and demanded to know if I was a member of the legal team and, if so, why I hadn't identified myself as such. Perelman and his forces were clearly rattled by the day's news coverage. It further showed in their actions later in the day.

After Perelman left the stand, Judge Weissberg called a recess. He wanted the parties in his chambers for one last attempt at settlement. Suddenly, the action came to a complete halt. As I recall, I waited for a good 90 minutes or so in the hallway of New York State Supreme Court, overcoat in hand, as the attorneys huddled behind closed doors. Rumors of a settlement began to circulate. As during the Marvel Comics fight with Carl Icahn, things had gotten too hot and Perelman wanted to end it.

Suddenly, Bill Beslow burst through the chamber doors, Patricia Duff at his side. They were obviously engaged in a heated discussion. Beslow had the habit of leaning in at the waist when making a point, legs as straight as boards. He was doing quite a bit of that now, as Ms. Duff continued their argument. I looked around to see several reporters lingering nearby.

Beslow came charging toward me, Ms. Duff directly behind.

"You've got to speak to her," Beslow yelled at me, saying that they were close to settlement but that "she is going to blow it." His exasperation showed, even through his usual dignified demeanor.

Before I had a chance to respond, Ms. Duff caught up with him and, quite literally, spun him around to face her. She stuck a finger in his face.

"Listen, you work for me and I am ordering you," she said. Beslow fumed and walked off, Duff following right behind.

I later learned the case was all-but-settled, but was hung up on the number of Jewish holidays Perelman would have visitation rights. Through some skilled negotiation by Bill Beslow, Ms. Duff would have retained custody, and—according to several sources I've spoken to, including reporters covering the case—would have received a monthly support payment close to $30,000. It would likely have been among the highest monthly support award in history.

This brings up an important point: When a party is weakened from a media onslaught and ready to settle—settle! Particularly if you are a David going up against a Goliath. Don't expect that the good publicity you've garnered that week is going to continue. It is a heady feeling to be winning the battle in the court of public opinion, but it is important to remember that this is just a tool you are using to influence the litigation, not an end in itself. Good press is not the goal here—positive resolution of your legal dispute is. When a party comes to the settlement table weakened, it is important to use your momentary advantage to hammer out a deal.

In Ms. Duff's case, she didn't seize the opportunity before her. More than two years of legal fees, court battles, and bad publicity later, she lost custody and wound up with a child support payment that was about what she was getting temporarily—and less than half of what Perelman was prepared to settle for in January of 1999. A shame really, since not only was Ms. Duff a good mother who deserved custody of her child, her daughter deserved better as well.

We continued to represent Ms. Duff through the first few months of 1999, but the relationship frayed as she tried to take more and more control of her publicity efforts. With bad advice from her political friends, she insisted on responding to every little attack, rather than (as we've discussed throughout this book) keeping to the game plan, keeping her eye on the ball. In the end, Perelman did exactly what he said he was going to do: He won.

An example of how far off track things were getting occurred at the end of February. I learned an important lesson in the process: We were losing control, making snap decisions regarding media strategy without proper information (remember the CIR process), and it showed.

I was in Las Vegas for a conference about my role as executive director of the International Lawyers Network (ILN), an association of approximately 75 law firms around the world. I received a call from a colleague in New York, letting me know that there was a court hearing scheduled on the morning of the February 26, to decide who would have custody of Caleigh over the Purim and Passover holidays. Patricia Duff, I was told, wanted the media to be alerted, since she was sure it was another opportunity to show Ronald Perelman for the hypocrite that he was.

"What's the value to our overall case?" I asked.

"She insists."

Now, Ms. Duff was a hard person to argue with when she insisted, so I figured what could happen? "Let the media know," I said, "but tell them not to expect much."

I didn't think much else of it, but as I was flying home on the red-eye flight from Los Vegas to Kennedy, the presses of the local New York tabloids were rolling—and "what could happen" did.

The article that greeted me as I got off the plane at JFK read as follows:

HOLIER-THAN-THOU RON WINS KID CLASH

A courtroom holy war broke out yesterday in the custody brawl over little Caleigh Perelman—with Dad winning visitation for most of next month's Jewish holidays by arguing that Mom's a phony Jew.

As proof of his claim, a lawyer for the father—billionaire Revlon CEO Ronald Perelman—said the little girl's mother, Patricia Duff, held Easter-egg hunts and baked leavened cookies when she had Caleigh at her Southport, Conn., estate last Passover.

Duff also concocted a story about having attended a seder ceremony at her rabbi's house last year, Perelman charged. The only reason Duff—an Episcopalian who converted to Judaism when she married Perelman in 1995—still doesn't go to church is because she "thinks her picture may be taken," Perelman charges in court papers.

"She spent the last Passover seder at an Easter-egg hunt! This is nonsense!" the makeup magnate's lawyer, Adria Hillman, shouted in the courtroom. "What happened last year was a sacrilege!"

Manhattan Supreme Court Justice Eileen Bransten agreed, saying, "It was a sacrilege" and ordering that Caleigh stay with her father for part of Purim and all of Passover.

Duff's lawyer denied Perelman's claims that Duff is a closet Christian and insisted that when Duff converted to Judaism, it stuck.

"She is absolutely Jewish," said Duff's lawyer, Bonnie Rabin, brushing off Perelman's attack as merely the prejudice of a born Jew against a converted Jew.

The holiday tug-of-war over the cherubic Caleigh is the latest round in the bitter, two-year custody fight between Duff and Perelman, who is worth an estimated $6 billion.

Perelman, 56, has been divorced three times. Duff, 44, has been divorced four times. Their daughter is 4 and must be raised Jewish according to the ex-couple's prenup and divorce agreements.

As the two sides hashed out a visitation schedule for next month, Duff's professed Judaism was what was really on trial.

In court documents, Perelman's lawyers quote a friend of Duff's—Connecticut neighbor Sissy Biggers—saying, "Patricia is a Christian and not a Jew . . . Patricia is afraid to go to church. We have asked her. She thinks her picture may be taken."

Her lawyers have claimed Duff is a devout Jew and full-fledged member of Park East Synagogue on East 67th Street—with enough religious heft to get invited to her rabbi's home table for seder, the Passover meal.

Perelman's people argued that Duff only recently paid up her $3,000 in overdue membership fees. Then they showed the judge a letter from Rabbi Arthur Schneier denying he had Duff at his home for a seder.

And if Duff is so Jewish, Perelman's side asks in court papers, why was she caught canoodling with her boyfriend, Sen. Robert Torricelli (D-N.J.), in George Steinbrenner's skybox for a Yankees-Texas Rangers game last Yom Kippur, the holiest day of the Jewish calendar?

Countered Duff's lawyer, "This is the most offensive micromanagement of Judaism I've ever seen!"

Afterward, Duff stormed out of the courthouse in apparent anger.

Source: Laura Italiano, " 'Holier-than-Thou' Ron Wins Kid Clash," *New York Post,* February 27, 1999, p. 3.

Lesson to be learned: Do not give up the Control, Information, Response (CIR) process, even in the heat of a courtroom battle. Even in the most chaotic of trials, you need as much *Control* as is possible over the messages being sent to the media, and enough *Information* to be able to make the right decisions regarding proper *Response* to each situation that presents itself.

MORE LESSONS FOR COURTHOUSE COMMUNICATIONS

Again, Perelman/Duff was an unusual case—but, as in all the unusual cases we've looked at, effective use of the systems and procedures developed in our business-related legal work had an immediate effect of the courtroom fight. Conversely, as the systems began to break down, we lost control of the message—and the overall course of the litigation suffered.

Let's look at some of lessons that can be culled from the Perelman/Duff courtroom dramas, and consider how they can be used in managing all manner of litigation that eventually winds its way to the courtroom. The primary lesson relates to speed of response: a litigant, his lawyer, or public relations representative needs to do all the things described in the rest of this book—and they need to do it faster. At lightning speed. Judges at trial, for example, have a tendency to dispense with all sorts of motions and other issues at the opening of each day's proceedings, in rapid-fire fashion. To ensure control and proper response:

- *You need to understand what is happening.* What issues have been decided, what motions have been dispensed with, and which are the most important to your side in making your case.
- *You need to prioritize.* What will tomorrow's news coverage be? What does your side *want* it to be? Sitting there in the courtroom, you need to immediately prioritize the story of the day—because they'll likely only be one story (or maybe two) dominating the coverage the next morning.
- *Message needs to be prepared and memorized.* Using the same techniques outlined earlier in this book, litigants, or their public relations representatives need to immediately jot down the *message,* then commit it to memory—so the spokesperson will be able to deliver the message seamlessly when there's a break in the action.

In the Perelman/Duff action, I needed to do all of these things, prioritizing my messages and realizing that I needed to "come out swinging" to ensure the $3-a-day story was the one that stuck. I needed to make a lower priority of other stories that were developing—like the disqualification of the Warners. Finally, I needed to ensure that our message was prepared and ready to deliver—even after our regular spokesperson had been thrown off the case . . . and out of the courtroom.

With laptops, portable printers, and cellular communications, you can set up shop in a corner of a courthouse hallway and have all the same tools at your disposal that you would have at the office. This greatly streamlines your message dissemination—especially if you also have folks back at the office who can assist in reaching those audiences who were not hanging around the courtroom that day.

In the end, the lessons of managing the courtroom drama are remarkably similar to the lessons learned throughout the litigation process: You need to have a clear strategy in place, an established system for getting your message to the right audience, in the right manner, at the right time, and you need to make sure that your side is not knocked off their game by the dueling antics of the other team. During the run up to a courtroom trial, litigation ebbs and flows, and the hardest task at times can be ensuring the case gets proper attention even during breaks in the action. But once you get to trial, the opposite happens—you have to be moving at 100 miles per hour, making decisions in a heartbeat, and ensuring that your execution is flawless to advance your case in the stifling heat of the media spotlight.

ACTION POINTS

✔ The same techniques that have served in other aspects of litigation are equally important once the case comes to trial, including the CIR system, Media Briefs, and message development.

✔ Speed is the major difference between communication in the courtroom and communication before the case gets to trial. While keeping your overall litigation communications program in place, you've got to have the ability to make quick decisions on all of the myriad issues that come at you at light speed during the trial phase of a case.

✔ Once your case moves to the courthouse, you'll have the distinct urge to hold a press conference on the courthouse steps. Resist! There are far better ways to communicate with the media at trial.

✔ Logistics become increasingly important at the courthouse, where you've got to figure out how to get in and out without sending a negative message. Moreover, when in the courthouse, there are many places to hide from the prying eyes of the media—so lawyers, clients, and everyone else involved with the case should be on their best behavior.

Afterword

But what about justice? my brother asked me after reading an early draft of this book. "Aren't you worried that the work you do skews the legal system in favor of those who know how to use the media to their advantage?"

It's a fair question. Many observers worry that, in using outside audiences to influence the course of the litigation process, justice suffers. Or, to put it more bluntly: Vicious, amoral spinmeisters use their "black magic" to tilt the scales of justice unfairly, twisting and bending the rule of law to meet their own nefarious ends; using media and other public audiences in legal disputes allows the waves of public passion that swell in the wake of a media barrage to engulf the reasoned, dispassionate dispensation of justice.

Well, if you've read this far, I'm going to assume you know that I don't believe this. In fact, I believe the opposite: Properly using the channels of media can actually level the playing field, eliminating many of the advantages that money, ideology, influence, and class have long brought to our legal system. I would argue that proper use of extrajudicial tools in the conduct of litigation and other legal disputes actually helps *ensure* justice in many cases. This is particularly true as both lawyers and their clients become more adept at properly using the tools of public relations to bring the case to the court of public opinion.

Many readers may now be imagining the giants of legal history turning in their graves at the mere thought. Remember, however, that some of the best legal theorists in history were legal realists as well. It was Justice Oliver Wendell Holmes who once said: "Theory is the dinner jacket you take off before changing a flat tire." The law has always been anchored in the practical realities of business, government, and personal life. We are a country founded on expediency; on compromise; on the realities of concepts such as property, regional loyalty, and economic practicality. Grand theories of jus-

237

tice are the foundation of our great legal system, but let's not pretend that extrajudicial realities have not, over the years, framed the judicial structure.

And there's no doubt that over the past two decades, media and other public audiences have assertively taken their place among all of the other real-world factors that influence the course of the law. Indeed, media and other public influences may now be among the most important of these factors.

That's the scary part. The rise of media and other public opinion influence on the court is threatening in that it circumvents many of the other real-world elements that have long held sway over our judicial system—particularly elements such as money and political and cultural influence. For decades, if not centuries, the course of litigation was guided by those who had the influence to properly frame the arguments and the resources to fight the battle and fight it well. The party with the greater resources usually won, while the poor, unrepresented or politically marginal usually lost. With this new ability to appeal to a broader public audience when addressing legal matters, parties to a legal dispute are able to short-circuit much of that traditional influence. To those that have traditionally benefited, it is a scary thing.

WHERE'S O. J.?

Which brings me to the O. J. Simpson case, since many of you may be wondering why that case doesn't play more prominently in this book. It was the "media" trial of the century, wasn't it? Why, then, wouldn't it be the centerpiece of a book on using the media to influence the course of litigation and other legal matters?

My reason is as follows: In my view, the O. J. Simpson case had far less to do with the effect of the *media* on legal processes than with the effect of *money* on legal processes. O. J. Simpson assembled a well-paid "dream team" of lawyers and experts and lined them up against earnest, but far less prominent (and well-paid) government employees, and—guess what?—the high-priced lawyers won. A commentator recently opined that Johnny Cochran successfully "manipulated" the jury in the O. J. case, but I think this analysis is wrong. Yes, O. J. Simpson probably got away with murder, but in my opinion it is not because of any media-laced manipulation. Instead, his lawyers and other experts successfully established reasonable doubt in the mind of the jurors. Whether you ultimately believe he was guilty or innocent, the fact of the matter is the criminal justice system worked exactly the way it was designed to—the way that it has worked for centuries for defendants who were well-known, well-financed, and (usually) white. The media had little to do with the outcome of the case—media attention mostly served to boost the egos and incomes of many of the players involved. In the end, money, not media-driven injustice, prevailed.

In most cases, however, I see the use of media and other public opinion techniques in litigation as a counterweight against power, money, and connections—shining light on cases that would otherwise fall victim to the existing proclivities of a system that tends to allow injustice to flourish under the right circumstances.

THE COST-BENEFIT OF
EFFECTIVE COMMUNICATIONS

Now, in fairness, let me punch a quick hole in my own argument. Some would argue that nothing has changed: Now the litigant with the greater resources can hire the best lawyer *and* the best litigation communications strategist to handle their case. The golden rule still applies, doesn't it—he who has the gold, rules? Well, yes, this is true to an extent, and certainly my hourly billing rate is the equal of many prominent litigators out there. But this obscures the simple fact that the volume of resources needed to effectively manage the communications aspects of litigation is far less, even if the intensity of communications strategy often rivals other aspects of the litigation. In other words, there are less documents, less procedure, and less billable hours involved when bringing your case to the court of public opinion. Moreover, you don't have to be a lawyer to press your case: The proper message and the proper approach (which hopefully you've learned about throughout this book) allows any litigant to proceed in the public arena. This is not meant to minimize the real costs involved with managing the communications portion of your legal matter (which, at times, can be considerable), I'm just suggesting that, compared to the costs of the litigation itself, the communications costs tend to pale, especially when potential return-on-investment is taken into account. Hence, a more level playing field.

Consider the Ford/Firestone product liability lawsuits, among the biggest legal stories of the year in 2000, involving the propensity of Ford SUVs to rollover after their Bridgestone/Firestone tires blew out. From the resulting media coverage of the case, one would have gotten the sense that these problems involving the Ford Explorer were recent and, if not exclusively, then at least in large part caused by faulty Bridgestone/Firestone tires. But this is not the case at all. SUVs have had rollover problems for years, and tire blowouts were only a small part of the problem. In the 1990s, there had been approximately 300 deaths caused by faulty Firestone tires on Ford SUVs—but more than 12,000 people died in SUV accidents unrelated to tire failure. Litigation relating to Ford SUVs, including the Explorer and its predecessor, the Bronco II, went back to the late 1980s and 1990s. Most of these cases were settled quietly and confidentially, without any public scrutiny of the results—or the underlying problems with SUV design. The SUV manufacturers and plaintiffs' lawyers worked together on settlements that brought money to the victims, but hid forever the danger of SUVs when compared to other automobiles.

But then, one plaintiff decided she wasn't going to play that game. Cathy Taylor decided to bring her case to court, and to the court of public opinion—and both Ford and Firestone were totally unprepared for the result.

To press her case, Mrs. Taylor—who in 1998 lost her 14-year-old daughter in the rollover of a Ford Explorer caused by a faulty Bridgestone tire—contacted Tab Turner, one of the leading plaintiff lawyers in the nation on these types of cases. After years of settling these types of cases confidentially, Turner made the most of the media opportunity, holding press conferences and interviews, and making available large amounts of information related to SUV rollovers—including timelines and summaries that made the reporter's job that much easier.

According to *New York Times* reporter Keith Bradsher, quoted in the PBS program *Frontline:* "We were offered not just 25-page chronologies with quotes from various internal documents that they have been gathering for the last four years, but even the documents themselves—huge, long lists of documents that we could order from the trial lawyers' warehouses, giving all kinds of missteps that Firestone and Ford took along the way. It was a story on a platter."[1]

The result was tremendous media coverage of the case and the issue of rollovers—coverage that shocked the plaintiffs' lawyers, the parties, and—not insignificantly—Ford and Firestone themselves. After a decade of covering up such lawsuits through confidential settlements, Ford and Firestone were caught flatfooted. Their mutual finger-pointing further stoked the media frenzy.

The fact that the media coverage focused *only* on the subject of tire blowouts, instead of the thousands of other SUV rollover cases, certainly warped the reality of the situation, and arguable lulled the public into a false sense of security that, once the tire problem was solved, the SUV rollover problem would be as well. But that's more the result of the years of confidentiality agreements than the one case that brought the truth to light. Was it unfair to Ford? On balance, I don't think so—after all, think of the media coverage they escaped in the years when the stories were hidden behind confidential settlements. It was like a shaken bottle of seltzer, ready to blow. Moreover, the argument can be made that the resulting media firestorm was as much Ford and Firestone's fault as anything else. They had grown so used to cover-up, they weren't prepared at all for the case that would thrust the company into the media spotlight. They were apparently under the impression that the secrecy would go on forever. That was a mistake.

Again, we do much of our work on the defense side, and had I been Ford's communications counsel on all of these many lawsuits over the years, I would have advised them to prepare for the suit that doesn't result in confidential settlement, because this is the one that will kill you. If the company had been properly using some of the tools discussed throughout the course of this book—including the Control, Information, Response (CIR) system, the Litigation Media Checklist, and the core Legal Communications Team—someone, somewhere, might have prepared the company for the day when one of these cases bubbled to the surface.

On the general issue of injustice, consider one more example, a criminal case involving a senior member of my firm, Richard Schrader. Schrader is a fixture in New York political and media circles, former New York City Commissioner of Consumer Affairs and campaign manager in Mark Green's ill-fated 2001 race for mayor. There are, arguably, few New Yorkers with better connections across a wide spectrum of business, legal, political, media, and community activist circles. For most of the 1990s, Schrader would need all of these skills as he became involved in the attempt to parole an inmate serving a life sentence after being convicted—most observers, regardless of political stripe, agree, wrongly—in the murder of an off-duty police officer.

The background: On a balmy May evening in 1970, a police officer was shot and killed trying to prevent a holdup. In less than a week, the police arrested Darryl King, a former Army MP and admitted heroin user. On the basis of the testimony of two eyewitnesses, King was convicted and sentenced to 25 years to life. By the end of the 1970s, King was represented by Myron Beldock, the attorney who had represented boxer Ruben "Hurricane" Carter and successfully proven that Carter's murder conviction was the result of prosecutorial misconduct.

As we're quickly learning in the age of DNA testing and other sophisticated crime scene investigative techniques, the wrong person being convicted happens more often that you might imagine. But even within that context, Darryl King's case was particularly compelling. King's appeal consisted of assertions that the Brooklyn district attorney's office withheld critical evidence about the case in the 1970 trial. At least four eyewitnesses described significantly different-looking suspects racing away from the crime. Several witnesses failed to identify King in a lineup. Some offered descriptions of the gunmen radically different from the prosecution witnesses. One of the key prosecution witnesses, Oliver Ross, a heroin addict, recanted his testimony, claiming that he had been coerced by the police interrogation. The sole remaining witness for the prosecution admitted that she had been given a $4,000 reward by the Police Benevolent Association for helping to convict King.

Which brings me back to my colleague Richard Schrader. In the late 1980s, Schrader met Myron Beldock, who subsequently asked him to help develop a communications strategy for the case. Beldock introduced Schrader to Bo Dietl, the colorful, highly decorated former New York City police officer who is now one of New York's premier private investigators. The flamboyant Dietl told Schrader he had never been so certain of someone's innocence as he was of King's—adding that he wanted to strap the "real killer in the hot seat" himself.

Key to Schrader's communications strategy was to convince high-profile columnists to get involved in the case, then use the "legitimacy" of those articles to forge broader media interest. The first columnist to take a public stand was Bob Herbert—then at New York's *Daily News,* now an opinion page columnist for the *New York Times*—who wrote a favorable commentary on the case. Schrader followed this with several dozen stories in the African American media.

After a tour in New York city government—culminating with his appointment as Commissioner of Consumer Affairs for the City of New York (during which time he wrote a favorable piece on the case for *Newsday*)—Schrader returned to consulting and called Beldock and offered to continue his work.

Interestingly, a turning point in the case came with the election of a Republican governor in New York State in 1994. George Pataki ran as a tough-on-crime, pro-death-penalty-candidate and his first order of business after election was to establish the death penalty. Schrader, representing a bar association, led the campaign to create a capital defender's office that would represent death row defendants. During that skirmish, he came to know several key Pataki aides, and his sense was that Pataki now had enough political capital to give a fresh look to pending parole cases.

Armed with this information, Schrader convinced NBC's *Dateline* to run the story in March 1995. It was a bombshell piece of reporting, and the resulting news coverage ricocheted in the print and electronic media for months. While King's conviction was never overturned, as a result of the media barrage he was finally released on parole in July 1995. To this day, none of the relevant observers, including Schrader, Beldock, and Dietl, believe the real cop killer has been found. Had it not been for the intense media coverage of the case—particularly the *Dateline* story that put all of the pieces together—Darryl King might still be serving his life sentence.

LITIGATION PUBLIC RELATIONS IS HERE TO STAY

The bottom line is this. Litigation PR is here to stay. The intermingling of public opinion and judicial processes is not going away.

Indeed, considerations as to the wider implications of court cases
are fast working their way into judicial deliberations themselves, as
courts attempt to grapple with this new powerful new force on the
legal landscape. Consider the following examples, all from the past
several years:

- In a major ruling in a 2000 lawsuit between fashion industry
  giants Calvin Klein and Linda Wachner, a New York federal
  court ruled that public relations advice that is only tangentially related to litigation strategy is not protected from discovery by the work-product doctrine. "The purpose of the
  rule is to provide a zone of privacy for strategizing about
  the conduct of the litigation itself, not for strategizing
  about the effects of the litigation on the client's customers,
  the media, or the public generally," wrote Judge William
  Rakoff. This is still, by the way, a very murky area of the law,
  so I tend to advise clients to consider all communications
  with myself and my staff subject to discovery—even if we
  are lawyers as well, and are working on issues directly related to the litigation.

- In an August 2002, case, a Michigan judge dismissed a sexual harassment lawsuit after the plaintiff discussed with reporters evidence that the court deemed inadmissible, even
  though much of the information was a matter of public
  record. How does this differ from all the cases discussed in
  this book? Or to put it more bluntly, why aren't my cases
  thrown out more often? Well, the Michigan case hinged on
  a past criminal conviction of the Ford executive that had
  been expunged from the record as part of a plea bargain
  settlement. There is a little-used Michigan law that forbids
  publicizing a conviction that has been expunged. Therefore,
  the judge ruled the violation of that statute was reason
  enough for dismissal. This, by the way, is a very different fact
  pattern than any discussed in this book, and an appeal is underway questioning the decision on both First Amendment
  and due process grounds.

- In the infamous Abner Louima torture case against New York
  City police officers, one of the officers, Charles Schwarz—

who continually proclaimed his innocence (and who had actually been tried four times)—accepted a plea bargain that included a requirement that at no time during his prison sentence could he publicly proclaim his innocence of the federal civil rights violations at issue in the case. Again, this ruling may be questionable with regard to the First Amendment—nevertheless, it is evidence of the impact of the media and other public opinion, not only on litigation strategy, but also on the settlement of both criminal and civil charges as well.

What all of these disparate court actions show is that the intersection of legal and extrajudicial concerns continues. Like every other weapon in the litigation arsenal, public relations techniques can be used to either enhance or derail the administration of justice. But make no mistake about it: Public relations *will be used*—and businesses and other organizations need to be ready. Indeed, everyone involved in legal disputes—from the clients themselves, to their attorneys, to their public relations advisors—should be well-versed in the management of communications aspects of lawsuits, lest those who find themselves seeking redress in the court of law fall prey to far broader injustice in the court of public opinion.

Notes

PREFACE

1. As quoted in *Lincoln the Lawyer,* by Frederick Trevor Hill (New York: Century, 1906).

CHAPTER ONE

1. 60 Minutes, "New Lease on Life" (April 7, 2002).
2. R. Lawrence Dessem, *Pretrial Litigation: Law, Policy & Practice* (St. Paul, MN: West Publishing, 2001).
3. *Daily News* (May 7, 2001), p. 6.
4. M. A. Farber, "Suit Against CBS Is Being Dropped by Westmoreland," *New York Times* (February 18, 1985), p.1.
5. Marie Brenner, "The Man Who Knew Too Much," *Vanity Fair* (May, 1996).
6. Suein L. Hwang and Milo Geyelin, "Getting Personal: Brown & Williamson Has 500-Page Dossier Attacking Chief Critic," *Wall Street Journal* (February 1, 1996), p. 1.

CHAPTER TWO

1. Edmund Morris, *Theodore Rex* (New York: Random House, 2001), p. 73.

CHAPTER FOUR

1. Dareh Gregorian and Dan Managan, "Lizzie's Dad's Defense: Victims Are to Blame," *New York Post* (September 5, 2001), p. 1.

CHAPTER SEVEN

1. William Manchester, *The Last Lion,* vol 2: Alone (New York: Laurel Trade Paperback Edition, 1988), p. 32.
2. See note 1, p. 34.
3. Bill Gates deposition in the Microsoft Antitrust trial, as quoted in "Microsoft Diary: Spin City," *Fortune* (December 21, 1998).

4. Rebecca Buckman and Nicholas Kulish, "Microsoft's Gates Has His Day in Court," *Wall Street Journal* (April 25, 2002).

5. Amy Harmon, "Gates Testifies of Dire Results if Penalties Stand," *New York Times* (April 23, 2002), p. C1.

CHAPTER EIGHT

1. Mark Gimein, "The Enforcer," *Fortune* (September 16, 2002), p. 77.

2. Tom Petruno, "Emails Open New Probe of Analysts," *Los Angeles Times* (April 14, 2002), Part 3, p. 1.

3. See note 1.

4. See note 2.

5. *Medicaid Fraud Report,* National Association of Attorneys General (March/April, 2002), p. 11.

6. "Merrill Enlists Giuliani in Bid to Battle Spitzer," *Wall Street Journal* (April 24, 2002), p. C1.

7. See note 6.

8. See note 6.

CHAPTER NINE

1. Margaret A. Jacobs, "For the Rich, Child Support Means Living in Style," *Wall Street Journal,*

2. See note 1.

3. Salvatore Arena, "Tycoon's Lavish Life: Peek At Perelman's $6b World," *New York Daily News* (January 21, 1999), p. 6.

4. Dareh Gregorian, "Perelman: It Won't Take a Lotta Bread to Feed My Kid," *New York Post* (January 21, 1999), p. 1.

AFTERWORD

1. *Frontline* program #2103, "Rollover: The Hidden History of the SUV" (February 21, 2002).

Index